CU00693362

I believe that our Heavenly Father invented man because he was disappointed in the monkey. I believe that whenever a human being, of even the highest intelligence and culture, delivers an opinion upon a matter apart from his particular and especial line of interest, training and experience, it will always be an opinion of so foolish and so valueless a sort that it can be depended upon to suggest to our Heavenly Father that the human being is another disappointment and that he is no considerable improvement upon the monkey.

From The Autobiography of Mark Twain

The Goblin Universe

Speculations on the Nature of Reality

By

Adam Rourke

Copyright © 2009 Adam Rourke

ISBN 978-1-60145-767-7

All rights reserved. No part of this publication may be reproduced, stored in a retrieval system, or transmitted in any form or by any means, electronic, mechanical, recording or otherwise, without the prior written permission of the author.

Printed in the United States of America.

BookLocker.com, Inc.
2009

Table of Contents

Introduction 1

The Real World 7

The Tip of the Iceberg.. 21

The Shadow World 37

Horton Hears a Who... 51

The Cat in the Hat 63

The Demon-Haunted World..................................... 73

The Two Hands of God... 91

The Golden Thread 101

The Technological Imperative 113

Faculty X... 123

The Tree of Life 135

The Eight Winds 147

The Double Truth... 163

The Damned Facts.. 183

Faith Healing 195

Forteana.. 209

Philip 225

Anima Mundi 241

The Eternal Present 255

The Goblin Universe 273

Selected Bibliograph 285

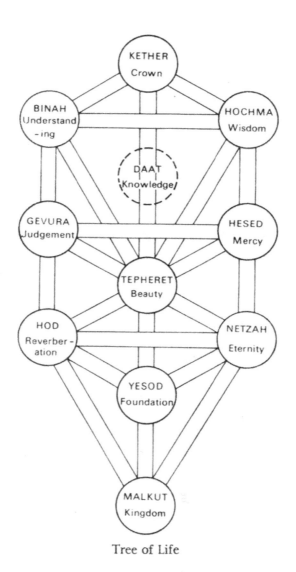

Tree of Life

Introduction

It is probably true generally that in the history of human thinking the most fruitful developments frequently take place at the point where two different lines of thought meet. These lines may have there roots in quite different religious traditions: hence if they actually meet, that is, if they are at best so much related to each other that a real interaction can take place, then one may hope that new and interesting developments may follow.
Werner Heisenberg

Throughout history, human beings have struggled to understand the world we live in. The finest minds the human race has ever produced have grappled with the problem of what it all means. Did some powerful God form the cosmos for reasons we cannot begin to imagine, or did it originate in a cataclysmic explosion for no reason at all? And in all this emptiness what place is man's? Does life have a meaning created with the universe itself, or only what we can give it from the way we live our lives? In searching for answers to such questions, humanity has utilized reason, mathematics, meditation and prayer. Each of these has its own truths to offer, but which is right? How, amid the plethora of systems and theories, is it possible to find a path that leads to the truth?

Faced with a choice of paths through a wilderness a good map is very useful. By giving a bird's eye view of the territory traveled, a map eliminates much of the element of chance from ones journey. A good map lets you know where you are and how to get where you wish to go. In just the same way a true understanding of the nature of reality is a tremendous help in understanding ones choices in life. This gives a basis for evaluating competing paths or theories without having to walk those paths themselves, very useful when it comes to charting a course through life.

Within Western civilization, science has come to dominate all attempts to understand the world. This has lead to some unexpected insights into just how reality is constructed. Still while science is a powerful method of discovery, it is still only one line of thought. Different cultures and different traditions have placed their greatest emphasis elsewhere, on religion, magic, or mysticism. By measuring the insights of science against the findings of these other disciplines, it should now be possible to sift through the competing theories and to find the thread that will lead us, like Theseus, out of the maze. As Dr. Heisenberg pointed out it is where these lines of thought intersect that "fruitful developments" are most likely to occur.

This domination of science is a direct result of its success in the material realm, with the opulent lifestyle of modern society as the result. This modernist view is of recent origins, however. For most of recorded history, other views have held sway. Even today, there are those who would not subscribe to it. Mystics, poets, priests and shamans have held different ideas on what constitutes valid knowledge. Are these alternative ideas valid lines of thought in their own right or just the delusions of ignorant people? In the end, to many people have believed these differing views for to long a time, to just dismiss them out of hand and any theory that is put forth as a valid explanation of all reality must be able to accommodate all of these varying views within its structure.

One of the cardinal sins of the scientific method is to select the data to fit the theory. To give preference to the scientist over the priest or the priest over the shaman is to commit this very error. Now it may turn out, within the perfected theory, that not all views are equal; but to give preference to one view over another at the commencement of ones search is sloppy thinking of the first order. It is only by diligently exploring all paths that the best one can be found. Any theory that purports to explain all of reality must be capable of accounting for the whole of the human experience. It has to be able to explain the subjective as well as the objective, the priest as well as the scientist, the things we understand quite well and the things we do not understand at all. Only a theory that can do all of this has any hope of being right.

We cannot find such a theory by confining ourselves to the methods and rules of any one line of thought. It is necessary to raise above all competing theories to find a viewpoint from which we can see all of them. This is the indispensable first step. If we confine ourselves to the methods and rules of any particular worldview it will inevitably be found that we will prove this view correct. Since all of these lines of thought are perfectly reasonable and consistent unto themselves there can be no other outcome.

Thinking is the only tool which human beings posses that can soar above all of these competing ideas. To the ancient Greeks thinking for its own sake was the ultimate expression of what it meant to be human, but in today's world thinking for its own sake is passé. Thinking today is a means to an end rigidly contained by the rules of whatever discipline one is using. Thinking that does not conform, that ranges freely wheresoever it will is dismissible as idle daydreams or mere speculation. The art of correct thinking took a step forward when Aristotle codified it into the rules of formal logic. These rules impart a rigor to ones thoughts that would otherwise be absent. The discipline of formal logic is now indispensable to correct thinking. The question then arises of whether formal logic is indispensable because it reflects the rules governing the creation of the universe or is it one more creation of the human mind; for there are other lines of thought that do not depend upon logic to validate them. With religious thought being a prime example, the basis of religion being revelation not logic. Still religion is a fact of life that generates physical effects that any "theory of everything" must be able to account for.

There will be no pretense that the present work is either scholarly or scientific. This is why there are no footnotes or any of the other trappings of a formal scientific paper. It will not conform to any other system either. By letting our thoughts go where they would and see what they will we can get on the track of the beast whether we bring it to bay or not. Still, lacking any formal base by which we can judge results, what we find can never be anything more than the musings of an armchair philosopher.

The very idea that thinking can be fun is one undreamed of today. As a pleasant way to spend some time it has gone the way of conversation. In this age of computers, video games and that sheep stare as we sit in front of the television any work that stimulates thought has value. If this book succeeds for even a little while in stimulating "the little grey cells", if it stimulates anyone's interest in philosophy or science to the point where they pick up a book instead of the television remote it will have done all I ask of it.

Very few of the ideas presented here are original. Instead, they represent a distillation of the ideas of some of histories finest thinkers. Occasionally I will inject an original idea, or at least it is original as far as I know. I have found that whenever I come up with an ingeniously clever idea and begin to dazzle myself with my own brilliance that I will inevitably find that someone else had the same idea years ago. Therefore, I have given up boasting that I myself am somebody and am content to set in my armchair and muse.

Join me now on a quest of understanding. I will do my best to keep it simple although understanding my arguments an agreeing with them may not, after all, be the same thing. In our journey, we will not bind ourselves to either logic or mathematics, which means our conclusions are not provable in any formal sense. Instead, we will have to rely on intuition and feeling as our guide. These can never have the certainty of a mathematical equation, but they can produce their own brand of certainty nevertheless. If nothing else, we may think some new thoughts, gain a few insights, and have a little fun as we take up the lance of reason and joust with the jabberwocky.

The Real World

Webster's New World Dictionary defines metaphysics as that "branch of philosophy that deals with first principles and seeks to explain the nature of being and the origins and structure of the world." Metaphysics is then that portion of philosophy that examines the nature of reality and tries to find the fundamental principles underlying that reality. As such it is synonymous with ontology, which is the study of the nature of being or of ultimate reality. Originally applied to that collection of Aristotle's works dealing with first principles it is usually thought of as including epistemology, which is the systematic study of nature. Traditional metaphysics is an attempt to discover why the world is the way it is by the use of reason.

Pioneered by the ancient Greeks, reason alone was believed to be capable of understanding the true nature of reality. Distrusting observation as crude and unnecessary these Greek thinkers laid the foundation for much of Western civilization. However, two thousand more years of experience has shown that this idea was too limited. According to Immanuel Kant (1724-1804) pure metaphysics "is a mere delusion arising from the fanciful insights of reason into which is in truth borrowed from experience, and to which habit has given the appearance of necessity," or in plainer English, Kant felt that metaphysics is purely speculative being isolated from the rest of philosophy by its complete independence from experience. Since "reason is a pupil of itself alone" Kant believed that metaphysics must be purified by criticism if it is to have any permanent meaning.

And it must be admitted that Kant was right. To find a safe path through a maze of competing ideas and theories does require observation an experiment if metaphysical thought is to be more than mere speculation. If metaphysics is to contribute to modern thinking it can no longer isolate itself from the empirical and must be willing to face criticism from any quarter. The danger, to which it has yielded in the past, is that it becomes so enamored with the experimental method that it begins to kowtow to it. This subservience has resulted in the low esteem in which metaphysics finds itself today.

For it cannot be denied that metaphysics has a bad reputation—the poor kid from the streets. No more deadly insult can be hurled at a scientist than to refer to his work as metaphysical. Yet if we apply the scientific method to metaphysical questions will not we lose the essence of what it is that makes metaphysics unique? With its heart gone, all that is left is simply poor science. If metaphysics is to contribute anything to today's world, it must first be true to itself. Today the scientific method so dominates the world that a problem is deemed real and therefore worthy of study, precisely because it can be studied empirically. Metaphysics cannot allow itself to be bound by any such limits.

Available to those of us who are mathematically challenged metaphysics is the poor man's physics. By combining reason and revelation metaphysics attempts to deal with questions of first principle that cannot be answered either experimentally or mathematically. Any attempt to apply these physical methods alone to non-physical questions can only yield meaningless answers or the dismissal of the question as unreal. Neither approach alone can hope to reveal all of the truth. Reason without intuition becomes narrow and dogmatic, while uncriticised intuition is indeed mere speculation.

Where empiricism fails the only path left open is metaphysical speculation. This is the only alternative to complete inaction. We will avail ourselves of it. Here we will try to unite the ideas and beliefs of science, philosophy, mysticism, theology and magic into a coherent worldview. In our search for this comprehensive theory thought will be allowed free-rein to go where it will and we'll see how what we find stands up to criticism.

As free spirits thought can go places inaccessible to empirical science. David Hume (1711-1776) established long ago that pure empiricism is not a sufficient base even for science and by so doing showed that whatever the explanation for the relative universe it is, at least partly, subjective. In subjective matters intuition must be our guide, although as John Locke (1632-1704) has said, it must still be judged by reason. Without such a ground it is very easy to have ones grand theories degenerate into sophism. We will encounter areas in our journey where Aristotelian logic does not apply. Still it is the best road map available and we will follow it wherever practicable.

What then is reality? Theologians have filled many volumes discussing this very question. Close behind come the philosophers filling many more volumes with theories of knowledge, theories of the nature of physical reality and theories of the ultimate. Within the last few hundred years' science has taken pride of place, shouldering all aside with its claims of a superior way of knowledge. What is one to make of all these seemingly irreconcilable views? Are they totally at odds, destined never to unite, or is there a golden thread that can lead us out of the maze? Can we combine all of these views into our own version of a Grand Unification Theory that will allow the underlying truths to stand forth?

For, after all, what the world is like should be perfectly obvious to anyone. To see the real world all you have to do is open your eyes and look. Out there is the real world of "shoes and ships and ceiling wax" while in here is the mind observing what is out there and, occasionally, thinking about it, all perfectly obvious to any right-thinking person.

Of course, no one can ever know exactly what another person is thinking; but the fact that each of us can understand the other is enough to show that both are experiencing, more or less, the same thing. If you ask someone to sit down in a chair, and he does so, the presumption is that what he experiences as 'chair' is the same as what you are experiencing. Anything else is nothing more than bohemian coffeehouse nonsense.

It is common enough knowledge that different people have different views of life. To see these differences one has only to talk to a Christian fundamentalist pondering how best to live in accordance with his beliefs and an east coast intellectual who believes in nothing. These underlying views are the conceptual framework upon which cultures are built and lives are lived. Put into words these concepts become ritual, art, myth and folklore. Different from culture to culture, changing through time, these conceptual frameworks are paradigms, which can be thought of as a model or blueprint. And just as a blueprint gives you the information needed to build your house, a paradigm gives you the information needed to build your world.

A paradigm is a shared set of assumptions, which govern the way we perceive the world. The picture built out of these assumptions allows us to explain the world, predict behavior, and to make choices. A paradigm constitutes a system for describing the world. From the time it is born a baby learns its native paradigm in the same way it learns its native language. For a child to be accepted as a full-fledged member of society it must capable of reacting to the world around it in the approved manner.

Today's paradigms find their base in a nature revealed by the methods of science. However, many people do not have what we might call the empirical temperament. These people are more comfortable within the shelter of religious thought or one of the New Age doctrines and feel alienation with the world they live in. The attitude of some scientists does not help. While the best scientists think of themselves as "humbly picking up shells on the shores of knowledge" not all are so restrained.

Immersed within the rightness of their paradigm the writings of some scientists take a condescending attitude toward ideas and beliefs that are often outside of sciences boundaries. To many lay people this smacks of arrogance. The result is a backlash that sometimes throws out the baby with the bathwater. No one people and no one age has a monopoly on wisdom.

Before we go any further, it might be as well to pause and discuss just what we mean by consciousness, as it will loom large in our discussion. Thought of in different ways by different people this is how we will understand it here. I may give some expert the apoplexy, but at least we will all be in one accord. We will begin with William James (1842-1910) who said consciousness is a process that involves awareness; you lose it when you go to sleep and regain it when you wake up. To James life and consciousness are the same; there can be "no experience except where there is life." Consciousness is then an outcome of life and without it there can be no talk of experiences.

Over the years all attempts to understand what consciousness is has resulted in a complete lack of consensus. Years of effort by the best consciousnesses at hand have failed to produce so much as a generally accepted criterion. In fact, the effort to discover what kind of thing consciousness is has proved so elusive that the suspicion is raised that maybe it is not a 'thing' at all.

For most people consciousness is the sum total of all mental processes. All that one needs to find consciousness is to close ones eyes, look inward, and there it is a continuous soliloquy streaming past the mind's eye. Here we do our thinking, make decisions, learn new skills and solve problems. This understanding of thinking goes back to Descartes (1596-1650) who considered consciousness to be the defining feature of thought. He used the term "consciousness to include everything that is within us in such a way that we are immediately conscious of it. Thus, all the operations of the will, the intellect, the imagination and the senses are thought." Each morning we get out of bed and face another day. Externally there are the tasks of the day, that unceasing round of doings, while internally flows a never-ending monologue of hopes, moods, musings and reveries, a place where your Walter Mitty self fearlessly faces down life's challenges. An organ called a brain is producing all of this, and in studying the phenomenon of mind it is here that science begins its search.

Remember that, although the brain receives the attention, it is only one part of the overall nervous system. Responsible for the control of all voluntary and involuntary muscular reactions the nervous system divides into two main divisions: the central nervous system and the peripheral nervous system. The central nervous system consists of the brain and spinal cord and is roughly speaking, that portion of the nervous system encased within a protective covering of bone; the skull and the spinal column respectively.

The peripheral nervous system is that part of the nervous system that is outside this protective sheath. These are the nerves themselves. In its turn, the peripheral nervous system also divides into two divisions: the somatic division and the autonomic division. The somatic division is responsible for acquiring sensory data and carrying the impulses that govern voluntary muscular reactions, while the autonomic division handles the motor impulses that regulate heartbeat, breathing, digestion and all of the other involuntary reactions. This overgrown swelling, known as the brain, is the site where consciousness traditionally resides. This brain divides into three parts: the hindbrain, the midbrain and the forebrain. The hindbrain is that part of the anterior portion where it first begins as a swelling of the spinal cord called the medulla oblongata. This is the part of the brain that most resembles the spinal cord in the organization of its tissues. Found here are the reflex centers where breathing, cardiac and alimentary actions are controlled.

Setting above the hindbrain, figuratively if not literally, is the cerebellum. The cerebellum controls equilibrium, co-ordination, balance and anything that requires precision of movement. We all have faced the challenge of learning a new skill. Initially each new action must be thought out, with will power applied to keep to the task of learning. This can be a long, difficult and tedious process, but given the necessary effort at some point what was hard will now be easy. The skill has become second nature with concentration being no longer necessary. In fact, thinking about ones actions will now inhibit rather than enhance ones performance. When we reach this stage the cerebellum is in control.

Medical science places the origins of consciousness in the operations of the forebrain. This divides anatomically into the diencephalons and the cerebrum. Composed of the thalamus, hypothalamus and epithalamus the diencephalons serves as a relay center for sensory impulses, reflex actions and controls some levels of emotion. Also controlled from here are water balance, fat metabolism, sleep, blood pressure and body temperature.

The other division of the forebrain is the cerebrum. When most people think of the 'mind', it is the activity of the cerebrum of which they are thinking. The pride of humanity it is here that conscious behavior and intelligence resides. The outer layer of the cerebrum is the cortex—the famous gray matter—that consists of about 10 billion nerve cell bodies. With each of these cells having the possibility of many tens of thousands of interconnections with other cell bodies, the brain has a complexity that puts a computer to shame, if there is such a thing as a soul, surely it in the cerebrum that it will found.

Exactly how all of this translates into the phenomenon of consciousness is not at all clear. Spiritualism along with some of the New Age doctrines sees consciousness as some kind of force field, such as auras, psychic vibrations, luminous vapors, halos or orbs. Magnetic fields also had their followings.

Not surprisingly, science will have no truck with any of this. True to themselves, scientific explanations try to ground themselves in physiology and to eschew all talk of outside forces. Sigmund Freud (1856-1939), for example, pictured the mind as producing waves of interference that caused psychic pressure to build up in the mind and to burst forth as awareness. While the Gestalt School of psychology thought of these waves as electro-magnetic fields that formed visual images on the surface of the brain. This idea fell out of favor when these fields where never found.

Theories that are more recent take their stand in mathematics and computer theory. According to this school, the brain is nothing more than the biological equivalent of a computer and all thinking is mere computation. What the brain does is to carry out sufficiently complex mathematical operations—called algorithms— and thought, feelings; everything in fact that is associated with consciousness appears. It is on thinking like this that the artificial intelligence people pin their hopes.

Many others have found the idea of the holographic mind attractive. According to this idea our brain, mathematically or otherwise, constructs reality by interpreting frequencies from a realm that transcends time and space. We will come back to this idea later. Current efforts aim at demystifying even this, and to make thought a straightforward result of the biology of the brain. Consciousness is, then, just a product of the interaction of the neural network and the external environment and nothing more. Free will disappears and what is left is a society that bears a close resemblance to an ant colony. In the end where all of these groups differ is in how much relative importance to attach to physical processes in the formation of that thing we call mind.

Philosophically these various positions run the gamut from materialism to idealism. On the one hand we have the consciousness does not exist at all school and on the other hand are those who feel that the mind is greater than, an inexplicable by any physical description. The most extreme of these views hold that the mind is a universal property of the cosmos like gravity or electro-magnetism. In this view, the mind is not a producer of consciousness but a receiver of consciousness; rather like a television set tapping into the TV signals that are all around it.

Within the last century the strides science has taken in understanding the workings of the brain have been stupendous. Science has teased its morphology, physiology, and the chemical reactions driving these processes into the open and pieced them together into a high level of comprehension. Of course, there is always more to learn, but a consensus would probably agree that the basic workings of the nervous system are now fairly well understood. Still this understanding is not perfect, there remain problems to overcome and one of the most challenging is to explain that most awesome of beasts, Mike the Headless Chicken.

It's September 1945, World War II had just ended and on his farm outside of Fruita, Colorado Lloyd Olsen is killing chickens. Along with his wife Clara, Lloyd is running a small farming operation. To supplement their income the Olsen's raise White Rock chickens, some of which they utilize themselves and some they sell at market. In 1945, killing chickens was a low-tech affair involving a chopping block and an ax. A bird would be laid across the block and one swift cut would severe its head. Some of the birds died instantly while others would get up and run a few steps before falling over dead.

Finally, the head was lobbed off a White Rock rooster before it was tossed down with the rest. This rooster, however, declined to die. When, after many minutes, it was still alive Lloyd began to feel sorry for it and instead of going ahead and finishing it off gave it some minimal first aid. And it lived!

Except for the little matter of having no head the chicken—who they named Mike—didn't seem any the worse for his experience. Fed crushed corn by having it poked down his esophagus and given water with an eyedropper Mike was a perfectly healthy chicken. Turned out in the yard with the other chickens he would try to behave in a normal manner. He would scratch about, try to preen himself and even was heard trying to crow, although the best he could manage was a gurgle.

It did not take long for news of the headless chicken to get around and soon the neighbors began to arrive, one of whom described Mike as "real peppy." By early October, the LA papers had picked up the story and the headless chicken was news. It was not long before a promoter named H.B. Wade contracted the Olsen's and with visions of wealth in their heads, Mike went on tour; being shown to paying audiences in LA, Fresno, Phoenix, Salt Lake, New York, Atlanta, and Seattle. He even made a triumphant tour of England.

Mike usually drew a good crowd, both of the curious and of those who thought it was all a hoax. Finally while on tour Mike died. With his passing went the Olsen's dreams of wealth. In the end they made enough to buy a new tractor and pay off a few debts, but that was all. In death Mike suffered the fate of many another of the near great and quietly faded from memory until today few have ever heard of him.

So what are we to make of Mike the Headless Chicken? To begin with it must be understood that this was not a tabloid hoax, but a well-documented story. Thousands of people went to see Mike, many with the avowed purpose of exposing the hoax. From our view today it is hard to see how such a hoax could be carried out. No conditions where placed on when or how Mike could be viewed. Many watched Mike right on the farm walking around with the other chickens. This would seem to rule out illusion, as the ability of the magician to control what the audience sees is the essence of illusion. The only alternative would be some sort of robotic device, yet even today's computer driven dinosaurs would not fool many people for long. In addition, if the whole thing was some sort of a trick, why declare Mike dead before the money was made? In view of these circumstances, we must accept the judgment of the time that all this was real.

This creates a problem for it goes against everything we think we know about the workings of the brain and the nervous system in general. I am sure someone will immediately point out that a chicken's nervous system is not exactly comparable to mammals. We will grant this. A chicken, which has very little brain to begin with, relies more heavily on ganglia and reflex action to control its bodily functions. This is how it can get up and run with its head chopped off. I have seen my father kill chickens in exactly this way so I have a little experience in this matter. Yes, I have seen chickens with their heads off get up and run, but a minute or two was all they would last before falling over dead. This is not the same thing as living for a year.

Well, you say, this was an anomaly, a once in the history of the universe event, comparable to a chimpanzee typing out the complete works of Shakespeare. This may well be, still it happened and therefore requires an explanation. And none of the currently accepted theories can provide that explanation. Somewhere in the workings of the nervous system is something not accounted for, somewhere a piece of the puzzle has been missed. For it is a plain fact that according to current theory it should be impossible for any creature of the cellular complexity of a chicken to live without its head. So what is this missing piece? I have no idea. Still it is a good story to keep in mind when someone is complacently expounding on how well we understand the workings of the brain.

Sciences method of dealing with the problem of consciousness is the physical approach. Here consciousness is linked to the physical, which is then broken down into parts. The premise being that if you can understand the parts you can understand the whole and that the whole cannot be greater than the sum of its parts. This attitude tends to concentrate on the origins of consciousness, but has less to say about what it is. It is to this question of what it is that we will turn in the next chapter.

Before we go further, however, a couple of more terms need defining. We'll be using the terms subjective and objective rather freely and it might be as well to state what they are; which, as before, will be a strictly working definition and may not fit every expert's idea of what is proper. When it comes to experts, however, a line of Mayor Richard Daily's of Chicago may be quoted: "experts, what do they know?" Within philosophy subjective theories of knowledge claim that we do not know an independent world as the basis of our ideas only feelings and thoughts are real and a subjective being is wholly a creation of whose feelings and thoughts. Subjectivism states that perceptions are all that can be known. These perceptions exist in the mind as ideas and it is impossible to go beyond them. Since all that can be known are the ideas of the mind then the world exists only within the mind of the knower and consists of "perceiver and perception, minds and ideas."

Objective theories of knowledge claim that we can know an independent world of material objects. An objective being is one where the object is perceived as real and existing independently of the perceiver. Matter is real and can be directly perceived through the senses. It is, as Bertrand Russell says; "what satisfies the equations of physics." Of course, both subjective and objective theories have many variations and competing schools of thought, but here it is enough to think of the subjective as the mental and the objective as the physical sides of reality.

Both of these ways of looking at reality have their champions. By and large the objective view of reality is the one held by the average person in Western society. This is an outgrowth of Western religious thinking. Within Judaic-Christian-Islamic traditions, God created a material world. "In the beginning God created the heavens and the earth (and) . . . saw that it was good." Eastern thought has leaned toward the subjective view that the world is maya, an illusion. Accordingly, eastern thought believes that there is only mind in a world of ideas. We will return to this subject later, but for now, we will carry on with our quest to discover the nature of consciousness.

The Tip of the Iceberg

Up until the end of the 19th Century the workings of the mind and consciousness where considered as being synonymous. When a judgment was made, when something was learned this was done in a conscious manner. All thinking was conscious thinking and the very idea of the subconscious—Freud had not discovered it yet—was unknown.

The first challenge to this idea of an all-inclusive consciousness occurred in an experiment conducted in 1901 by the psychologist Karl Marbe. What Dr. Marbe discovered made the Marbe experiment psychology's Michelson-Morley experiment. The experiment itself was a model of simplicity. A subject sat at a small table facing the experimenter. On the table in front of the subject were two weights, one heavier than the other was. What the subject had to do was pick up both weights and decided which was heavier. Easy enough but when looked at closely the data revealed a startling fact, one that left the psychologists of the day dumbfounded. This was the finding that consciousness played no part in the decision making process at all.

Doing the experiment yourself easily proves this. Pick up any two objects and judge which is heavier. If we pay strict attention to how we get this answer, it will be seen that a decision is made without any awareness of how it came about. The answer is just presented to the conscious mind; no discernable thinking goes on at all. In fact, if you consciously try to determine which is heavier it will be found that the answer takes longer to arrive. Consciously trying to arrive at an answer seems to inhibit rather than enhance the process.

Further thought shows that the same thing applies to the formation of concepts and ideas, to reasoning and to the learning and performance of a skill. Examine the common experience of driving to work each morning. There you are peacefully driving along your mind occupied with this morning's sales presentation, or listening to the radio, or replaying lasts nights big game, anything but driving. Yet, in the end, the car pulls into its accustomed parking space and you are there. During the drive you may have focused your attention on your driving at intervals, but this attention will not have lasted long. No, your subconscious mind drove the car to work; consciousness was not required for the task at all.

The ability to function better with 'no mind' is a feature of most activities. By letting your consciousness go your body reacts directly and enhances your performance. Developing this ability is one of the goals of the martial arts. Learn to make your mind like water and your skill will be at its greatest. Address a golf ball with grim determination to consciously make that perfect shot and watch the ball slice into the trees. Then something distracts you, your mind wanders and your body smoothly executes its swing and straight down the fairway goes the ball. And this is not just confined to golf, it can be seen in all types of activity; playing a musical instrument, bike riding, tennis, painting, writing, anything at all involving skill. Consciousness plays a role in the learning process, but we can say that a skill is learned only when it becomes automatic.

Everyone has had the experience of wrestling with a problem that just seems to defy solution. Finally, you give up and go on to other things and then the answer just pops into your head, seemingly from nowhere—Archimedes running down the street naked shouting eureka. This is such a common experience that it has prompted the British physicist Wolfgang Köhler to talk about the three B's, the Bus, the Bath and the Bed as the places where the greatest discoveries are made. What this shows is that consciousness is not required for creativity either.

Indeed, it is possible to envision an intelligent being capable of performing any of the tasks of an ordinary person who is not conscious at all. Given all this, it becomes difficult to imagine what the properties of consciousness might be.

Before a thing can exist it must have some properties, extension for instance. Yet we have already established that consciousness does not extend into any other of the mental processes. If none of the other mental processes imposes a limit upon consciousness then the only thing that can impose such limits is consciousness itself. And therein lies the secret of how it can be so limited within the minds functioning's and still appear so dominant, for consciousness can only be aware of what it is aware of and it is for this reason that it looms so large in its own estimation.

If consciousness has no great extension then what about continuity, we may not understand much about consciousness; but, at least, we can know that it is always present when we are awake. And right away we run into exactly the same problem as before. Just as a flashlight must be turned on to enable you to see in the dark, so you can only know you are conscious when you are conscious.

Once, many years ago, I was waiting in line at the license bureau when a young man came walking down the sidewalk opposite the window where I was standing. This young man—who looked to be in his early twenties—was, presumably, an epileptic. For as he passed by the window he suddenly stopped in his tracks remaining completely immobile for several minutes before continuing on his way as if nothing had happened. He was completely unaware of having missed a step. For him his walk had been perfectly normal and if no one told him of his episode and he did not notice the missing time he would have never known that anything was amiss.

The problem faced by that young man on that long ago sidewalk is the same one we face here. Think of what it is like to go to the movies. The picture on the screen appears continuous although it is really being created by a series of still pictures projected so rapidly as to appear continuous. Who's to say that we do not produce consciousness in the same way? It may be continuous or it may not, but the fact that we can only be aware of being aware when we are conscious means that it is a question without an answer.

If consciousness is not necessary for any of the mental processes then the only thing left is the act of perception itself with consciousness being a phenomenon not a thing. Roger Penrose in *Shadows of the Mind* (Oxford University Press, 1994) considered this phenomenon to have both an active and passive aspect. Awareness itself is the passive aspect, but the ability to know carries with it the implication of choices. It is this increased ability to choose that forms the active aspect of consciousness. With the freedom to choose comes the feeling of free will. Once free will appears, it is only a short step to a feeling of self.

If we concentrate upon the act of perception then surely something is learned. We learn where consciousness is located. Be conscious of being conscious and, if you are like most people, it will seem as if consciousness is located in the head just behind the eyes. Not only do we locate it here in our own heads, but we do so in others as well. You can see this assumption in the age-old practice of making eye contact with the person with whom you are speaking.

When ask to describe what they see when they turn their eyes inward most people will give some variant of the movie theater analogy. In this simile consciousness becomes you seated in a movie hall while the picture passes on the screen before you. Contained within this analogy is the implication of space. The theater represents the 'space' within which the action takes place since the idea of a screen and a watcher implies a space between them. All of this is produced by the fact that the easiest way to think about something is to make it a 'thing'. And by the rules of the everyday world a thing must exist in space.

Considered rationally it is obvious that there is no space behind the eyes. What we are seeing here is the mind creating space and, by extension, time. With the separation of space and time, geometry comes into existence. Geometry, however, implies three dimensions, which means that a three dimensional hologram makes a better analogy than a two dimensional movie. In this scenario, the subconscious mind takes all incoming sensory data, filters it through all the other workings of the mind and produces this hologram. And just as it creates space and time 'in here' so it create space and time 'out there'. What this does is give us our first glimpse of the mind creating reality.

While we are on the subject, please note that locating consciousness behind the eyes is only a convention. Aristotle, for instance, located consciousness in the upper chest just above the heart, the brain being thought of as a mere cooling organ and even today there are people who would locate their consciousness there. There is, however, no necessity for it to be located in any one place and, in fact, it does not have to be located in the body at all. Take the famous out-of-body experiences (OBE's) many people have had due to injury, drugs or meditation. In a typical episode, people will find themselves floating above their own body that they can see with perfect clarity. Their perceptions seem normal in every way; they 'see' what is happening and later are able to describe the actions of anyone who was present quite accurately. If not for the unusual point of view, the experience would appear normal in every way.

Let us take a minute to examine an out-of-body experience and see what light it throws on the nature of consciousness and the workings of the mind. The traditional explanation for an OBE is that every mortal possess an inner spirit or soul. Thought of as having an independent existence, this vital force or élan vital is capable, under exceptional circumstances, of leaving the body. Although always attached to the body by an invisible cord the astral body can go anywhere and is still capable of perceiving its surroundings in a normal manner. This explanation has generated considerable heat between those who believe in this ethereal being and those who dismiss the whole business as superstitious nonsense.

To date neither side has been able to muster an argument of sufficient weight to force the other side to change their minds. Why is this? Is it because the whole phenomenon simply does not exist or is it, perhaps, that both sides are wrong and there is some third explanation for the whole business? It turns out that there is such an explanation and that it has something to say about the nature of consciousness and the nature of reality as well. To begin to understand what this is lets look at one of the most common of these experiences; that of the patient under anesthesia.

The purpose of anesthesia is to render someone unconscious so as not to feel any pain during an operation. However, as more than one study has shown, only the conscious mind shuts down; the subconscious goes right on functioning as usual. Normally the mind takes all incoming data and processes it into a holographic image. When you gaze out of your eyes at the "purple mountains majesty", it is this three-dimensional hologram that is being seen. This is not just true for seeing; hearing, touch, taste and smell are all expressed within the hologram in exactly the same way. And remember that this hologram is not attached to anything, locating it in the head is just a convention.

While under the knife the subconscious is still functioning, is still taking in sensory data just as it does when awake. Normally we remember none of this, but under certain conditions the mind can take all of this data and produce a hologram just like when it is awake. Of course, the eyes are closed and it is not seeing directly, but it has enough information to imagine what the scene should look like. A nurse is heard to walk across the room and pick up an instrument from a gurney and this information is converted into a mental image of the nurse walking to the gurney. This created image may or may not correspond exactly with what the conscious tenets of the room observed. When the patient later tells of seeing the nurse cross the room it is going to be assume that what she saw was the same as what everyone else saw and as long as there are no glaring inconsistencies whose to know?

The mind has now created a holographic image of the room and the people in it. However, it cannot project this image from its ordinary point of view. To do so would mean you could again feel pain. It, therefore, projects it from some other viewpoint and since your body would be in view from that viewpoint, it duly includes it within the picture. And understand that what the mind is doing here is exactly the same thing it does while awake. No psychic powers are needed whatsoever. What you are seeing while reading this book is just as much a construct of the mind as the experience of floating in the corner of the room. Thought of in this way the holographic image and reality itself become difficult to distinguish.

All of this is interesting because, at last, we have learned something about the nature of consciousness. This is that the hologram the mind creates and the state of being conscious cannot be separated. When the hologram is present—whatever the viewpoint—you are conscious, when it is not you are unconscious. Forcibly stopping the mind from generating the hologram is how you render someone unconscious. The world we live in and the knowledge of that world then become two aspects of the same thing.

This, however, raises a problem for if an OBE is just consciousness displaced why do we not feel pain while it is occurring. And the answer seems to be that the relation between consciousness and pain is more complicated than it appears at first sight. Of course it is well understood that consciousness plays a role in voluntary actions but the idea that it might have a role to play in involuntary actions is certainly counter intuitive, for by definition an automatic action is done without conscious thought.

The first thing to notice if we are to understand how the mind can appear to be conscious while the body appears unconscious is to note that there seems to be two types of pain. The first kind is an ordinary involuntary automatic response, while the second is—so to say—a voluntary automatic response. The first is what might be called ordinary pain. People dying from chronic illness will, while seemingly unconscious, moan and toss around and show every sign of suffering pain, although it is possible that these people are not unconscious but semi-conscious. Be that as it may, perhaps the point can best be shown by looking at ordinary reflex action.

We are all quite familiar with the physical sensation of being hurt. Single-celled organisms exhibit avoidance behavior toward adverse stimuli that is, if not a sign of pain itself, certainly its precursor. In humans pain, and the attempts to avoid it, are just as basic as breathing. Still it has long been known that there is more of a connection between pain and the mind than the simple fact that pain isn't felt while unconscious.

The yogis of India have known for a 1,000 years and the medical profession for a 100 years, that it is possible to mentally control pain through various meditative and bio-feedback techniques. Within all this is a curious feature that is not often mentioned.

Reaction to pain is usually thought of as being controlled by the subconscious mind. The fact that organism that cannot be said to be conscious appear to react to pain can lead to no other conclusion. However, consider this, if you touch your hand to a hot stove it will instantly jerk away. This is what my high school biology teacher called a reflex action. Touching the hot stove generated a signal in the nerve endings of your hand that passes along the nerves of your arm to the spinal cord where a nerve center processes it and sends out the signal to retract the hand. So efficient is the process that the hand can jerk away from the heat before the mind is even aware of the pain. No reaction could be more fundamental, yet be it noted, if you are unconscious it does not work.

Well of course it does not work your unconscious. True enough, but there still seems to be a little more going on than just being unconscious. If an experimenter where to take a frog and apply some kind of irritant to one of its legs that leg will jerk away. Now render the frog unconscious and repeat the stimulus, the leg will no longer react. Cut that same frogs head off, however, and the leg will once again react to the stimulus. Somehow what little brain a frog has is controlling whether this reaction occurs or not.

In considering this problem, it is first necessary to make a distinction between being unconscious and being asleep. If you are asleep and your little brother jabs you with a pin you jump up and start pummeling him. But if you are unconscious the same jab will have no effect at all. Indeed, this is a classic test to see if someone is really unconscious. Simple organisms do not exhibit this trait, only when an organism has evolved to a level of complexity that allows it to be rendered unconscious does this trait appears.

This reaction, or lack thereof, to pain is such a fundamental feature of living things that it could almost be used to define when the first glimmerings of consciousness appear. This cannot have happened by accident, but could only have come about through the forces of evolution. This can only mean that this reaction has some purpose, in a Darwinian sense, in the struggle for survival. What can this be? How can channeling reflex actions through the conscious mind increase an organism's chance for survival?

If attacked while asleep your reaction is to wake up and fight or flee. However, if you are unconscious you do not have this option. Say you are being mauled by a grizzly and have been knocked unconscious. Now your best chance of survival is to remain absolutely still and play possum. If, however, while unconscious your reflex actions continued to cause your limbs to jerk and twitch your chances for survival would go from not very good to zero.

The mind generates consciousness to perform specific functions one of which is to experience pain and to guide the bodies external reaction to that pain in a manner best suited to survival and it is this same reaction that is showing up in OBE experiences. There is more than one tale from the hunting literature where someone being mauled by a lion calmly stood off to one side and watched it happen.

In an out-of-body experience the ordinary senses seem to be working and yet one feels no pain. Data collected by the senses is utilized, but data generated within the body itself is not. The reason for this can only be the same reason your hand does not jerk away from a hot stove if you are unconscious. If, while floating disembodied, you continued to react to pain this would be identical to the problem encountered during the bear attack. What this is showing is that being aware of pain and having pain is not necessarily the same thing. The physical sensation of pain and the mental awareness of pain decouple with each being able to exist independently of the other. This forces us to consider the possibility that some, at least, of the body's workings that have always been considered as physical reactions are actually part of the paradigm and that the paradigms role is greater than it first appears.

Having trouble following all this? It is easy enough to say that the world one sees is analogous to a hologram, but comprehending it is another matter. Let us think about it for a minute and see if we can be make it a little clearer. Pick some object, a chair lets say, and look at it. And while you are looking, consider what is happening. Light is reflected off the surface of the chair enters your eyes and strikes the retina. Here the energy from the photons is converted into a signal that is passed along the optic nerve to the brain. The brain then processes this signal, using all its preconceived ideas of what a chair should be, to create a three-dimensional picture of a chair.

The mind then projects this 'holographic' chair into the conscious mind and perceive this picture as real. Whether or not there is an exact correspondence between the chair 'out there' and the chair 'in here' is an unanswerable question because the chair that the mind has formed is the only chair you will ever see. Not only is it not possible to know what the external chair is really like, it is not even possible to prove that there is an external chair at all.

We have been rather free and loose with our use of the word consciousness. There is really no generally accepted definition for the term consciousness and I will not try to supply on here. Rather we will simply take it to be the commonly held experience of awareness and to note that what I have been calling consciousness most people would divide into consciousness and self-consciousness. The difference between the two is subtle and debating the proper definition for each has kept several generations of psychologists gainfully employed, but we will take a stab at it anyway.

For many people the most familiar of the schemes proposed for understanding the structure of the mind is the one created by Sigmund Freud. Within this scheme, the mind is divided into four parts: the ego, the id, the superego and the libido. His ideas have been attacked by many and are not generally accepted today, but they are still a perfectly serviceable way of dividing the workings of the mind.

Our own scheme, which replace Freud's terms with the subconscious, conscious and self-conscious, runs something like this. Think of the mind as an iceberg. The subconscious represents the vast bulk of the iceberg that lies beneath the surface of the water forever hidden from view. It is here that most of the actual workings of the mind take place. Here all bodily functions are controlled and much of thinking transpires. Characterized by the kind of thinking found in dreams, here our impulses push for gratification and the rules of logic do not apply. All of which has serious implications for the mind-world interactions.

Directly above the waterline sits the conscious portion of the mind. The division between the subconscious and the conscious minds is not a sharp one and it is not always easy to know with which one is dealing. And above this, at the tip of the iceberg, sits self-consciousness. Return to our analogy of the movie theater. Consciousness is then the picture on the screen, that continuous stream of pictures and dialogue that is forever passing through ones mind. With the appearance of consciousness the individual is now aware of what is happening. Consciousness and awareness is then the same thing.

Self-consciousness is the watcher seated in the movie hall observing the picture on the screen. This is the mind watching itself. When we ask the question of "Who am I", we mean this watcher. Where a conscious being is aware, a self-conscious being is aware that it is aware. Self-consciousness then is the watcher.

Remember a time when you were completely immersed in whatever it was you were doing. As you concentrated your attention at some point you lost consciousness of self. Now you are only doing, not watching what you are doing, until you come to yourself with a start and realize that a considerable time has passed without your knowledge. When you were in this state you were conscious and when you are again aware of self you are self-conscious and this is the difference.

Whichever theory you like you will find that most try to understand consciousness by stating what it does. And by adopting this line of thought psychologists have revealed not only what it does, but also what it is. Consciousness is the quintessential functional entity—a term we will be seeing a lot more of later.

A functional entity is a 'thing' that can only be said to exist while it is performing its functions and which has no independent existence beyond those functions. The reason that trying to decide what consciousness is has proved so difficult now becomes clear. Consciousness is not anything at all, it has no physical existence in the classical sense and when you are passed out drunk or otherwise unconscious it does not sit around a quiet room somewhere waiting to be called.

Consciousness does not create the worldview—that is the job of the subconscious—it is only to be aware of it. Tradition links consciousness to intelligence with consciousness being a by-product of that intelligence. The Marbe experiment has shown that there is no necessity for this link. It is possible to imagine a being with a very advanced intelligence that is still not conscious. What then does consciousness contribute to the struggle for survival?

The function of the brain, reduced to its lowest common denominator, is to make choices. It maintains physiological control of the body too, of course, but it is when it begins to make choices that a mind is present. The more complex the mind the greater the number of choices that are available and the greater likelihood of making a correct choice, this gives any creature a tremendous advantage. It is no coincidence that the most advanced thinker on the planet is also its dominant life form.

When, in that long ago Precambrian sea, the first single-celled organism deliberately turned toward the light mind had its beginnings. The human mind is, however, a lot more complicated than a heliotrophic bacterium. As it stands, the theory indicates that when complexity reaches a certain point, when intelligence rises above a certain level, some sort of critical mass is reached and—like wetness from water—consciousness appears. While it is possible to imagine an intelligent being that is not consciousness, its role in establishing dominance is to great for it to be a mere by-product. Somewhere, somehow being conscious must confer some advantage in the struggle for survival.

Several ideas have been put forth as to what this might be. Right now the idea that consciousness enhances ones ability to plan is in favor. I believe, however, that there is a little more to it than this. I submit that this advantage is an increased ability to concentrate, which in turn allows the brain to utilize its increased complexity more efficiently. Being consciously aware of a problem brings the power of the will to bear on its solution.

This heightened level of awareness concentrates all of the minds abilities and by so doing enhances it ability to make choices.

Consciousness does not do the thinking, what it does is to focuses the world picture into a sharper image. An enhanced ability to concentrate results in the enhancement of all other abilities be it will power, creativity, or any other. The ability to keep after a problem, to worry about, fuss over and plod along until the answer is found gives the bearer a priceless evolutionary advantage. This problem solving ability has placed mankind on the top of the evolutionary ladder.

With the insight's provided by modern physics it may now be possible to begin to find the place of consciousness in the scheme of things while bringing something more solid than just endless argument to bear on the problem. Using this knowledge as a base some of the old problems of philosophy, mysticism and magic take on new meaning. Freely ranging through whatever discipline that has an insight to give it should be possible to create a synthesis among these widely differing views and to use it, like a beacon of light, to illuminate some of life's most perplexing problems. And since we are going to use the findings of science as our base for this synthesis we shall begin there.

The Shadow World

Modern science began when Galileo Galilei (1564-1642) combined the empirical methods of observation and experimentation with mathematics. This happy combination has proven so successful at problem solving, improving the standard of living, and generating new knowledge that it has become the dominant fact of life on earth. Science is responsible for almost every characteristic of modern life. Where is the tribe so remote that it is untouched by science, what philosopher is so brave as to expound a theory that contradicts it, even the most conservative of religious fundamentalists hold their views in defiance of science. From humble beginnings, science has expanded until no corner of the globe has been left untouched.

Between the dawn of the Twentieth Century and its close, the old, predictable, stable world of Newtonian physics gave way to a much broader vision. The clockwork universe was replaced by a universe of the infinitely strange that Sir Isaac might fail to recognize. With its coming, the Newtonian concepts of time and space vanished into to the realm of the quaint; OK for dealing with ordinary problems of the sub-light world, but hopelessly unable to probe into the true center of reality.

Much has been made of this revolution and the great strides it has made, which is true enough when dealing with the abstract mathematical formalism of these theories. It is less so when it comes to forming this new knowledge into a coherent, understandable picture of reality. For, like everyone else, the only world these scientists have ever experienced is the three-dimensional world of everyday life. Living in a three-dimensional world, our language and thought patterns are three-dimensional as well and adapting them to describe a four-dimensional reality is no easy task. How well they have succeeded is a matter of some debate.

It is not too much of a stretch to see the concept of the space-time continuum (we will get to this shortly) as nothing more than a mathematical description of the mystic's idea of the unity of existence. The similarity of these two points of view has not escaped notice and whole books have been written on the subject, although there is a conservative faction within the scientific community that denies any such relationship. For them the equations revealed by relativity and quantum theory imply no such conclusions.

The mention of the word mysticism strikes fire for these scientists. Unfortunately, for their position the similarities are so great that no amount of mathematical manipulation has made them go away. No, the coincidences are too great to ignore. The Heisenberg lines have crossed an opened a window into the heart of reality.

As any scientist would be quick to point out, science is a method not a philosophy. Science has no philosophy or creeds and the only belief required is belief in the method. This method is a strictly rational one of dealing with facts that can be proven or disproved. Its main weapons in this empirical approach are experimentation, observation and reasoning from known causes. When dealing with objective reality it is the most effective method known for solving problems.

It is upon this foundation that the whole of science rests. Attempts to understand the physics underlying the workings of the world began with the Greeks, but took a giant step forward with the work of Isaac Newton. Traditionally this became classical physics. If you want to get technical, however, classical physics is actually composed of Newtonian and relativity theories, all science, in fact, from before 1924 and the advent of quantum mechanics.

Driven to the country by the plague Newton is said to have gotten the inspiration for his theory by seeing an apple fall from a tree. At that moment, the realization flashed into his mind that the force that made the apple fall and the force holding the planets in their orbits was the same. From this insight he went on to create the mathematics of a theory that is one of the great triumphs of the human mind and in so doing he brought order out of chaos and secured man's place in the universe.

Newton's world is a clockwork world. This is a deterministic world where every effect must have a cause with the laws of motion precisely controlling all future behavior. This mechanical universe operates independently of any observer or any human choices. If a thinker, with sufficient brilliance was given enough information he could, in theory, work out the entire happening of the universe from beginning to end.

If determinism is one plank of the theory then objectivism must be the other. The whole premise rests upon the idea of solid objects moving in empty space. There objects exist apart from any human desires or perceptions. Called "the zone of the middle dimensions" this realm of the big and slow is identical with the ordinary world of our daily experiences. Within this zone classical physics is still a perfectly valid way of describing the universe.

Albert Einstein, doodling mathematical equations in his spare time at the Berne Patent Office, laid the groundwork for the theory that would topple Newtonian physics from its throne. Usually thought of as the Theory of Relativity, Einstein's thinking actually manifested itself as two theories. First published in 1905 the Special Theory of Relativity deals with uniform motion, while the General Theory, published in 1915, deals with non-uniform motion. There is a lot of experimental evidence in support of the Special Theory of Relativity and it has been pretty well proven to everyone's satisfaction. The experimental evidence in support of the General Theory of Relativity is weaker, but it is so elegant it is used extensively anyway. Curiously, when Einstein won the Nobel Prize it was not for either one of his relativity theories, but for an earlier work on light quanta that is considered one of the founding papers of quantum mechanics.

Relativity theory has a reputation for being esoteric and abstruse, but the difficulty arises not from the fact that the ideas themselves are so hard to comprehend as from the fact that they contradict common sense. In our everyday common sense view of the world we know what the shape of a coin is or the length of our own foot, space conforms to Euclidean geometry and time flows perpetually onward. All of this is so obviously right that there must be something wrong with anyone who questions it. There is a truth lying behind everything we know and our task as human beings is to discover this truth. And therein lays the problem, for what relativity theory is showing quite clearly is that this concept of a concrete world forming the framework of our beliefs and understanding is an illusion.

The universe as viewed through the lens of relativity theory is a strange place. Here the speed of the light coming out of the headlights of a speeding car never increases rather it is the car that gets shorter. Acceleration becomes indistinguishable from gravity, while matter and energy are interchangeable, one into the other. The idea of cause and effect loses its meaning with the order of any set of events depending upon where you are standing when you see them, and that independent, objective world that we know so well begins—like the desert seen though heat waves—to shimmer.

Special Relativity—with, which we will be primarily concerned—is, based upon two postulates with the first being that the speed of light is a constant. Within Newtonian physics, velocity is the distance traveled divided by the time it takes to cover that distance. Here both time and distance are thought of as constants. A minute is a minute and a foot is a foot and remains the same no matter how one looks at them. Einstein turned this on its head.

Within the new system it is the speed of light that never changes and time and distance that are the variables. What this means is that the speed of light will never be observed to travel at any other speed than 186,000 miles per second. The light coming from the headlights of a car traveling at 60 miles per hour is not the speed of light plus 60. No matter what the relation between you and the light source the recorded speed of light will never vary.

From the first postulate flows the second postulate that simply says that all motion is relative, hence the name. This means that movement can only be considered as moving in relation to something else. If you are in a spaceship in a completely empty universe there would be no way of telling if you were moving or not. Indeed, since there would be nowhere to move to the very idea of motion is meaningless.

But, you say, if you accelerate then you can feel that you are moving. And this is true; you would feel an increase in g load, as an astronaut would say. However, in this situation it is always possible to argue that you are motionless and that it is the force of gravity that is increasing. Without a point of reference that allows a judgment to be made, there is no way to decide which alternative is correct.

This idea of relativity extends to more than just motion; rather it is a property of all physical existence. Nothing—nothing— exists except in relation to something else. Once it is realized that these two postulates do not contradict each other the entire logical structure of the theory will appear and all the unfamiliar features of a relative universe will follow.

So what are these strange features? We will begin by asking a very simple question. How long is a one-foot ruler? A no brainier right, a foot long ruler is 12 inches long and this is easily verified by anyone who cares to measure it. What was not understood before Einstein was that all of the people doing the measuring were doing so from the same frame of reference. And that it is this similarity of viewpoints that creates the illusion of uniformity.

Within a relative universe there are no privileged frames of reference, up-down, in-out, moving-stopped all of these things are dependent upon the frame of reference of the observer. All experience loses its absolute significance being true only in relation to something else, if everything in the universe instanteously doubled in size how would you ever know it. Up-down, in-out is observer dependent and cannot be decided by experimentation.

Einstein's eureka moment came when he considered what would happen to a measurement if velocities approaching the speed of light were involved. Imagine yourself standing on the observation deck at the airport watching a plane fly past. For you, standing firmly on the ground, it is the plane that is moving. However, there are no privileged frames of reference. One person's experience is just as true as another's. To someone on the plane it would be just as true to think of themselves as being at rest and that the airport is moving. Thinking of the plane as moving and the airport as stationary is only a convention.

Now let us perform an experiment. As you watch the plane fly by imagine a friend is holding up a ruler in one of the windows. Further, imagine a supercharged plane capable of reaching speeds that are a sizable percentage of the speed of light, and that you have a very quick eye. As you stand watching you measure the ruler you are using as the control and find, as expected, that it is 12 inches long. However, when you measure the ruler in the window of the plane as it passes by you find that it is only 10 inches long. Moreover, it is not just the ruler that has gotten shorter, your friend, the plane, everything in fact will be found to have shrunk by the same amount.

To your friend on the plane making her own measurements everything is perfectly normal. Her ruler is still 12 inches, she is still the same size and the length of the plane has not changed a bit. From her point of view, your ruler is 10 inches long. The question of how long a standard ruler is now has two answers. And the thing that must be understood is that both answers are right.

How can this be? You quickly recheck your measurements, but they are accurate. The answer lies in the invariability of the speed of light. Since the speed of light cannot change in our equations, the other factors must. In fine, this means that as any material object accelerates it will get shorter and its mass will increase. The true nature of reality is then the exact opposite of what common sense would dictate. Einstein summed up how this is possible when he said; "Length is what we measure with a measuring rod and time is what we measure with a clock." If a ruler is measured as being 12 inches long then that is its true length, but if it is measured as 10 inches long then that is its true length. There is nothing else.

Moreover, what is true of its length is just as true of all aspects of an object. Take a fifty-cent piece and hold it out in front of you. Held upright it is a circle, but rotate it 45 degrees and it is an ellipse. Of course, everyone knows that the 'true' shape of a coin is a circle, but just like the idea that the plane is moving and the airport is not, this is only a convention taught to us in childhood. Just as the true length of a ruler is whatever it is measured to be, so the shape of a coin is whatever it is perceived to be. To assign the coin a circular shape is an arbitrary act that gives us another glimpse of the minds role in creating reality. Or, as James Jeans put it: "As the subject [relativity] developed it became clear that the phenomena of nature were determined be our experience rather than by a mechanical universe outside of, and independent of, us."

All of which means that in the final analysis ultimate reality is a personal affair. This in turn leads to the conclusion that any idea we may have of reality as an amorphous mass within which all of humanity lives and breathes is wrong. Instead, it would be more correct if we were to use the simile of a honeycomb in a beehive to describe realities structure. A honeycomb is composed of innumerable cells, each slightly different, yet with none more right than the other. Reality is then not continuous, but is composed of individual realities all united to make a whole.

Within relativity theory, space and time are no longer considered separate things. Rather—like two sides of the same coin—they are what Herman Minkowski called space-time. He then elaborated this idea into the concept of the space-time continuum. In this continuum, there are no events, no causes and no parts. This is a united whole where individual events lose there meaning. This "astral world embraces all that was, is, or will be and people like us, who believe in physics know that the distinction between past, present and future is only a stubbornly persistent illusion."[1]

While this four-dimensional space-time is considered by physicists to underlie reality it is not the world we live in. This is the "middle dimension" where space-time splits into space

---

[1] Albert Einstein

and time, an evolutionary necessity for survival. This three dimensional world of the middle dimension is, of course, the holographic world we have already spoken of. So accustomed are we to living in this three-dimensional hologram that it is very difficult to conceive of any other.

As consciousness focuses on space-time, the three-dimensional world emerges like a wave from the ocean. The wave is a distinct entity, but it must not be confused with the ocean. Think of our daily world as the shadow of four-dimensional space-time. A shadow is a projection of a three-dimensional object onto a two-dimensional surface with its shape varying as the angle of projection varies. This analogy—used by mystics, philosophers and now physicists—has its origin in Plato's parable of the cave.

When his students would ask about the true nature of reality Plato would tell them this parable. Imagine a cave in which there is a man chained to the wall. His position in the cave is such that he can never see the entrance, all he can see are the shadows cast on the wall in front of him. Of the beings that pass the entrance of the cave and cast the shadows, he can know nothing. Their true nature must remain a mystery to him. All that he can ever know about the real world outside is what he can deduce from watching the ever-changing shadows.

All of which bears more than a little resemblance to the esoteric ideas of mystical thought. So much so, that it makes many scientists nervous. For them mysticism is an esoteric delusion whose tenets cannot possible be accepted. The idea that the findings of physics can be used to understand mysticism or for self-examination causes their hackles to raise, mysticism is speculation science is fact. To them the theory of relativity is concerned solely with the measurements of external data. The vehemence of some of the statements used in support of this idea, however, raises the strong suspicion that their reactions owe more to bias than to reasoned argument.

To these scientists the mathematical formalism of physics has nothing to say about mysticism and those who do try to show such a connection have been "smitten" by Eastern religious thought. Nevertheless, if these writings are read with attention it will be found that the arguments as to why the statement of a physicist is an insight into the true nature of reality and the exact same statement from a mystic is nonsense are not conspicuous. More often ridicule is simple heaped upon those who are trying to find some common ground between the two and this cannot be said to add weight to their position.

To be fair what is found so objectionable is a lack of logic. Logic after all is the foundation of science, allow logical contradictions and it becomes possible to prove anything and rational thought is at an end. Within the rules of science, anything that cannot be dealt with rationally is automatically suspect. This is the problem intuition has to face whenever it is offered as evidence. Still it is the judgment of humanity that intuition is a valid way to gain knowledge. The insights of Einstein, Heisenberg and Bohr owe at least a nod to intuitive perceptivity.

Still great effort has been expended to show why the plain evidence before our eyes just is not so. This has proved a difficult task for the simple reason that these two lines of thought do not just seem to be saying the same thing; they are saying the same thing. As Lawrence LeShan has shown it is perfectly possible to take statements made by mystics and statements made by physicists, mix them up, and then be unable to tell who made which statement. To disallow the insights of one group while allowing those of the other is to base your decision upon who made the statement rather than its contents. No, the inescapable conclusion is that if one is right they both are and the overwhelming weight of evidence says that physics is right. The Heisenberg lines have crossed.

Before moving on to quantum mechanics we should point out that the revelations of relativity theory lead to even stranger conclusions than are usually supposed. To get an idea of what these may be lets look at one of relativities best-known consequences, which is that the speed with which time passes is inversely proportional to velocity. This is the well-known fact that the faster one goes the slower clocks will run until at light speed they will stop completely. To see what this means for ultimate reality as a whole let us look at relativity's most famous contradiction, the twin's paradox.

We begin with identical twin brothers. One twin—we will call him Larry—becomes a schoolteacher and stays at home, while his more adventurous brother—we will call him Darryl—becomes an astronaut. When the brothers are 30 years old, Darryl goes off on a spaceship capable of traveling at a large percentage of the speed of light. For stay at home Larry celebrating his 60th birthday 30 years has passed. However, upon his return home Darryl will find that for him only 10 years have passed. Due to the slowing down of time at ultra high speeds, Darryl is only 40 years old. And this is not just a figure of speech. The clock on the spaceship showed that 10 years had passed and the crew duly aged 10 years. The clocks on earth showed that 30 years had passed and everyone there aged 30 years. "Time is what you measure with a clock."

The mind rebels at this. Surely no two such different answers can both be right. One has to be right and the other wrong and the simplest way to find out which is which is to check the age of the universe. Did this wonderful, galaxy filled, ever expanding universe age 10 years or did it age 30 years? And the answer is, it did both. Larry, at home, aged 30 years and no matter what measurements he makes or where in the universe he makes them he will always find that 30 years have passed. Darryl, who aged 10 years, can make the same measurements and he will always find that 10 years have passed. This must be so; no single person can measure time as passing at different rates within his own life.

Not only are the twin's now different ages, but also two alternate histories of the universe have been created. Now suppose there is a third brother who also made a journey in a spaceship so that—for him—15 years have passed, now we have three different histories of the universe. The honeycomb structure of reality once again reveals itself. This is why there is no such thing as the age of the universe.

Now wait a minute this can't be right, after all scientists have measured the age of the universe, haven't they? They have indeed with the current estimate being between 10 and 15 billion years. And the key word here is estimate. Lets suppose that two scientist decide that instead of measuring the age of the universe in billions of years they will measure it to a billionth of a second. Further, suppose that both are using identical atomic clocks. One of these scientists does her work in a laboratory on earth, while the other does his work aboard the space station. Due to the different speeds of one lab relative to the other each will arrive at a different answer. The same thing would happen if the two scientists were on different planets with different rates of rotation.

No matter who measures the age of the universe they can only do so using their own clocks that will always give an answer consistent with the experience of the person making the measurement. This is why there is no correct answer to the question of the age of the universe. The age of the universe does not exist independently of the one asking the question. While we are here, please note that when someone takes a measurement—and this is true of all measurement—then all of the reality that this person can experience will reflect this measurement. When the mind creates a reality by taking a measurement it creates all of reality. And, just like in the twin's paradox, when a history is created, all of reality must conform to that measurement.

What this means is that our analogy of the honeycomb is too limited. There we tried to show that reality is composed of the individual realities of everyone living. The twin's paradox is showing that each of these cells is a universe unto itself. At any given moment every person is creating their world out of the measurements, i.e. experiences, of their lives. Moreover, since no two people's experiences are identical no two universes will be either. Nevertheless, what must be understood—what the twin's paradox is showing clearly—is that the two universes are equally true. There is no privileged frame of reference.

Relativity has stood on its head the common sense daily world we live in. At the same time, it gives us a mathematical basis for the Eastern concept of maya, which is that the world we live in is as much mind created as not. With the discoveries of Einsteinian physics the idealism of philosophy and the illusions of mysticism have found their mathematical expression.

All of this is a little more complicated than just taking measurements. To begin to appreciate what these other complications are we will look at that other great achievement of 20th Century physics, quantum mechanics. What relativity does for the macro-universe quantum mechanics does for the micro-universe. And what it reveals is even stranger than what relativity shows. Any effort to understand this shadow world must consider these findings. This is the task of the next two chapters.

Horton Hears a Who[2]

We come now to the quantum world and the quantum world is a weird world. In Newtonian physics, it is theoretically possible, given sufficient knowledge of initial conditions, to calculate the entire history of the universe. Quantum mechanics has disproved this idea. At the atomic level, the world is shown to consist of probabilities that deny any possibility of completely calculating this history no matter how much information is available. Here matter cannot be shown to definitely exist at all. The best that we can say is that it has a likelihood of existing. Its properties like these that cause quantum mechanics to do even more violence to common sense that relativity does.

Quantum mechanics is often referred to as quantum theory—something I will do myself—but strictly speaking this is not correct. It is not so much a theory as a framework or guideline for the construction of all modern physics. First formulated in 1924 it has had great success and no contemporary scientist now seriously doubts it, although its full implications have yet to be worked out.

The basic tool of theoretical physics is mathematics. That "all things are numbers" is an ancient idea that says that mathematics is not just a useful way of describing nature, but is an intrinsic part of nature itself. A consistent mathematical description then becomes the high road to truth.

However, as with relativity theory, translating the essence of the relevant math into words is another matter. For "as far as the laws of mathematics refer to reality they are not certain; and as far as they are certain they do not refer to reality."[3] Several

---

[2] Dr. Seuss
[3] Albert Einstein

51

models have been proposed to fulfill the need for this 'metaphysical' description with the most widely accepted being the Copenhagen Interpretation developed by Niels Bohr and Werner Heisenberg.

Simply put the Copenhagen Interpretation divides the world into an observed system and an observing system. What it says is that the act of observing has consequences for the experiment being performed. Unlike classical physics, where he can be disregarded, in quantum mechanics the observer must always be included. This idea of the crucial role of the observer is one we have seen before. We encountered it first in our discussion of the nature of consciousness. It crops up again in relativity theory with all three being similar enough to cause one to suspect that once again the Heisenberg lines are crossing.

When discussing quantum level particles it must not be supposed that they are real in the same sense as a billiard ball is real. In the quantum realm particles cannot be said to exist, they only have "tendencies to exist." In the everyday world a ball has position. Struck by a cue the ball now has position and momentum, both of which can be calculated with great accuracy. Not so in the quantum world, if one tries to calculate an electrons exact position and exact velocity it will be found that the more certain one becomes the more uncertain the other becomes.

The inability to specify both the position of an electron and it's velocity at the same time is known as the Heisenberg Uncertainty Principle after its creator, Werner Heisenberg, although technically, the uncertainty principle doesn't apply to a single measurement on a single particle, but is a statement about the statistical average of lots of measurements. What this is saying is that over a large series of measurements it will be found that it is impossible to produce a product that is equal to, or greater than, Planck's constant.

It is the indeterministic nature of these particles that are responsible for the probabilistic nature of quantum mechanics. Just like in relativity were one cannot specify events in space-time the quantum level has no events either. Here are only probabilities that propagate from point to point through space and determine the future. These are the Schrödinger Waves. In the quantum realm, ordinary ideas of an isolated material object lose their meaning. What is left is "a dynamic web of inseparable energy patterns."

The Schrödinger Wave is very basic to understanding the true nature of reality. Conceived by Erwin Schrödinger as a way of testing the probability of subatomic events the wave is actually the key to understanding events at all levels of reality. These waves are roughly analogous to ripples spreading out in all directions like those created by a pebble tossed in a pond. As these ripples spread out over the surface of the pond, sometimes they cancel each other out and sometimes they reinforce each other. Where the interaction is strongest is where there is the greatest possibility of an event. What then turns a possibility into a real event is the act of observation.

Before going any further, it might be as well to clarify what we mean by an observer. The scientific understanding of an observer is any information gathering and utilizing system. This includes human consciousness, animal consciousness and information gathering machines. Sidestepping the question of the validity of machine intelligence, we will define the observer as being synonymous with ordinary human consciousness.

Physics began to break out of its Newtonian shell with the work of Michael Faraday and James Clerk Maxwell. Working in the Nineteenth Century Faraday and Maxwell revolutionized physics by showing that the concept of a force could more accurately be viewed as a force field. Following Newtonian thinking a force was something that could cause motion or cause motion to cease. Faraday, through his experiments on electricity and magnetism, concluded that this was not the whole truth. He could not explain the data his experiments were yielding using conventional ideas of a force. Only when he added the idea of a field did it all begin to come together. In the new model, force became a force field of electrically charged particles, with these particles being the points where the fields became infinitely large.

A field is then a space within which magnetic or electrical lines of force are active. This is a concept that is easier to illustrate than to explain in words. And the way this is always done is with some iron filings and a magnet. Put a small amount of metal shavings on a piece of paper and hold it over a magnet. When this is done the shavings will form into a series of concentric lines anchored on both poles of the magnet, thus are the lines of force revealed.

James Clerk Maxwell then reduced these ideas to mathematical form producing the electromagnetic theory of light. In Faraday's thinking, the idea of an electromagnetic field had been just an aid to understanding the data generated by his experiments. After Maxwell's work, the field was no longer a fanciful aid to understanding, but was considered physically real. The essential reality of nature was now understood to be a set of fields. Within Newtonian physics, fields and particles were distinct things. Particles were immutable and eternal, while fields emanated from particles and were responsible for the forces between them. By combining these ideas the nature of light now became clear. Light was an electromagnetic field with wave-like properties. This became the established wisdom. It was for this reason that Einstein was dismissed out of hand when he proposed that light was a particle-like bundle called a quanta.

Einstein's ideas about light had their origins in a brilliant leap of the imagination by Max Planck. This was contained is his solution to the black body radiation problem. No material object—say a metal bar —glows in the dark at room temperature. In a dark room a metal bar will be black and invisible. If heat is applied the bar will begin to glow, brighter and brighter as the temperature increases until it is white hot. By the end of the Nineteenth Century this radiation curve had been precisely measured.

Planck set himself the task of understanding the physical basis needed to produce these measurements. In an act of sheer inspiration he realized that the material body consisted of atoms—he called them "vibrating oscillators"—whose energy exchange was discrete and not continuous. This is the smallest unit of energy possible. Called Planck's constant this unit of energy is very, very small, but it is not zero. To understand what this means think of the world as made out of oats. What quantized energy shows is that the world resembles a pile of individual grains of oats rather than oatmeal. This is one of the most important insights ever gained.

It was by applying this idea to the problem that allowed Einstein to come up with his theory of the particle-like nature of light. In the years that followed these ideas would provoke a storm of contention between those who were sure it was a wave and those who believed in its particle nature. The solution, when it came, turned out to be one neither party had expected. The unlooked for result was the discovery that light has a dual nature, it is both a wave and a particle.

Developed by Niels Bohr into the idea of complementarity, i.e. two properties that exclude each other, this can be a hard idea to swallow. For Bohr the wave-particle aspect of light was "two complementary descriptions of the same reality, each of them being partly correct and having a limited application."

That is if light is treated as a wave it is a wave and if it is treated as a particle it is a particle.

This idea takes a little explaining. The theory makes a clear distinction between light as a wave and light as a particle. When light is treated as a wave it is a wave, it is not part wave and part particle, it is not a wave made up of particles. It is a wave. Similarly, when light is treated as a particle it is a particle it has no wave-like properties. The two properties exclude each other with whichever one it is being observer dependent.

The findings of quantum mechanics have a reputation for being so fantastic and bizarre that it is pointless to try to understand them. However, throwing up ones hands is a serious mistake. For it often happens that the stranger a finding the more insight it will offer for as Sherlock Holmes explained to a long-suffering Dr. Watson: "It is a mistake to confound strangeness with mystery. These strange details, far from making the case more difficult have really but the effect of making it less so."

To see what the strange has to tell us lets visit an astronomer studying the light from a distant galaxy. Now between this galaxy and earth is a second galaxy that the light from the first must pass on its way here. While studying this incoming light the astronomer has two choices, the light can be studied as a wave or as a particle. Remember, if viewed as a wave light will behave like a wave and so as it passes the intervening galaxy it will pass around it on both sides. If, on the other hand, this self same light is viewed as a particle it will behave as a particle and pass by the intervening galaxy on only one side. Now think about what this implies.

The galaxy being studied is many millions of light years away and the intervening galaxy itself is ten million light years away. This means that any light seen passing this galaxy did so ten million years ago. Understand that this business of taking different paths is not just an optical illusion. As a wave ten million years ago, it really did pass by this galaxy on both side and as a particle; it really did pass it on only one side. This raises an interesting question, for how did the light know ten million years ago what choice the observer was going to make today? For know it must have for it to assume the proper physical configuration to conform to the thoughts of the observer. To say that this is a paradox without explanation is no explanation. Taking our cue from Sherlock Holmes, we will think of this paradox as a guide and see where it leads. To begin to get a handle on how this is possible we will look at another experiment: the Einstein-Podolsky-Rosen (EPR) thought experiment.

Although one of the originators of quantum mechanics Einstein was never comfortable with some of its implications, to him there was an objective reality consisting of "independent spatially separated elements" and he never could accept the indeterminism that quantum theory implied. He expressed these doubts in his famous dictum "that God does not play dice." Since he thought there was some external reality underlying the quantum realm and since quantum mechanics denies this he felt that the theory was incomplete.

With the help of two colleagues, he devised the EPR thought experiment to try to show this deficiency. And the way they tried to do this was to show that quantum theory—as it was understood-—violated local causality. What this means is that events that happen far away cannot have an instantaneous effect on a local event, to do so violates the rule that no information can be transmitted faster than light, something expressly forbidden by relativity theory. Until Einstein pointed it out the idea that quantum theory seemed to allow local causality to be violated had not been generally understood.

Quantum theory allows for a rather mysterious interaction of particles called quantum entanglement. Once entangled the interactions of these particles lies somewhere between direct communication and complete separation. The strangeness lies in the fact that the mere choice of parameters for one particle appears to fix the parameters of the other. There is no classical analogy for this phenomenon whatever.

A simplified version of this thought experiment begins with two electrons spinning in opposite directions. Although the Heisenberg Uncertainty Principle does not allow us to measure any single particles position and momentum at the same time, it does allow us to measure the sum of the momentum. Here the two particles are spinning in such a way that the sum of their spin equals zero. Since the two spins cancel each other out the two electrons can be thought of as spinning in opposite directions. Once these two particles have entangled their spin will always equal zero. Now the two particles can be separated to any distance—across the room or to the orbit of the Moon—and their spin will still equal zero.

We now have two entangled particles, it is not know exactly what they are doing, only that the sum of their spin must equal zero. For either electron the chances of finding it to be spinning in any given direction is 50-50. Once electron A has been measured and a direction of spin established then electron B—wherever it is—will be found to be spinning in the opposite direction. This appears to happen instantaneously, faster than the speed of light can carry the news.

This posed a formable challenge to the theory, which was answered by Niels Bohr. Bohr's solution was that once the two particles become entangled through interaction they form an indivisible whole. Being a whole the system can no longer be analyzed in terms of its independent parts: it has no independent parts. Thus, any measurement performed on one electron "will instantly determine the direction of the other." Since we are dealing with one system there is no violation of local causality. Einstein, in accord with his line of thinking considered the two particles to be objectively real. Bohr's solution denied any objective existence without actually measuring it. The prize was awarded to Bohr and the whole thing put down to one more example of quantum weirdness. The question was not forgotten, however, and physicists went on debating its pros and cons.

Then John Bell—a physicist working at CERN near Geneva, Switzerland—decided to try and settle the matter by direct experiment. He rigged up a device that fired photons derived from positronium atoms in opposite directions toward slits in two sheets of metal that acted like polarizers. Behind the slits were photo multiplier tubes to detect the photons. It was a long and complicated experiment that involved changing the angle of the slits to see what effect this had on the behavior of the photons. If the world is completely objective then what happens to one photon will have no effect on the behavior of another photon.

Bell found that this was not the case. His findings showed "that either the assumption of objectivity or locality or both are wrong." Since then several other experimenters, notably Alan Aspect and his colleagues in Paris in 1981 have confirmed Bell's findings. In the end, the experiment showed that if there is an objective reality it has to be non-local.

And here matters have rested. Yet the meekness with which Einstein accepted Bohr's solution is rather surprising considering that it has a couple of weaknesses. In the first place, to say that the parameters of the second particle are determined instantaneously no matter what the distance is only an assumption. Since the limits of our experience can never exceed the speed of light, however we experience these entangled particles we must do so within those boundaries.

Secondly, Bohr's solution does not explain how these two particles entangled in the first place. Just to put it down to an unexplained act of quantum weirdness is no different than saying it's magic. What is needed then is an explanation that not only predicts the results, but also explains how they came about. It turns out that there is such a solution, although it lies not in quantum mechanics, but in relativity theory.

To try to see what this explanation might be let us begin by simplifying the EPR experiment even further. First, we will replace the electrons with two spinning tops. To simulate quantum uncertainty we will place each top in a black box. Now there is no way of knowing which way each top is spinning. The tops entangle and the boxes are separated. According to Einstein, we have two separate objects widely spaced. According to Bohr, the two tops form a single system that cannot be meaningfully thought of as separate.

Now for the experiments, a scientist makes the appropriate measurement with box A and finds that top A is spinning clockwise. When box B is opened its top is found to be spinning counterclockwise as expected. As with the electrons it seems that either local causality has been violated or that the two tops must be thought of as one system.

So which is right? Well, Bohr was right when he said that they could be thought of as forming a single system, but Einstein was not wrong when he said they were two separated objects. Since the two tops were separate objects before they entangled they can still legitimately be thought of as separate objects. To give preference to one view over the other would be a violation of the relative state of nature. Nevertheless, no information has been exchanged between these two objects, at the speed of light or any other.

To see how this is possible let us return to the twins paradox from relativity theory. Remember in this paradox one twin aged ten years while his brother aged thirty years with each brother's experience of how much the universe had aged being a reflection of his own age. No matter how each brother measures the age of the universe he will find that it has aged in accordance with his own experience. When the mind creates reality, it creates all of reality. Each brother has created his own cell that is consistent unto itself. The same is true of the tops.

Top A—in its closed box—has a 50 percent chance of spinning in either direction. The same is true for top B. However, once box A is opened and its spin is determined to be clockwise the direction of spin for top B is no longer a probability. It is a 100 percent certainty that it will be spinning counterclockwise and this is so in spite of the fact that no information at all has passed between the tops. Just as the first twins measurement of his age created a universe that aged thirty years, so the observer's measurement of top A as spinning clockwise created a universe in which top B is spinning counterclockwise.

That is all well and good, but doesn't this create a loophole that does allow for faster than light transmission of information. Suppose box A is on earth while box B is on a spaceship in orbit around Mars. At that distance, any signal will take over eight minutes to travel from the earth. At a prearranged time the scientists on earth open box A and find the top to be spinning clockwise. One minute later a colleague aboard the spaceship opens box B and sees that it is spinning counterclockwise. She now knows what the result of opening box A was seven minutes before the information could have reached her at light speed.

Unfortunately, a strict adherence to Relativity Theory rules this out for it is here that the light speed barrier imposes itself. Confronted with a sealed box each scientist knows that the probability of finding any given spin is 50-50. If box B is opened within the eight-minute gap it may be found to be spinning opposite to top A, but it may not. The odds are 50-50. There is an equal chance that it will be spinning in the same direction as top A. Now, from the perspective of the spaceship, the truth as revealed is exactly the opposite of what was found on earth. There is a subtle point here that must be understood. If any of the scientists on earth could transport instantaneously to the ship, they must find top B spinning the opposite of top A. In the universe created by the earthly observation this must be so. Within this eight-minute gap the universe inhabited by the shipboard scientists does not contain this knowledge. In their universe, the direction of spin is still a probability. It is only when that knowledge has been received at the speed of light that their cell of reality will conform to the one on earth.

Two diametrically opposed histories of the universe have been generated. Just as in the twin's paradox, where you cannot specify the age of the universe without including the observer, here the observer must be included as well. And just as each twin created all of reality so do the observers here. Once again, we are faced with two contradictory histories that are both right and once again, the central role of the mind in creating reality is revealed.

This business of entanglement is not the only strange feature revealed by quantum mechanics. What it has to say about the relation of probabilities to the creation of reality is equally as strange as entanglement.

The Cat in the Hat[4]

What quantum theory reveals about the nature of reality is the same thing relativity theory reveals. Any measurement or choice one makes is reflected in the whole of reality: past, present, or future. When a mind, by observation, creates reality, it creates all of reality. A little piece of reality is not created within absolute reality. There is no absolute reality. This is how our two tops entangled and this is also how that stream of light 'knew' ten million years ago whether to pass that galaxy as a wave or a particle, all of reality includes all of time.

Of course, everyday life is not this simple. Say that box A and box B where opened in such a way that two separate histories where created. We are now faced with a paradox, but practically it will not last long. What will happen is as people talk about the results the difference will smooth out and what will be left is an explanation acceptable to all. That a paradox has occurred will be acknowledged; but this will be assimilated into the existing paradigm, just as the twin's paradox was.

We now need to look at one more thought experiment. Like many others, Erwin Schrödinger found the implications of the Copenhagen Interpretation troubling. He devised the cat-in-the-box thought experiment as a criticism of that interpretation. In challenging, the idea that the world does not exist without the observer Schrödinger was addressing the same question Einstein had with the EPR experiment. This is the idea that we live in a non-objective world. With the weight of the Bell experiment behind it, the ball now seems in the Copenhagen court and Schrödinger's cat has ended up being a brilliant illustration of the very thing it was meant to disprove.

---

[4] Dr. Seuss

Like the EPR thought experiment we will simplify the cat-in-the-box to the point that it will give a true physicist fits. We begin by taking a cat and sealing it in a box along with a weak radioactive source and a detector of radioactive particles. At some point in the experiment the detector is turned on for exactly one minute. While it is on there is a 50 percent chance that the radioactive source will emit a particle. If a particle is detected a poison gas is released killing the cat. We can now assign probability waves to the state of the cat, one probability wave for the live cat and another for the dead one. The correct description of the cat is then not an actuality but a probability. Quantum weirdness has spilled over into the macro-world.

At this point the scientists conducting the experiment do not know if the particle fired or not and so it is meaningless to speak of the cat as being alive or dead. Such is quantum weirdness that the cat may legitimately be thought of as—in some sense—alive and dead at the same time. To factually determine the state of the cat one scientist is now designated to open the box. When he does the cat is found to be alive. For this scientist the condition of the cat is no longer a probability, for him the cat now has a definite state. However, this knowledge is only valid for the scientist peeking into the box. Only when he communicates the state of the cat to his colleagues does it becomes an actuality to them. Now instead of one cell knowing the state of the cat several do, but it is only when this knowledge is relayed to the general public that all cells realign in conformity.

What the cat-in-the-box thought experiment ends up showing is that the world is a non-objective world of probabilities that the act of observing turns into reality. In addition, an observer dependent world carried to its logical conclusion implies that ordinary everyday reality—the chair you are sitting on or the book you are reading—lacks definite exist when it is not being observed. Those bohemian coffeehouse ideas may not be so crazy after all.

Not surprisingly, this view has provoked resistance with much energy being expended in an effort to explain it away, for even if this matter/mind stuff is alright for the quantum realm it surely can have no relevance for the world of the everyday. After all common sense would seem to show that there are things that must exist in the absence of any observer. Perhaps doubt can be cast on the existence of any object but surely, the underlying laws of nature must still exist.

To see how this idea might be more apparent than real let us take a look at one of sciences most basic discoveries, the concept of entropy. Few things could be more fundamental than entropy for it forms the basis of our understanding of time. What makes entropy a particularly good choice is that what we learn about entropy will apply equally well to both time and space. Let us then look at the relationship between entropy and time.

To begin you must understand that the idea of time can be thought of in several ways. Time as understood by a physicist studying her equations is not the same, as the nonprofessional understands it. Ask anyone how he experiences time and the answer will very likely be that it is unidirectional, that is it flows in only one direction. The question now arises as to where this arrow of time comes from? There is nothing in the equations of classical physics—either Newtonian or Einsteinian—that demands it. These equations are symmetrical as regards time. Quantum theories ideas about time more closely resemble the everyday experience than does relativity theory, yet even here there are postulated particles that can move backward in time. Time, as understood by theoretical physics, lacks this quality of movement. It is only in the middle dimension that the 'arrow of time' appears.

Scientific understanding of this phenomenon centers on the laws of thermodynamics. The first law of thermodynamics provides the theoretical foundation for our understanding of the concept of energy. In physics, energy is defined as the capacity for doing work or overcoming resistance. What this law says is that energy can neither be created nor destroyed; it can only be converted from one form to another. That the energy of any reaction must be conserved is the origin of the idea of the conservation of energy with the form of energy most familiar to the average person being heat.

Your body has a temperature of 98.6° F with this heat residing in your body in the form of molecular motion. Increase the motion of these molecules and your temperature goes up. If two bodies of different temperatures come into contact, the energized molecules of the hotter body will collide with the molecules of the cooler body and communicate energy to them. In isolation from any outside source heat will conduct from a higher energy state to a lower one until the temperature of the two bodies become, more or less, equal. The reverse never occurs making heat transfer irreversible.

This asymmetry of the movement of energy becomes the second law of thermodynamics. Left to itself energy progresses from a more excited state to a less excited state, and to reverse the process energy must be added from outside the system. Transfer this idea from energy to matter and you have the quantity of entropy. Defined, as being a feature of 'information', entropy is that quality of disorder or messiness of a physical system. An ordered system of physical objects is in a higher energy state than a disordered one. Obeying the first law of thermodynamics, this more ordered system can only move to a state of greater disorder.

This finds expression in the middle dimension in the simple fact that it is hard to keep things neat. Think of your bedroom, left to itself it tends to get messier and messier until it resembles the proverbial pigsty. Straighting up your room requires you to do some work. To create greater order out of disorder energy must be applied. It is upon this increase of disorder that our concept of time rests, which makes this concept very important for our understanding of the relation of the micro-world to the middle dimension of the human experience.

The middle dimension is that portion of the continuum that the mind can experience directly. Moreover, since entropy is only found in the middle dimension the suspicion arises that it too must have some connection to the mind. So what is there about the middle dimension that could allow entropy to arise? And the first thing that comes to mind is that the middle dimension has a 'now'. The equations of theoretical physics lack this concept and the reason that this is so is that 'now' is thought itself. The act of thinking creates this 'now' from which flow the past, present and future.

Thoughts cannot be described mathematically and this is why the concept of 'now' finds no expression there. No, thought is only found in the middle dimension because thought and the middle dimension are the same thing. When the first brain began to form in that long ago sea it found itself faced with a set of fields. As any high school science student knows it is very difficult to think about fields. To think the world must be broken up into parts and with this break up before and after came into existence.

Entropy is, then, an evolutionary adaptation for survival that bears the same relation to reality as time and space does. When that first mind began to interact with space-time to create reality it had to structure that reality in such a way as to allow for personal survival. The world may be an illusion but it is not a Bugs Bunny cartoon. There anything goes here it does not. A symmetric world would be unlivable. Entropy is the minds solution to this problem. Whatever entropy has to say about the workings of the middle dimension; it can have nothing to say about objective reality.

Another idea that is trotted out in opposition to the matter/mind problem is that of decoherence. Arguments for this commonly begin with the idea that the cat-in-the-box has a memory while a subatomic particle does not. Having a memory gives the cat a history that makes it a unique sentient being. It therefore knows if it is alive or dead. Or, at least, it knows if it is alive. Furthermore, the cat interacts with the rest of the world. It breathes, gives off heat and responds to sense data. Even a dead cat interacts with the world to a certain degree.

Within this scenario, the two waves of probability form coarse-grained histories. A coarse-grained history is compiled by using the high points of the available data as opposed to a fine-grained history where as many points as possible are used. The idea being that the interaction of these two histories causes them to decohere, that is to fall apart. Since the two waves of probability no longer interfere with each other the state of the cat is no longer a probability. And this is true, this is the way the cat knows it is alive. However, this tells the scientists conducting the experiment nothing at all.

What all of this appeal to the cat interacting with the world and coarse-grained histories really shows is sloppy thinking. First off, the question before us is not what the cat knows; the question is what the observer knows. Note that decoherence assumes the truth of its own postulate. For until they are observed the air the cat is breathing, the heat it is giving off, the box itself are all just as problematical as the cat is. In a relative universe, every person lives in their own cellular world with its base in their own experience. Yes, the cat knows if it is alive since its reality is based upon its own experience, but this does not tell the scientist conducting the experiment anything. The only way for the scientist to know if the cat is alive is to open the box and no amount of decoherence can change this.

Schrödinger went to great lengths to invent a suitably quantum sounding situation for his cat. But in the end there is no difference between Schrödinger's cat and one that arrives from the pet store in a box. Until the box is opened, the probability waves apply to this cat just as surely as to the other. What we are seeing is not just some unique feature of quantum theory, but a fundamental feature of all life. Until the box is opened, not only can we not say whether the cat is alive or dead, we can't even say positively that there is a cat in the box at all. To assume that the cat is there when it is not being observed is only "our expectation of its existence." This inability to prove the reality of an unobserved event is then not just a feature of quantum mechanics but of reality everywhere. What we have in the cat-in-the-box is a mathematical base for the philosophy of transcendental idealism—of which more later.

Or take another example that illustrates the same thing. One of today's greatest unsolved mysteries is whether there are other sentient beings on other planets. Of course, everyone has an opinion, but mathematically the probability of their existence can be described in exactly the same manner as the cat.

The usual response to this question is to compute the odds of their existence as well as we are able. A number is assigned to as many variables as possible; how many stars in the galaxy, how many stars have planets, how many planets have atmospheres and so on for as many as can be thought of. The answer will depend upon what variables were chosen and what values were assigned to them. Estimates run from a very high degree of probability to practically nil.

However, these extraterrestrials are breathing (presumably), they interact with their world; they have a memory and know that they themselves exist. So what does this tell us about the likelihood of life on other planets? Nothing at all, it has not changed things in the slightest. In the end extraterrestrials will only be known to exist when we meet one. Until that time it is not possible to say that they exist and it is not possible to say that they do not exist. No, the probability waves mean exactly what they say and the cat really is both alive and dead at the same time.

Nonsense, a cat is either alive or it is dead whether we know which it is or not. All this business about probability waves is just talk, right? Wrong! Quantum mechanics says that it can be both at the same time and it has experimental evidence to back it up. This is the famous two-hole experiment. In this experiment a sheet of metal containing two holes is set up between a light source and a detector. Now fire a single photon at the detector, in the common sense view the photon must pass through one hole or the other. The only way it can possibly pass through both holes at once is to divide. However, this is not what happens. A single photon fired at the sheet of metal will pass through both slits at the same time and it will do so without dividing.

Remember that on the quantum level there are no events, only waves of probabilities. If only one slit is open then the probability of the photon going through it is 100 percent. However, if two slits are open there are now two possible choices, two waves of probability. Just like the cat-in-the-box, these waves will interfere with each other. This interference may be either constructive or destructive, but the result is that it cannot be said which hole the photon passed through.

And this is exactly what is seen. When one slit is open the photon goes through one hole, but when both holes are open the interference pattern indicates that the photon has gone through both holes at the same time. When the experiment is performed—as it has been—this is what is seen. And here is the really interesting point, the thing that links the phenomenon to the mind. If a detector is present at one of the slits so that it is possible to see which slit the photon goes through then it only goes through one hole again. A photon has only "tendencies to exist"; it is only a probability to begin with. By adding a detector at one of the holes probability is eliminated and a fact is born. The photon is now a 'thing' and a 'thing' can only go through one hole at a time. In this way is reality formed.

Our treatment of quantum mechanics is a coarse-grained history if there ever was one. Still it is enough to give a sense of what quantum theory has to say about the nature of ultimate reality. The micro-world is revealed as a random place of probabilities that lie beyond the range of our sensory perceptions. And this is the most interesting finding of all for with it the true nature of reality is revealed. The micro-world is made up of probabilities while the middle dimension is made up of facts.

A fact, then, is a probability observed. Facts and sensory perceptions are linked; where there are no perceptions there are no facts. This perception created world is the everyday world of cause and affect we all live in. This is the world of classical physics, which is the cellular hologram, which is conscious awareness. Quantum mechanics agrees with relativity theory in showing the role of the observer. It also agrees in showing that when an observer creates reality he creates all of reality. Quantum mechanics confirms relativity theory's findings of the relative nature of reality and in a relative universe; one person's world is just as true as another's is.

This translates into different created realities that contain different possibilities and different limitations. Since the Copenhagen Interpretation was created as an explanation for what has been revealed by quantum mechanics there has been controversy over how the interpretation should be interpreted.

What isn't generally realized is that the meaning of the Copenhagen Interpretation—and with it the way the mind creates the middle dimension—has already been worked out in great detail. Philosophers did this 200 years ago.

The Demon-Haunted World

Philosophy began when the first cave dweller looked up at the night sky in wonder. We have no way of knowing if the world that person saw resembled our world, but it is almost a certainty that the questions being ask were ones we could understand. Who am I? What is man and what is his place in the scheme of things? What do the gods demand of me if I am to win their favor? Humans have been asking these same questions throughout all of history and it is not too much to suppose that here is where they originated. Their answers would not be our answers, but in asking the questions philosophy was born.

Look somewhere between theology and science, out on the periphery of ordinary thought and you will find philosophy. Raised to a discipline of its own by the ancient Greeks, the basic premise of philosophy is that nature can be understood by reason alone. In pursuit of its goals philosophy has created a bewildering prolixity of claims, counterclaims, competing schools of thought and opposing points of view. Descartes is quoted as having said: "That one can imagine nothing so strange and incredible but has been said by some philosopher."

What all of these competing ideas represent is an exploration of reality from every possible angle. In our day, however, philosophy seems to have lost its vital spark. Today it is more of an academic endeavor focusing on theoretical topics of technical and mathematical interest rather than a vibrant search for guidance and practical understanding of the common human experience. Still throughout history, it has uncovered some important truths that have to be woven into any theory of the ultimate nature of reality. The study of philosophy is a lifetime occupation and we can do no more than give yet another coarse-grained history. In fact, we will do for philosophy what we did for physics. Fortunately, it is not necessary to understand the whole of philosophy to pursue our goal. Here we can confine ourselves to ontology and epistemology and pass over all problems of values, morals or ethics and we will begin by looking at the most commonly held theories, which breakdown naturally into three divisions: monism, pluralism and dualism.

The first of these is monism, which is the doctrine that all of nature is made of one ultimate substance, one being, one principle or one ground. To the monist change is an illusion stemming from recollections of descriptions of events. Any attempt to distinguish between the description of a thing and the thing itself becomes an exercise in futility. Behind this illusion of change there is something changeless and eternal that makes these changing descriptions possible, but what this is must remain forever unknowable. As well as being popular with more mainstream philosophers the idea that ultimately all is One and that reality is composed of different aspects of that One also forms the basis of all mystical thought. Taken up by Hegel (1770-1831) the world was held to be "the manifestation or unfolding of an all-inclusive or absolute spirit realizing itself in time."

Standing opposite monism is pluralism. Traced in part to Democritus (c. 460-360), pluralism thinks of reality as consisting of an infinite number of parts, infinitely rearranging themselves in space, which is easily recognizable as the basis of Newtonian physics and is the viewpoint of modern atomic theory. Unlike monism, which looked upon reality as an unchanging eternal whole, pluristic beliefs behold a world that is incomplete and forever changing. Where monists see unity and harmony, the pluralists see struggle and discord. Such different views lead to very different ideas about the proper way to interact with one's world and with the people in it.

Where monism sees the world as essentially one and pluralism sees an infinite number of parts, dualism sees the world in terms of opposites. Where pluralism sees infinities of atoms swirling in space dualism sees matter and empty space, the material and the non-material. The classic example of dualist thought is the Tao of Chinese philosophy. According to the Taoist, all things are composed of a positive and a negative element or father and mother elements, which in combination create the extant universe. These are the famous Yin and Yang. Science too has adopted elements of dualistic thought with its division of reality into energy and matter. The dualists tend to treat the physical side and the mental side as just two more opposites with both being necessary to the act of creation.

This physical side and mental side are what we have been calling the objective and subjective sides of reality. Within philosophical thought the subjective is considered "just the mental state of conviction." The objective side is the "content of what is believed." This content is a claim or representation about some aspect of the physical that is referred to as a proposition. As an aspect of the physical a proposition, in theory, can be proven or disproved.

Whichever view is favored speculation about them tends to fall into two classes. Either emphasis is placed upon the role played by the mind or the emphasis is on things that are more material. These two points of view naturally fall into the metaphysical distinctions of idealism and realism. To the idealists the basis of reality is the mind and it is only ideas produced by the mind that make things knowable and since ideas are all you can know it is never possible to know if these ideas are accurate or not. Think back to our discussion of how the mind forms an image of a chair. What idealism says is that this image is all you can ever know about a chair.

No way says the realists. Objects exist in and of themselves apart from any mind observing them. The mind 'in here' and the objects 'out there' are two separate things. For the realist there is an objective world that exists independently of any mind. While the mind may color what it sees or put its own slant on events reality itself is not dependent upon the presence of any observer. The mind plays no part in creating what is real; it only observes what is presented to it. Reality, then, has an independent existence that the mind records like a fancy camcorder.

Followed to the end realism becomes materialism. To the materialist the basic substance underlying reality is matter. To the strict materialist there are no minds, no souls, no immortal God, no subjective reality at all. Only objective, concrete objects an events exist and to postulate the non-material is unnecessary and since it is unnecessary it would be irrational to belief it. This is not a very widely held view today.

While the sparring between the idealists and the realists goes back to the Greeks, pragmatism is a more modern approach. Principally associated with William James, pragmatism rejects any distinctions between the knower and the known. This is a system of "pure experience." Here relationships are still present; but there is no duality present, consciousness and its contents are the same thing.

Despite 2,000 years of effort, philosophy has produced no canon or theory continuing the same disagreements ad infinitum. Pragmatism was conceived as a way to break this impasse. Here the validity of a concept is tested by its practical results rather than by abstract speculation. Pragmatism is a way of settling metaphysical disputes that cannot otherwise be settled. Rather than appealing to reason disputes are settled by considering the practical consequences of one alternative to another in the life of the individual. Not generally used today it nevertheless has a direct practically that I find useful.

Before we move along there are a couple more ideas we should glance at since we will be seeing a lot of both later. These are the theories of mysticism and supernaturalism. Although grouped within philosophy technically mysticism is not a philosophy at all. A philosophy is a set of beliefs about the way the world works arrived at through the application of reason. The answers in philosophy are arrived at by thinking, but the answers in mysticism are arrived at by not thinking.

Through various mental disciplines, the mystic tries to achieve a direct union with reality that allows him to rise above the metaphysical distinctions of monism, pluralism and dualism. Technically a monism, mysticism sees ultimate reality as ineffable and the union with this nameless unity is the goal. Once this unity has been achieved, knowledge is acquired directly through intuition.

Supernaturalism identifies the ultimate substance or ground of reality with God. God or His thoughts are the substance out of which reality forms with His Divine Will being the force that sustains it. Within Western religious tradition, God is conceived as wholly transcendent, i.e. existing apart from His creation. These ideas are held in opposition to the idea of pantheism where God and His creation are One. Combine the two viewpoints and supernaturalism becomes the dominant philosophical view in the world today.

All of the theories we have dealt with so far have been ontological theories of the nature of ultimate reality. Epistemology, the other branch of philosophy, is not concerned with knowledge itself; but with the origin, nature of and limits of knowledge. Epistemology divides naturally into two rival schools called empiricism and rationalism. The empiricists believe that ultimately all ideas and concepts derive from experience. These ideas and concepts are the basis for the laws of thought, which are useful but apply to the way we think not to what we think. Or, to quote John Locke: "No mans knowledge can go beyond his experience." One's experience is all there is.

Rationalism holds that knowledge is based upon ideas and concepts that are innate with the most famous rationalist of all being Plato and his idea of "forms." Within Platonic thinking these "forms" inhabit a world of their own that is eternal, perfect, and timeless, without physical location, underlying yet independent of reality. Unchanging these forms make change possible. Reality is a manifestation of, though not identical with, the "forms", which are not a part of our experience, but exist a priori to that experience. These a priori concepts embrace, but are not bound by, logic.

Rationalism today tends to focus on the rarified heights of pure mathematics as forming that timeless world of "forms." This last viewpoint is expounded today by no less a person than Roger Penrose, the Rouse Ball Professor of Mathematics at the University of Oxford. For him the elegance and beauty of mathematical concepts are to perfect to be a mere by-product of human thought. Experiences, therefore, derive from these concepts and not the concepts from our experience.

Having trouble sorting all of this out? It is really not very hard. Throughout our whole discussion of empiricism vs. rationalism we have actually only talked about three things: 1) the mind, i.e. our conscious perceptions, 2) the physical world, and 3) Plato's world of forms. The difference between empiricism and rationalism is that rationalism recognizes all three of these concepts as being valid: while empiricism only recognizes the first two. The empiricist does not deny the idea of the concepts, but for them these concepts are a product of our thoughts rather than being a cause of those thoughts. In other words, the rationalists feel that the forms represent contact with a reality that exists a priori to, and independent from, human thought. To the empiricist these same concepts are a creation of the mind and nothing more.

Of course, the problem of the ages has always been which of these theories is right. Does monism, pluralism or dualism best reflect the true nature of reality, do the empiricists or rationalists have the better grip on reality and how do you prove it? For the problem that arises is that you run straight into the philosophical concept of skepticism. What skepticism says is that it is not possible to provide a single piece of undisputed evidence that will prove the reality of anything. This makes skepticism the philosophical equivalent of the Heisenberg Uncertainty Principle.

To see how this works lets look at three common sources of knowledge: experience, testimony and memory. Of course, a little thought will show that all of these are just different forms of experience, but we will do the conventional thing and treat them separately. Let us begin with experience; choose an experience from the common flow of events that is your life. Now try to prove that it is real. The first thing you will notice is that the only thing that any given experience can be measured against is another experience. This creates the situation where one is trying to prove the reality of one experience by using another experience. This is circular reasoning. The proposition that any given experience is real cannot be proven in this fashion.

Testimony, which is any statement made to establish a fact, frequently with some avowal of veracity attached, runs into the same problem. Trying to prove a testimony with a testimony is just as much circular reasoning as it is with experience. Therefore, of our three examples we are left with memory, which is in some ways, the most important of all. This is because almost everything we think about is a memory.

Now wait a minute, I am thinking now and these thoughts are not memories. And this is true enough, thoughts are not memories when you are thinking them, but they are memories when you think about them. 'Now' is a property of the thinking mind, a point without dimension that is the interface between the past and the future. Say the word 'now'; from the instant you finish enunciating the final 'w' it is a memory. Trying to prove a memory with a memory puts us right back on the same circular track we were on before. Moreover, since no one claims memory is completely trustworthy the uncertainty of our efforts is magnified.

But all of these things; experience, testimony and memory are all mental activities, but what about something that is not necessarily a mental process, but can be thought of as an innate part of the universe such as mathematics. After all, it is possible to prove the truth of a mathematical statement. However, is proving the truth of a mathematical equation the same as showing an objective truth? After all when you try to prove anything in mathematics from the grandest theorem to balancing your checkbook you can only do so by using mathematics itself, which leads right back to the same problem of circular reasoning that all the other examples encountered.

When it comes to using mathematics as some kind of proof of reality we are face with yet another problem. This is Gödel's theorem. The Austrian mathematician Kurt Gödel, then at the Institute of Advanced Studies at Princeton University, developed this theorem in 1931. What Dr. Gödel was able to show with his work is that it is possible for a theorem to be both true and false at the same time. This is known as Gödel's Theorem of the "excluded middle."

Note that Gödel's arguments are not saying that truth is completely inaccessible to mathematics. What this does say is that since not all propositions are provable then human insight into the true nature of reality must be greater than mathematics. This was an idea already familiar to philosophy as the Verification Principle. This principle also recognizes the fact that there are statements that can be neither proven true nor proven false. Both of these ideas are just two more indicators of the uncertainty that lies at the heart of reality, showing that the uncertainty of Heisenberg's Principle and of Schrödinger's Waves is not just a property of the quantum realm but permeates all of reality.

Remember one of the basic tenets of logic says that a proposition cannot be proven based upon an assumption. However, if the sources of knowledge are not reliable, if there is no way to prove which is true and which is false then the truth of any statement can never be proven in any absolute sense. A strict adherence to the rules of logic will lead to the conclusion that no equation, proposition or statement can ever have more than a subjective truth.

To try to illustrate the unreliability of our beliefs and the uncertainty it entails some philosophers have taken a more radical path. This is called—not surprisingly— radical skepticism. What is done is to suggest a radical hypothesis, one that cannot possibly be true, and then dare all comers to refute it. The point being that by failing to find an answer a radical rethinking of our most basic beliefs becomes necessary. The two most famous radical hypotheses are Bertrand Russell's "The Five Minute Hypothesis" and Rene Descartes' "The Demon."

The Five Minute Hypothesis asks the question what if, like a subatomic particle springing into existence out of the void, the entire universe sprang into existence just five minutes ago.

Moreover, this virtual universe is created exactly as we see it now; fossils in the ground, tree rings in the trees and that bald spot on the back of your head. Even memories are the same. If this is true then everything we think we know is wrong. There is no past at all and the entire universe is constructed quite differently than anything we have imagined. It is also a brilliant example of the pitfalls encountered when one tries to use ones experience—in this case memories—to prove another experience.

Rene Descartes "The Demon" made the same point in an earlier day. Imagine a demon with the power to influence the mind however it wishes and that this demon is directing ones actions by inducing all sensations, thoughts and experiences to lead to belief in an objective world. However, this world is a fiction, in the entire universe there is only one's self and the demon. How then, in the face of the demon, can an objective world be proven to exist since no argument can be found that can slay the demon?

This has not stopped people from trying. There have been claims over the years from one philosophical school or another that the demon has been slain. But demons are tricksters, there is no argument however brilliant the solution, however intricate the thinking or however tight the reasoning that cannot be a ploy of the demon. Since the demon resides outside of our experience, no argument based upon that experience can ever disprove its existence. The demon is immortal.

The bottom line is that in all of human knowledge there must always be an element of doubt that reason can never overcome. All of which is a direct consequence of living in a relative universe. For what skepticism, Gödel's theorem and all the rest is showing is nothing else than the relative nature of reality. To prove anything in the manner desired would require the viewpoint of a transcendent god. Ordinary mortals, bound within the confines of our own experience, will never know such truth. A truth relative to what we are experiencing is all we will ever have.

What does all of this tell us about the nature of reality? What kind of structure must the universe have to yield the observed results? If the materialists are right and the physical is all there is then it should definitely be possible to know something. After all, if the subjective side of reality is an illusion then the doubt generated by that side should also be an illusion that we can reason our way out of. Human knowledge would then be positive. The fact that thousands of years of effort has failed to prove an error in the skeptics point of view is strong evidence that no such error exists. In the end this entire squabble over the reality and complexion of truth only serves to place the ball firmly in the subjective court.

To see where this leads we will adopt a very artificial way of looking at the problem, which has the virtue of simplicity, if no other. This will give us three possible ways that reality can be structured. The materialists can be right in which case our knowledge should be positive. The idealist can be right and reality is nothing but a mental state in which our knowledge can never be positive. Or, the realists are right and the world is a mixture of the two.

Since the debate is still raging after all these years, the conclusion must be that uncertainty is a fundamental property of reality. Such a conclusion means that the first proposition cannot be correct. The idealists position yielding a subjective reality can be correct. By mixing the two the realists have created a world that has a subjective aspect, which means that it too can be correct.

However it is viewed the conclusion is inescapable that some form of subjective reality must exist. Moreover, since the mind generates subjective reality it therefore follows that the mind exists and participates in the formation of reality. This is the position arrived at almost a hundred years ago by physicists and several hundred years ago by philosophers.

During these few hundred years the main stream of philosophy has tended to converge on one of its currents. This has been a trend away from materialism toward a realization of the importance of the mind to the phenomenon called reality. From the pure idealism of Berkley (1685-1753), who held, along with the eastern sages, that reality is an illusion philosophy has come to conceive of reality as composed of both subjective and objective elements with all of these currents culminating in the work of Immanuel Kant.

The Copenhagen Interpretation was a profound insight into the true nature of reality, but it was Immanuel Kant's Transcendental Idealism, from his book *A Critique of Pure Reason*, that provides the most detailed description of the workings of the mind in creating reality. Transcendentalism is considered a very difficult philosophy to understand, a difficulty not helped by Kant's style of writing.

To begin to get a handle on what it all means perhaps the best place to start is with the term transcendental itself. Kant, himself, defined it in the following manner: "I apply the term transcendental to all knowledge which is not so much occupied with objects as with the mode of our cognition of these objects, so far as this mode of cognition is possible a priori." In English all this means is that true knowledge consists not of objects themselves, but with understanding how we know that object and just as Plato can be thought of as the embodiment of rationalism so Kant can be thought of as the embodiment of empiricism.

The Critique of Pure Reason is a work of such erudition that it is almost incomprehensible. This is the book that, when it was published, it was said that there were only ten people in the world capable of reading it and they didn't understand it. So masterly were his insights that philosophy ever since has been filled with commentaries of Kant, variations of Kant or disagreements with Kant. No philosopher since has been able to ignore him and none has surpassed him with the added problem that Wittgenstein, the Logical Positivists, the Vienna Circle and the rest now must also face the findings of modern theoretical physics.

Now it may be argued that of all philosophers past and present the choosing of Kant was an arbitrary act. That in picking Transcendental Idealism over any other system one is picking the philosophy to fit the theory. And this is why it was picked only it was not arbitrary. Transcendental Philosophy was picked because it is almost a mirror image of the Copenhagen Interpretation. In fact, the resemblance is so strong that the suspicion arises that the originators of the Copenhagen Interpretation had more than a little knowledge of the works of Kant. Of all the various schools of philosophy transcendentalism is the only one that can cite physics in its support.

Kant begins by pointing out that all we have to gather information about the world around us is our senses. And since all the senses can gather is "the mere representation of relation", all we have is the relation of one thing to another and to the thing doing the sensing. In other words, there is no fixed point of reference against which we must judge what our senses reveal. A 'thing' can only be known relative to something else, what its underlying essence is can never be known. The construction of the form of this thing is the product of the minds relationship to the object, with other objects and with the minds own mental concepts. This "mere representation" is all we can ever be know about anything.

This thing-in-itself, the whatever it is that lies behind an observation Kant called the unconditional. This unconditional thing lies beyond the range of our senses and there is no reason why it should resemble our perceptions of it in any way. In kantian thought the immediate object of perception emerges from a synthesis of the external and the internal. The external is the underlying thing-in-itself about whose true state we can know nothing. Kant called this realm of the unconditional the noumena. The internal is our perception apparatus, which we call the mind. The joining of these two creates the world we perceive. This created world is called the phenomena.

Once created these phenomena cannot be understood by the use of the intuition alone or by the use of the intellect alone, both are needed. One of the functions of the brain is to think. A thought is a discrete entity having a beginning and an end. Thoughts strung together equals thinking, which is all we have to try an understand experience. Conversely, the only thing we have to think about is our experience. Truth is then not some discovery of an outside reality, but is true by its "coherence" with the system of thought—i.e. the paradigm. This paradigm is not an objective array of facts standing outside our thoughts, but thought itself made real.

For the mind to function it must employ fundamental concepts. Kant called these basic concepts "categories." These categories are things like substance, quality, quantity, causality or relationships. Everything flows from these categories. These concepts act as the template that allows the mind to create the phenomena out of the noumena. Kant's concept of the categories is then very similar to Plato's idea of forms with the difference being that Kant does not grant his categories any innate existence.

Within Kantian thought space and time are neither absolute nor relative properties of things-in-themselves. The outer world—the noumena—cause only "the matter of sensation", while the mind, by using these concepts, brings about order.

Space and time themselves are not substances, however, and cannot be described by these categories; they are rather a part of our "apparatus of perception." Space and time (and yes entropy too) is then a by-product of the way the mind works. Whether the mind was created within space and time, or whether space and time were created within the mind becomes a meaningless question. Whichever is true all experience must conform to the characteristics as expressed by space and time.

If space and time are neither absolute nor relative properties of the unconditional does this mean that they are unreal? For Kant (agreeing with Roger Penrose) the mathematics that dealt with space and time were a priori. The mathematics of space and time are not part of our experience, yet we can have no experience without them.

Space and time are, therefore, empirically real, but transcendentally ideal. If we delete the mind then space and time disappear. Space and time can only be experienced as phenomena. Their true nature being unknowable space and time can only exist in us. We may think of space and time as 'out there' independent of our experience, but Kant did not. To him they are "forms of understanding and therefore forms of intuition." It is these "forms of intuition", i.e. space, time and the categories that, when applied to the noumena, produce the everyday world we live in.

By showing the importance of the mind we return to the age-old question of whether the world exists apart from our thoughts. Kant's answer is "if we use the concepts we must deploy the categories. If we deploy the categories we must assume the distinction between how things are and how they seem. If we make that distinction we commit ourselves to an objective reality and aim our discourse towards it. Even to deny the existence of reality is to think, and therefore to assume its existence. In other words although there is no way to prove that the world exists we must act 'as if' it does. We must "believe without believing"[5] and when we've done that we've done all we can do.

If a tree falls in the forest and there is no one to hear does it make a sound? This little phrase is many peoples only brush with Immanuel Kant and his theories. Here is transcendentalisms most famous conclusion. If the logic of the theory is followed to the end then the conclusion must be reached that, as we live in an observer created world, nothing can be proven to exist when it is not being observed, although it should be noted that the theory does not actually say that nothing exists when it is not being observed. What it says is that there is no way to prove its existence.

What Transcendental Idealism has shown is the role of the observer in forming the world we live in. To Kant a thing can only be realized in relation to some other thing. Things exist only as relationships and it is for this reason that the thing behind it is forever unknowable. This is relativity theory practically word for word. In fact, to understand Kantian thought requires the same level of intellectual effort needed to understand modern physics. Moreover, the fact that three such diverse lines of thought all converge on the same point is strong evidence for its validity. This is circumstantial evidence, to be sure. But, like the "trout in the milk bucket" it is hard to ignore.

With the works of Immanuel Kant the search for the origins of everyday reality reached its peak. His theories have been chewed up, mulled over, criticized and modified, but not overthrown. Philosophy since has moved on to what is essentially an analysis of the phenomena, what we today would call the paradigm. It is this analysis that has produced most of modern philosophy. Nevertheless, on the question of where the

---

[5] Carlos Castaneda

paradigm comes from Kant still rules. Moreover, all of this is not just an interesting intellectual word game. As we will see the consequences in ones daily life can be very far reaching. It is time then to move on to the paradigm, what it is and what it can do. As we leave the works of Kant to take up this question you might pause for just a second and glance into the branches of that tree that fell in the forest. If you're very quick, you just might catch a glimpse of the smile of Schrödinger's cat as it slowly fades away.

The Two Hands of God

Two Zen monks were out for a stroll. As they walked along a flag, fluttering in the breeze arrested their attention. One monk said, "Look at that flag waving in the wind." The other monk shook his head, "No, your wrong, the flag isn't waving it is the wind that is waving." The first monk stuck to his guns and an intense argument ensued. Finally, they appealed the question to the abbot. This worthy listened patiently and then delivered his answer, "You are both wrong, it is the mind that is waving."

Everything we have talked about up to now has only served to show the importance that must be attached to the observer. The role of the mind is so inescapable that the eminent physicist John Wheeler has proposed changing the word 'observer' to "participator." Moreover, the interactions of this participator extend across all of reality. On this the philosophers and the physicists agree.

When we think of objective reality it is normal to think of the solid, material, physical world in front of our eyes as that objective reality. In a participator world our perceptions of any object is a combination of the incoming sensory data and our mental conceptions. Analogous to the Hindu concept of maya, it is the mathematical world of space-time and the subjective activities of the mind working in concert that create this three-dimensional picture that we call objective reality. Objective reality and the paradigm then become synonymous.

And the interesting thing to notice is that there is no necessity for one person's mental contribution to be exactly the same as someone else's. Each of us brings our own unique set of experiences and memories along with possible variations in our understanding of the categories themselves. Still since each person's experiences are based upon the same underlying reality, a constraint is place upon how widely these two pictures

91

can differ. But differ they can and in a relative universe neither is, a priori, invalid.

Interesting but what has this to do with me? A great deal as it turns out. The importance lies in the fact that different worldviews hold different possibilities. Very useful when one is trying to decide on the best course of action. To understand how this can be it must be understood that each of these differing viewpoints is just as 'real' as any other. For now it is enough to realize that increasing the number of viewpoints increases the number of choices available and this can have serious implications for how we relate to each other and how we should live our lives.

Democritus declared that the world we perceive is only "conventionally true." The everyday world is not formed from reasoned argument nor rational thought, neither is it true in any independent sense, but is only true by custom. Belief, filtered through the sieve of biological survival becomes the customs of society.

By Roman times Seneca (4 B.C.-A.D.65) had developed this idea into the concept of the paradigm, although he did not call it that. The most common analogy used to try to clarify the idea of a paradigm has been that of a map. However, for the modern mind, a DVD player may prove more useful. Here the DVD disc stands in for space-time with all possible events—past, present and future—stored in it. The mind then becomes the beam scanning the disc. As the beam moves across the disc a picture springs onto the television screen only to fade back onto the disc as the beam passes by.

All the information needed to create the movie is on the disc, but it is inaccessible until the beam scans it. Only while the beam is focused on it does a meaningless jumble of encoded information assume recognizable form. And while it is conventional to scan the disc in a certain order, there is no necessity to do so. This order of scanning can then be likened to the conventions of society. In this way the proper picture is generated. This analogy becomes even more useful if we add the idea of the hologram from chapter one.

When faced with probabilities the mind must choose. It does this by focusing its attention on one and ignoring the other. However, the mind does not stop at experiencing; it also talks about what it has experienced. A dialogue develops with other people, observations are made and opinions given. Different perceptions by different people are mulled over until a consensus is reached as to which is the proper way to think. Once this occurs the possibility of choosing one or the other is no longer 50-50. Convention has been established, seeing the world as the group sees it will be rewarded and anything else will be discouraged. The plane will fly past the airport and not the airport past the plane. And it is this general understanding of what is real that will be taught to the children. A paradigm has been created.

When the first paradigm began to distill out of early hominid minds the underlying forces driving it were not rational thought or scientific understanding, but folklore. Included in this are myths, legends, folktales, fables, superstitions, ballads, proverbs and parables. This living tradition stretches from the shadowy past to today's technological society. It is here that the concepts underlying all societies are found and it is here that our world took shape. Codified into the paradigm they have become the map that guides us through life.

Of course, humans are not the only beings that think. Any mobile organism must be presumed to think at least to the degree necessary to control its movements and anytime thought appears some sort of paradigm must be postulated as well. Although the less the mental powers the less rich and varied will be the paradigm. With their more complex brains, human beings should have the most complex paradigms. All of which is postulated on the premise that there is something special about the human mind.

Remember that the human brain is based upon the same DNA and is a product of the same evolution as any other mammalian brain. As a mammal people have a brain whose physiology is not fundamentally different from any other mammal's brain. Yet it cannot be denied that man is different. The human mind is capable of feats of which other animals cannot even dream. Debate about what this difference is has a long history and—so far—no answer.

Homo sapiens—Man the Wise—so mankind has named itself. If there is one thing that humans have always gloried in it is their perceived mental superiority. And humanity can, with some justification, take pride in its mental prowess. What other creature can boast of creating language or science? What other creatures can boast at all? This same power has allowed the human race to colonize every available niche and to become the dominant force on the planet.

Recent studies of animal behavior have shown that the gap separating us from them is not as great as was once imagined. Yet even this smaller gap is still unbridgeable. To appreciate just how absolute this gap is it is only necessary to look at the closest equivalent to humans, the so-called signing apes. These unfortunate creatures—usually chimpanzees, although other species have not escaped altogether—have been subjected to experiments designed to teach them to speak. Since their morphology precludes ordinary speech they are usually taught either one of the sign languages for the deaf or to form words and sentences by punching symbols on a keyboard. And some of their accomplishments have been remarkable.

But it must be remembered that all of these accomplishments, be it learning the words and syntax of language or generating original sentences came about through the prompting of their human captors. No chimpanzee, gorilla or orangutan has ever achieved any of these things spontaneously. Even Kanzi—the most accomplished of all—is still many orders of magnitude removed from an Einstein or a Newton.

For many years the ability to make and use tools was considered the dividing line. Field studies of chimpanzees dashed this idea. In the wild chimps were found to be quite capable of making and using simple tools. Even some species of birds have now been found to be toolmakers. So if not tools what about brain size? Surely, the one thing that sets humanity apart is the size of the brain. But, of course, this all depends upon what is meant by brain size.

If by brain size you mean absolute size by weight then the smartest creature on earth would be the sperm whale. And if you mean the ratio of brain size to body weight the winner would be the mouse. OK, then how about language, surely this is the one unique property of which humans can boast. Well maybe, but there are other species with quite elaborate means of communicating with other members of their species, so whether mankind's linguistic abilities are all that special really depends upon how language is defined.

Although language itself may not be unique, it can be argued that humans have developed it to the point that it may legitimately be considered as a defining characteristic. For humans language is more than just a mechanism for intraspecies communication, it is an expression of mankind's ability to reason symbolically. And it is this ability to use symbols—to think abstractly—that many regard as the true defining characteristic. Yet even here the old saw "beasts abstract not" is not completely true. Dolphins and whales have been shown to have the ability to reason abstractly, as have the great apes.

Chimpanzees—besides their tool making talents— even have shown signs of self-awareness. In fact, the more we learned about chimpanzee's abilities and social life the more they begin to look like our own.

Still, while man may not be the only animal that can think symbolically humans have carried this ability far beyond that of any other species. And it is in this quantitative and qualitative superiority that the dividing line between humans and animals occurs. Of course, in achieving this level of activity brain size played a role. All available evidence indicates that before a mind can begin to think abstractly a certain size is needed, but more is needed than just size. To develop its full potential a mind also needs a certain structure. Complex thought requires complex physiology.

The most unique feature about the structure of the human brain is that it is, in a sense, split in two. Or, more accurately, the cerebral cortex, the thinking part of the brain, is divided into right and left hemispheres. So well developed is this asymmetry that it can be seen while still in the womb. In fact, humans can almost be thought of as having two brains.

These hemispheres have a cross-court connection with the body. The left hemisphere controls the right side of the body, while the right hemisphere controls the left. This placing of the control centers in the brain as far away as possible from whatever it is that is being controlled is a common feature. The region that controls the feet, for instance, is situated at the top of the brain, while vision is processed in the rear. What the significance of this is—if any— is unknown.

The two hemispheres do more than just control the body, however. The left hemisphere is verbal, logical and practical. It deals with the rational aspects of reality. The right side is intuitive, spatial and artistic. It specializes in realties intuitive aspects. And the interesting thing about these two brains is that, under certain circumstances, they can operate independently from each other.

This has been demonstrated in people who have—for medical reasons—had the connection between the two sides severed. When this happens the two sides will go right ahead experiencing the world individually, although since language is confined to the left hemisphere it is the only one who can talk about those experiences. In this situation, one hand can—literally—not know what the other hand is doing.

Humanity's ability to think, while unique in complexity, is a natural outgrowth of mammalian brain evolution. Traced backward it is easy to show that the more primitive an organism the more primitive its mental processes. Such simple reactions are considered nothing more than pure instinct. Yet, once again, things are not that simple. Instinct is defined as an inherited habit or reaction that occurs spontaneously in a completely mindless fashion, but how often have you heard of instincts being associated with plants.

When a sunflower turns its head towards the sun it is considered a straightforward chemical-physiological reaction. A single cell organism moving toward the light is hardly more complex although its actions would be more likely to be described as a reflex action. By the time cellular complexity has risen to the level of a moth reflex action no longer seems an adequate description. When a moth comes to a flame, the term instinct now seems more appropriate with the difference being that the moth has a brain—such as it is. Moreover, what a creature with a brain has that plants and microbes do not are emotions. This then is the difference between a reflex action and an instinct. For emotions are the vehicles by which instinct functions.

To see this in action one has to look no further than good old fashion sex. Sex is one of the primary instincts being, in some cases, even more powerful than the instinct for survival. Now think about the last time you meant an interesting person at a party. Did you think, "I am required to procreate and this person seems suitable." No, there was something about this person you liked, their looks or personality. There was an attraction; maybe even love and the sex act flowed from those emotions. The same is true for any sentient being be it mouse, moose or mallard duck. Emotions are the psyches expression of instincts.

When a deer runs from a cougar, this is a natural result of the instinct of self-preservation. However, the deer is not a mindless automaton; it runs from the lion because it feels fear. The advantage such an arrangement gives the organism is that instincts are more flexible than reflex actions and when emotions became conceptualized thought had its beginnings. Just as thinking increases the choices available over emotions alone so emotions give instinct more varied responses. The whole of the evolutionary process results in the brain increasing its ability to make choices.

According to the anthropologists while human ancestors of 150,000 years ago were anatomically human certain traits one would expect to find in a fully developed human being were missing, art being one of those things. While there are some objects d'art from earlier than 50,000 years ago, they are few and far between and in many cases equivocal. Another of the things that was not quite right was tools. Early humans had tools, to be sure, but for at least 100,000 years their tool kit was very standardized and invariant. It just did not show the inventiveness that one would expect from a fully-fledged human being. From this, we can infer that the ability to think had not yet reached modern levels. Then, at about 50,000 years ago art, diverse tools, body ornamentation, elaborate burials and all the other things we associate with minds like ours appeared.

This can only mean that at approximately 50,000 years ago some critical threshold was passed. Some key piece of the puzzle clicked into place and modern man was born. And the only thing that could possibly have produced this was some sort of a mutation. Before this mutation people could think. They had abstract thoughts and some sort of self-awareness; but this awareness was not fully developed, they were still less than modern humans.

After this mutation fully developed language, tool making, art, all the things, in fact, put forward as the definition of a human being were in place. Of course, it is possible that each of these features had a separate origin, but in the spirit of Bishop Occam, it seems more reasonable to postulate one. This single mutation pushed the mind over the top and all the rest followed. Whatever this mutation was it must have expressed itself on the physiological level and this could be considered as the defining trait of mankind.

This last evolutionary step to modern man has been called a "fortuitous mutation." So what could this fortuitous mutation have been? Humans have a brain build on the standard mammalian model. What evidence there is seems to indicate that this splitting of the brain goes back to the very beginning, so far that it is possible that even dinosaurs had it. One is tempted to wonder, however, if this split was complete. Did a dinosaur's brain work just like ours or was it only with mankind that the double truth appears. If so it then becomes tempting to wonder if this was not the fortuitous mutation.

Could the final splitting of the brain into symmetrical hemispheres be the crucial mutation that lifted man to the top? Did the interplay between the rational left and the intuitive right produce the final step toward abstract thinking on a grand scale? Did it accomplish this by elevating the objective thinking abilities of the mind to a par with the subjective abilities? Or is a divided brain just a more efficient way of organizing neural tissue? Whatever the explanation it worked, no other creature has it and no other creature can think like a man. It was with this mutation that man became "man the wise."

Among many religious and mystical traditions the beginning of reality is not the formation of a substance, but the formation of opposites. The relative universe begins with the appearance of the positive and negative, the mother and father, the Yin and Yang, being and non-being. The tendency to explain the world in terms of opposites became the philosophy of dualism. This idea of opposites—what Alan Watts called the "the two hands of God"—is a valid and insightful idea that finds its origins in the very structure of the brain.

The net result of all of this was to give humans a much greater range of options. This is the advantage of intelligence, exercise your prerogative to choose and you become more human, do not use it and you become less so. Couple this with a greater memory capacity and the result is a more highly developed picture of the world. Such a universe has a structure and objects have meanings unimaginable to an animal. All of which is predicated on an enhanced ability to make choices. Differing viewpoints are now possible and with differing viewpoints different paradigms emerge.

At 50,000 years ago the human brain was as large as it is now. At the dividing line it did not get any bigger, what it did was reorganize. The morphological differences between a human and an early human are not overall brain size and it is not brain to body ratio, it is structure. This was something new upon the planet. The basic engine had been retooled to give more power and a new force had been let loose upon the earth.

The Golden Thread

All of these advances in mental powers find a reflection in language, which can be thought of as the external manifestation of thinking with the rise of language and the rise of thought being parallel. This connection is so intimate that it is very difficult to even conceive of thinking in the absence of words. It is no coincidence that the structure of reality and the structure of language so closely mirror each other. The simple act of giving everything a name allows for a more rich and varied understanding of that thing and its place in nature. This cannot help but find expression in the construction of the paradigm. The richer the internal thoughts are the richer will be the paradigm these thoughts produce. It was no accident that the first thing Adam did was to give everything a name.

To understand this better imagine a man and an antelope standing side-by-side looking out across the African savanna. Now we will ask the question, what does the man see and what does the antelope see? Before proceeding, we must admitted that it is difficult enough knowing what is in the mind of another person let alone an antelope. However, since both are based upon the same DNA and have been subjected to the same evolutionary process we will assume that what they see is similar.

And what is the man seeing? Not much. As he looks out across the veldt he sees grass bending in the wind and a few trees scattered here and there, nothing else is in sight. Now what does the antelope see? First off it does not see 'grass' or 'trees' since it has no concept of either and without these concepts there is no reason to suppose that it differentiates between them. The same is true of the wind. The antelope can see the grass moving, it can feel the breeze, but the idea of 'wind' has never occurred to it. The antelope experiences its world, it knows to eat grass and to watch the trees for leopards but it does not think about any of these things. The very thing that humans do unceasingly—the internal dialogue describing and categorizing the world—the antelope does not do at all.

Without an internal dialogue it can have no concept of self and with no concept of self the antelope will not differentiate between what is 'in here' and what is 'out there'. The antelope will have no idea of a consciousness looking out of its eyes. The man, on the other hand, does have such ideas. He will see himself as in the world, while the antelope will experience the world as a totality of which it is a part. This is such a fundamentally different way of looking at reality that it is no wonder that humans have such a tough time imaging what is going on in an animal's head.

An animal's mind cannot be thought of as just an uneducated human mind. Perhaps the closest anyone can get to seeing the world as an animal sees it can be found in the dream state. More closely resembling the world of magic than the skeptically rational, this state is described by Carl Sagan in the *Dragons of Eden* (Random House, 1977) in the following way:

> . . . *waking states of other mammals is very much like the dream state of humans---where we can recognize <u>signs</u>, such as the feeling of running water and the smell of honeysuckle, but have an extremely limited repertoire of <u>symbols</u> such as words: when we encounter vivid sensory and emotional images and active intuitive understanding, but very little rational analysis; where we are unable to perform tasks requiring extensive concentration; where we experience short attention spans and frequent distractions and, most of all, a very feeble sense of individuality or self, which gives way to a pervading fatalism, a sense of unpredictable buffeting by uncontrollable events.*

A beautiful description of how a mind lacking fully developed consciousness interacts with its environment, this is the world as the subconscious mind experiences it. Remember, this subconscious part of the mind creates the paradigm. The paradigm is then a consequence of thinking and not of consciousness per se. This is the reason that creatures without consciousness still have a paradigm.

A paradigm is a way of structuring reality. As the design of a building determines what use it can put to so the design of a paradigm determines what use it can be put to. Whatever shape a paradigm takes all have one thing in common. All valid paradigms have a clearly defined set of implications and laws. Like different systems of geometry each is self-consistent and perfectly logical within its own rules. Just as the universe can be described as concave, convex or flat depending upon which system of geometry is being used so the questions that can be answered and the goals that can be reached will vary within the different paradigms.

One trait that all paradigms share is that each considers itself the only valid way of viewing reality so that everything must conform to its rules. Within these paradigms—or modes of being—certain questions can be answered and certain goals accomplished while any that falls outside of these rules are considered either irrelevant or impossible. So basic is this tendency for one paradigm to regard all others as illusions that this may be considered the primary rule governing their operation.

True enough that different modes offer different possibilities, but there is an important limit to what is or is not possible within each of these modes. It is not possible to do anything in one mode that will disprove the claims of any other mode. An ordinary road map and the one used by geologists look very different, but they all must reflect the same mountains and the same oceans.

This is just one more example of the fact that we live in a relative universe without any preferred point of view. Relativity theory has shown quite clearly that it is possible for two people to look at the same thing and to get two different answers. The length of a ruler is whatever you measure it to be and in this truth lays the origins of the paradigm. Just as it is not possible for our two observers, measuring the length of a ruler as it flashes past, to prove that the other is wrong, so it is not possible for one paradigm to prove another wrong. And the reason this is so is that the other is not wrong, there is no right and wrong only measurements. To see how this works out in real life lets turn to yet another example, this time we will look at the phenomenon of levitation.

There are stories coming out of many different schools of mystical training of adepts who can—by putting their minds into a trance—levitate off the ground. Within the mode of reality in use today this is a flat out impossibility. Yet sages of saintly disposition and impeccable character say that, on rare occasions, it does occur. I am not prepared to call these men liars so we will assume some phenomenon does occur that can be interpreted as levitation. Whatever this phenomenon may be the second rule says that it will never be possible to perform it in such a way so as to prove or disprove its reality. Nothing overt will be involved; circumstance will simply arrange themselves so that no one point of view is more valid than another. The relative nature of reality will come into play in such a way that science will never be able to prove that levitation doesn't occur and the mystic will never be able to prove that it does.

But of course, science can disprove levitation. Nothing could be easier than devising an experiment to prove just that, should one be so addlebrained as to disbelieve the mathematics. But the problem science faces is that it can only reach conclusions by applying its own rules. Just like the philosophers before them, when scientist use the methods of science to prove the conclusions of science they are dealing in circular reasoning. What has been shown is not that levitation is impossible under all circumstances only that it is impossible under these circumstances. As a valid paradigm this mode has shown itself to be self-consistent. Relativity prevents the conclusions of one mode from disproving another by using the rules of that mode. There are no preferred points of view all modes are equal.

OK, so what are all these different modes of reality we keep talking about? There are many variations, but they all tend to fall into four main divisions. In his book, *Alternate Realities* (Ballantine, 1976) Lawrence LeShan gives the following list:

1) The Clairvoyant Modes of Being
2) The Sensory Modes of Being
3) The Transpsychic Modes of Being
4) The Mythic Modes of Being

This is a useful list. However, Dr. LeShan said later that if he had it to do over again he would have called the clairvoyant mode the flow-process mode of being or the mystical mode of being. He felt that by using the term clairvoyant he was giving to much importance to what is really a minor feature of this mode. We will adopt this idea and hereafter the clairvoyant mode will be referred to as the mystical mode of being.

Each of these modes will rate chapters of their own; here they will be discussed in the most general of terms. If, as the cabalists say, reality osculates between two poles then the mystic and the sensory modes might be thought of as those two poles. The mystic mode would represent the illusionary intuitive side of reality, while the sensory mode represents the solid rational side, all and nothing if you will. All paradigms have their base in one or the other or some combination of the two. Being the only two means by which the mind can understand reality it can be no other way.

Reality as understood intuitively yields the mystical mode of being. Here there are no individual objects or events; there is only the total fabric of being. Since all things are part of a single whole boundaries do not exist, either in space or in time. Any attempt to divide events into individual 'happenings' is an error. Here valid information is gained through revelation not through the senses, which by dividing reality into parts paints a false picture. It is into this realm that the great saints enter. Sheltered within this mode can be found the greatest men and women the human race has ever produced. Here we find people like Jesus and Buddha, beings so great that they are not even considered to be human.

At the opposite extreme, the sensory mode represents the rational pole. The realm of classical science, here there is no totality of being only objects and events. Space has structure and time flows forever onward. All events happen in space and time. An event can occur only by direct interaction of objects or forces. This is the realm of logic; here a thing exists only if it, or some effect it generates, can be directly measured. Primarily responsible for biological survival this realm has given us such benefits as television, airplanes and easy spread butter. This is the dominant mode of being in the world today.

Midway between the mystical and the sensory modes lays the mythic mode of being. The worldview of the shaman and the hunter-gatherer this is a place where logic does not apply, within this mode can be found the play of children, magic and the occult sciences. What is 'in here' cannot be differentiated from what is 'out there'. Here the connection between thing and events is not cause and effect; here all events are governed by a specific act of will. If two things are connected in the mind then space cannot separate them and anything that affects one affects both. Power is exercised through the will and to gain power is the goal of the magician. It is through the power of their wills that the witchdoctor and the wizard seek to control their worlds. This is probably the oldest mode of being in existence.

The transpsychic mode of being is similar to the mythic mode only with more logic. It is within this mode that religion has its origins. Here all things are separated into individual objects, but are so connected that they may be considered One. Each object is separate enough to know its own wishes, but connected enough to communicate those wishes to the whole. Here space and time exist, but are unimportant. Since all parts are connected what is done to one is done to all. It follows that anything that disrupts this harmony is bad and from this flows ethics and morals. Within this mode lies great power that can—through devotion and single-mindedness of purpose—be brought to bear on life's problems.

In looking at each of these ways of viewing reality we see that each is associated with a particular discipline. These represent the major ways that humans look at their world. By pairing everyday concepts to their respective modes it becomes easier to understand how each is related to daily life. Let us recap our list:

1) The Mystical Modes of Being - Mysticism
2) The Sensory Modes of Being - Science
3) The Transpsychic Modes of Being - Religion
4 The Mythic Modes of Being - Magic

Put like this it can be seen that these modes are not just some esoteric play on words. These modes represent the underlying thought patterns upon which all of human society and all of human culture is based.

All well and good but what does all this have to do with me? I'm a practical person with a family to raise and bills to pay. How can shifting from one view of reality to another help me? How can shifting from one mode to another make something real that was not real before? And even if all this where possible how does one go about making such a shift?

In trying to explain this Lawrence LeShan used the analogy of the boardwalk and I think we cannot do better, although in fairness I should say that my use may not be the same as his. Imagine a large circular, enclosed area surrounded by a boardwalk with four viewing portals spaced an equal distance from each other. The view the boardwalk encloses is the everyday middle dimensional world with each portal representing one of the modes of being. In keeping with the primary rule each of these four viewing portals considers itself the only valid place to stand.

Now imagine that directly in front of the portal where you are standing is a large hill. And on the other side of this hill—completely hidden form view—is a target with a bull's eye painted on it. If someone where to hand you a rifle and ask you to shoot the bull's eye you would find it an impossible task since you regard your present point of view as the only one possible. You might even argue that the target does not exist at all. However, by shifting your point of view—by walking around to the opposite side—it now becomes possible to hit the target. What was impossibility is now easily and the secret to the whole thing was just to realize that it was possible to shift ones perspective.

All normal people are capable of making these shifts to a certain degree; which, in most cases, they do so easily and naturally that they are completely unaware it is even happening.

When speaking of shifting paradigms it must be realized that paradigms divide into two forms. There is your personal paradigm unique to you and the larger paradigm of the society in which you live. All personal paradigms are found within one of the larger modes of knowing, which offer room for spontaneity in ones personal variations.

Although long known these differences in personal paradigms are more commonly described as simply a difference in attitudes. Most of us know—to our disgust—one of those positive type people who succeed at whatever they try without seeming to put forth the least effort and a negative type person who never seems to win no matter what. OK, so one of them is lucky and the other is not. But, then what is luck; what is there about one person that brings luck that another person doesn't have.

And what luck is is a function of your personal paradigm; the lucky ones picture themselves as winners. The three-dimensional hologram in their minds creates a world in which they are lucky. This is the secret of those self-help tapes you listen to on the way to work. They have many approaches, but what they are all trying to do is to get you to picture yourself as a winner. If you can change the paradigm to one in which you are a winner you will be a winner. Winners picture themselves as winners and all reality conforms to this belief. This is also a good demonstration of the fact that all of this is not just some clever play on words. The world, as created by the mind, is the world we live in.

Understand, however, that while we can shift from one mode to another not all modes will be given the same weight. The average person is raised within one of the paradigms. The emphasis in your family may have been on science or it may have been the church. Whichever it will form the underlying beliefs of your life. Learning a paradigm is very similar to learning language were the child picks up the language it hears spoken around it. For the adult, however, learning a new language is a long and difficult process and no matter now many tongues you learn your native tongue will always feel the most natural. In just the same way what may be called your native paradigm will always be your most natural way of viewing the world.

So how does one shift modes? It is not that hard, most people are able to shift between modes and not even be aware of having moved. Think of the busy executive, her working day spent making decisions—the sensory mode—for her company. Her evenings are spent in the backyard playing—the mythic mode—with her children. Or, perhaps, she relaxes by meditating—the mystic mode—or reading the Bible—the transpsychic mode. Each of these activities requires a shift in perspective, yet the executive does it so easily and naturally that she is completely unaware that any shift has taken place.

Shifts in paradigms can occur in other ways as well. Many people have had the experience of trying to solve a problem for which the solution just will not come. You wrack your brain for hours and nothing, and then at some point you lose consciousness of self. When the self disappears so does the boundary that separates you from the rest of reality. The pluralistic universe disappears and only the whole is left.

Now, seemingly without effort the answer appears. This state of mind is productive, but ephemeral. Any intrusion of ordinary thought and it is gone, but while it lasts it is great. Afterward you are left with feelings of exhilaration and accomplishment. Or, perhaps, you are sitting in church, your mind only partly following the sermon, when suddenly you are filled with feelings of exaltation and a union with something greater than you are. Both of these experiences represent a shift in paradigms. These experiences—and more like them—are the common lot of all mankind.

While shifting between modes is easy on a superficial level to fully utilize any of these modes requires one to be fully immersed in it and to believe absolutely that it is true. To try consciously to learn a new paradigm, in the sense that it is now the primary guide for one's life, requires extensive training. Think of the years of struggle required for the yogi to find Samadhi, the Buddhist to find Nirvana or the Christian to find the Kingdom of Heaven. For all the path is long and the way is hard and in the fierceness of the struggle needed to learn a new paradigm the hold the old paradigm has on us is clearly shown.

To delve deeper into the implications of these perceptual shifts it will be necessary to look more closely at just what each paradigm is saying. This is complicated by the fact that not all paradigms have been studied with equal thoroughness. In addition, it is not uncommon for one mode to be confused with another mode. Untangling all of this will be the subject of the next few chapters.

The Technological Imperative

The physicist Robert W. Wood was once asked to offer a reply to the toast, "To physicists and metaphysicists." His answer was that it "is not that the practitioners of one are smarter than the practitioners of the other. The difference is that the metaphysicist has no laboratory." Science does indeed have a laboratory, but this laboratory is not a place it is rather the whole approach of observation and experiment that is the hallmark of science. Traditionally this approach and the mind-set it engenders have found its most complete expression within the bounds of the sensory modes of being. Adapted, as it is, to answering questions beginning with the word 'how' the sensory mode of being is the paradigm most homologous with scientific thought.

As has been said, science is a method not a philosophy. So what is this scientific method? Ideally, the process works something like this. A scientist will begin by identifying a problem that he feels is important enough to warrant his attention. Once the problem to be studied has been decided upon the next step is to formulate a hypothesis. A hypothesis is simply a tentative explanation of the problem and provides a base for further investigation. To be of value the hypothesis must make a prediction about some unknown fact or behavior that is testable.

Once the hypothesis has been postulated and predictions made it is time to devise an experiment to test it. The correctness of the prediction now either validates or invalidates the hypothesis. The more correct predictions that can be derived from the hypothesis the more likely it is to be correct. For it to have any meaning in a scientific sense the results of this experiment must be repeatable. Repeatability is the essence of

<u>science</u>. No conclusion can be accepted that cannot stand up to repeat testing.

If a paradigm is looked upon as a genes attempt to insure personal survival then the sensory mode must be looked upon as the most successful mode of all from a biological point of view. Seen in this way the different paradigms become evolutionary attempts to construct more efficient worldviews to increase reproductive success. The four modes we shall look at have been nature's answer to this challenge.

It goes without saying that each of these paradigms must be valid and functional in their own right or they would not have survived until the present day. This is not to say that one mode is better than another is in any absolute sense, but, rather, that one mode is more efficient under certain conditions of culture and levels of knowledge than are others. As human societies have evolved forms that are more complex based on greater levels of knowledge the paradigm has evolved along with it.

As we have seen, right up to the beginning of the Twentieth Century thinking was considered synonymous with rational thought. This has been shown not to be the case yet it persists in lay thinking about the workings of the mind. The rational part of this thinking process has been codified into the rules of formal logic. Which along with the logic of mathematics—which strictly speaking is not identical— is the foundation for the sensory modes view of the world.

This classical view of nature is a pluralistic one based upon the idea of solid bodies moving in empty space, a deterministic world governed by precise mathematical equations. Physical reality exists independently of the human mind. This thing called 'mind' is a consequence of the morphology and physiology of the brain and nothing more while the world is ruled by consistent, unvarying natural laws. This is the common sense world of everyday life, the Leberswelt of Edmund Husserl (1859-1938).

All of this is predicated upon a belief in an objective reality. Here an object or event has to be observable, for without this it is not testable. To be real a thing or event must be available upon demand, which allows it to be quantified, measured and subjected to experimentation. By so doing the criteria for what is considered real is set. Anything that does not possess the necessary qualities to meet these conditions must be—by definition—unreal.

It does not take very much experience in life to realize that many things that the average person would consider both real and important do not meet these conditions with God being a good example. God cannot be quantified, He does not occupy space and no one—at least since Moses—has actually seen Him. Moreover, this is true of the entire subjective side of reality, none of which can be proven by the scientific method. Any individual scientist can and will have their own personal opinion on any of these questions, but science, as a body, can have nothing to say. Science deals with only that segment of reality encompassed by the sensory mode with other paradigms being responsible for the rest.

Take the case of a rising young doctor who is studying a particularly disagreeable disease. This illness causes great pain and suffering and has no cure. After years of labor a medicine is developed that will prolong the life of the patient indefinitely, what it will not do is relief any of the symptoms, the patient suffers just as much as ever. Ask the question of how to determine correct dosage or side effects and there is nothing better than the scientific method. If, however, the question of should this medicine be given is ask science has nothing to say. This question is simply not amendable to the scientific method. Religion, on the other hand, can provide an answer to this question. It has nothing to say about drug performance or procedures, but it can provide an answer on a moral question. A very powerful method for studying nature science has its limits.

Still to give the impression that scientists are rigid hidebound materialists oblivious to all but the tenets of the sensory mode of being would be completely unfair for scientists have done some of the most brilliantly innovative thinking of the last century. This thinking has changed the way we view the universe in a profound way and forms the basis for our present discussion.

What the Church was to the Middle Ages science is to our own time. Almost every attribute that characterizes the modern world is a product of science. The results of all of this rational, logical, left-brain activity have been an outpouring of new products and services without precedent in history. Although your household may lack slaves and body servants from the point of view of medical care, nutrition, entertainment opportunities and ease of travel people today live at a level unimaginable to the ancients.

Advances in medicine and agriculture have probably saved more lives than have been lost in all the wars ever fought. While 30 years of age was a good life for a Roman life expectancy today is now pushing 80. Supersonic aircraft whisk people anywhere in the world, while the Internet may make the journey unnecessary. In today's world the average person, living in a developed country, lives better than kings did in the past, this is no small achievement.

During the last century science completed the job of ousting the Church from the top rung of the ladder. The Church is still very much with us, but it is no longer the final authority on all matters. If you doubt this begin to count how many times you run across the phrase "scientists say" in magazines, newspapers or on the airwaves. Now try counting the number of times the Church is quoted as the final authority. Even in areas where it has no special expertise science is still expected to supply the answers.

Only information obtained through the senses is valid, hence the sensory mode. Ideas may be generated through mathematics and reason, but they only become valid when some proof is offered to the senses. A cause must precede any event or effect. No event can occur without a cause and since intuition cannot be shown to have a cause it must be, by definition, non-existent.

Space and time exist and all events occur within them. Objects in space have a definite shape governed by the rules of geometry. All physical objects must obey these rules. That the cause must precede the effect gives time a direction, events in the past can be remembered, they cannot be changed. Future events can theoretically be changed.

Boundaries separate each event or object into individual events or objects unconnected to each other. Any event separated by space is a separate event just as any event separated by time is a separate event. Any interaction between objects or events must be due to contact, either of the objects directly or by forces produced by the objects. The universe is composed of parts that, in turn, have smaller parts. These parts can be dealt with separately or they can be arranged into groups and classes that also function as parts. The world as experienced in the sensory mode is a pluralistic reality of bits and pieces where no object is greater than the sum of its parts.

Perfect for manipulating the material world it is through the production of material goods and not by the acquisition of knowledge per se that sciences attained its present eminence. In fact, it has been so successful and material goods have become so plentiful and easily acquire that they now define what it means to live the good life. The desire to live a comfortable and secure life has been replaced by ostentation. Whether life is even worth living is now considered directly proportional to the number of things possessed.

While this has lead to a steep rise in the standard of living the inner qualities of life cannot be said to have kept pace. Science is brilliant at building a better mousetrap, but the question of whether the mouse's life has value is one it cannot answer. This has led to widespread feelings of emptiness and disaffection and a yearning for something that should be there, but isn't. Placing a monetary value on the quality of ones life has led to the hordes of angry young people who are a threat to others and to themselves. No hope of attaining all the goods desired is equated with no hope at all. Without hope moral restrictions lose their force and any means of gaining wealth becomes legitimate.

So what kind of life does following the logic of this mode lead to, physical comfort of course, but what about the great subjective questions? Some of the worst examples of excess can be found in societies that relied on reason and excluded more spiritual or philosophical thinking with the Soviet Union being the prime example. It is true that there have been a great many scientists of high moral character, but the question arises as to where this moral character came from. Was this strong character and moral strength a result of the rules and tenets of this mode of being or do they have some other source?

Since only what can be experienced directly and repeatedly is real it follows that God cannot exist. Only real objects having real causes exist and it is sciences job to explain these connections. There is nothing more. When Napoleon asks Laplace why he had left all reference to God out of one of his works Laplace replied: "I have no need of that hypothesis." As epitomized by this reasoning God becomes a hypothesis whose existence must be proven before He can be considered real. God is reduced, therefore, to just one more object among many. Within a paradigm where only physical objects and the interactions between them are real the concept of God can find no place.

Yet the logic of the sensory mode, if carried to its conclusion, produces a small conundrum. It is not enough to shake the paradigm, but it is curious nonetheless. The basis of the problem lies in the fact that every effect must have a cause. When medieval philosophers tried to use Aristotelian logic to prove the existence of God one of the first and, as they thought, most powerful ideas was that of the First Cause. This is the idea that if one goes back far enough ultimately the beginning, the something that started it all, will be reached. To those philosophers that something was God.

Science, unable to prove the existence of God on other grounds, has discounted this argument. Pushed science traces the origin of the universe back to the Big Bang, that instant when a singularity containing the entire universe began to expand by an unimaginably violent explosion. When ask what caused the Big Bang the most frequently given answer is that this question is unanswerable. Since space, time and all possible causes did not exist before the Big Bang; since time itself did not exist before the Big Bang, the question becomes meaningless.

The same reasoning that applies to any concept of God holds true for life after death. Since only what the senses perceive is real, life lasts only as long as the senses perceive signs of life. Moving, talking, breathing, all of these things are signs of life, when they are gone so is life. Yet most people do not find this a very comforting idea, at a gut level it feels wrong. Reason is saying one thing and your feelings another, are these feelings just wishful thinking on the part of someone who is afraid to die or is there a way around the logic of this conclusion. It turns out that—as with the First Cause—there is a loophole.

Think back to a dead body you have seen say in a funeral home. What is the difference between this body and a living person? Most people have no trouble telling the difference, but when ask to state what this difference is many find this an awkward task. It cannot be a simple matter of physiology. A dead body has the same chemical make up as when it was alive. Well, you say, a living person is animate while a dead one is not. True enough, but most people would feel there is a little more to it than this. The feelings you get while looking into the eyes of another person are not the same as when you are looking at the energizer bunny. With a living person there is a presence, a personality, a psyche or a soul.

This presence has many names, but within the language of the sensory mode the word that most easily springs to mind is energy. A living body radiates an energy that a dead one does not. Now remember what your high school science teacher said about the law of conservation of energy. This says that energy cannot be destroyed it can only change forms. When the body stops generating this energy what happens to it. Does it just dissipate? This is possible but there is no logical necessity for it. Since the fate of this energy cannot be directly traced ideas on its fate must remain speculation. As with the idea of the Divine, the logic of the sensory mode does not absolutely forbid the idea either of a soul or of an after life. Once again, the door is left ajar.

All modes have their own unique slant on viewing nature and our relationship with it. As a pluralistic outlook the sensory mode divides man and nature. Nature is 'out there' something we live in, but are not a part of. Living and dying in such a society is not easy. In a culture that prides itself on its sophistication and on having vanquished all such primitive thought finding the fulfilled, contented life has proven rather difficult. For when one is faced with suffering and death logic offers no answers.

The benefits that science has bestowed upon the human race have been tremendous and yet it has shown itself to be a two-edged sword. The list of areas where science has produced a situation capable of destroying humanity, or at least civilization as we know it, is long and growing longer. We are all to familiar with the threat of nuclear war, add to this the threat of overpopulation, global warming, deforestation, the possible collapse of the ecosystem and the ability to genetically engineer humanity into something no longer human. For these reasons, and many others, clouds have begun to darken the bright sunshine of the scientific promise.

Having ousted religion from the top of the hill science has become more powerful than the Church ever was in its claims to hold the key to truth. What science lacks are the curbs the Church placed upon its members. The Church, regardless of the excesses of some of its members, imposed at least a veneer of restraint upon the actions of the clergy. Moreover, these limits where stronger than mere group disapproval. This is lacking in science.

Science today acts upon what has been called the "technological imperative," what can be done will be done. Any limits are up to the conscious of the individual scientist and if there is money to be made or academic stature to be gained what one does not do another will. As soon as the realization penetrates the public mind that you too can have your very own Elvis clone someone will begin production.

The reason for this is embedded within the rules of the sensory mode itself. Within this paradigm the concept of values based upon subjective judgments of right and wrong find no place, something works or it does not. These values—which any society must have if it is not to crumble—must come from somewhere else. While there is no room for subjective values in the sensory mode there is such room in other modes. It is to these modes that we must turn if we are to find the origins of ethics, morals and values. All those things, in fact, that gives life meaning.

Faculty X

While the sensory mode is the mode of logic, the mystic mode is the mode of non-logic. On the subject of logic, Albert Einstein had this to say; "Pure logical thinking cannot yield us any knowledge of the empirical world; all knowledge of reality starts from experience and ends in it. Propositions arrived at by pure logical means are completely empty." Apply this to science Richard Maurice Burke said: "He believes in science, but science is constantly changing and will rarely tell him, in any case, anything worth knowing." It is this realm, where logic does not apply, that we will now enter.

The mystic mode of being is so named because the reality described is the world as seen by the mystics in the rapture of their altered states of mind. To the sage knowledge cannot be gained through experience or logic, but only by a direct encounter with reality. Where the self ceases to be and the knower and the known are One true knowledge can be found. To accomplish this adepts try to calm the mind by stopping the internal dialogue. For it is in the space between thoughts that the One is encountered. Called by many names—the Tao, Brahma, the Absolute, the Godhead or God—something is being encountered that cannot easily be described by words.

Mystical experiences are, by their very nature, ephemeral and esoteric. Within modern society mystical experiences are looked on with distrust as mysterious, arcane and incomprehensible. Loose and sloppy thinking is its hallmark making it the very opposite of scientific thought. Yet, curiously, mysticism also has a reputation for the profound coupled with a depth of experience denied common mortals. No one who has ever had one would call such an experience shallow, frivolous or meaningless. Even a minor moment of mystical union has the power to shake someone to their roots.

Why is this? What is there about a mystical experience that can generate such widely differing views on its meaning and why is the experience itself so difficult to describe? Men of great literary ability have been mystics and yet they seem to have no easier a time than anyone else in putting what they have seen into words. Their accounts run heavily to metaphor, paradox and the negative statement.

This inability to describe what is seen in words is the hallmark of the mystical experience. With the left-brain shut down and the right-brain dominant one is left with an over view of all experience. This is what the British author Colin Wilson has called Faculty X. The experience is had by the silent intuitive right-brain, but it is the language using left-brain that has the chore of expressing this experience in words. Moreover, since this experience takes place outside of reality as structured by language, and therefore outside of the paradigm, this is no easy task.

Yet to say that these experiences are incomprehensible may to be to say too much. The language used is paradoxical to be sure, but this may be because what is encountered is paradoxical. Perhaps one of the functions of the "categories" is to eliminate the appearance of paradox and so create a coherent world. Paradox may be a fundamental feature of reality in which case these statements become only the simple truth.

It must be realized that any statement or idea can sound like nonsense for one of two reasons. One, it can sound like nonsense because it is nonsense. Or, two, it can sound like nonsense because you are not smart enough to understand what is being said. Albert Einstein himself provides a good example of this second statement.

When, in 1905, he finished writing his paper on Special Relativity he submitted it to a German physics journal for publication. At that time all papers submitted for publication where reviewed by a panel consisting of a certain number of fixed members and one guest member who changed periodically. When Einstein's paper came up for review none of the fixed members on the panel could make heads or tails of it. To them it seemed to be just so much gibberish and they voted to reject it.

It just so happened, however, that the guest member then serving was Max Planck and while he did not claim to understand it fully either, he did understand that here was something extraordinary and it was through his influence that Einstein's paper on Special Relativity was published. Without his presence on the committee it would have been dismissed as recondite foolishness. This is a good story to keep in mind when thinking about mysticism.

In all societies mystical union with the One has been considered the highest possible goal with the term most used to typify this experience being ecstasy. What follows is a feeling of rapture or a flash of light illuminating the darkness that reveals that you and the universe are One and that—as someone once said— "out of this world you can never fall." All feelings of self are lost and with them go fear, longing and want. What is left is peace, contentment and joy. People who have found this are called saints. They have found the secret of life, what greater goals can anyone achieve.

So what are the basic principles of the mystic modes of being? What does an intuitively experienced world look like? According to Spinoza (1632-1677), the Western philosopher most often associated with mysticism, the world is a whole composed of a single substance whose parts are not logically capable of existing alone. Reality is a seamless whole with all events and objects being a part of that whole.

It is meaningless for someone to view reality as being separated in any way, as much an error as viewing the front and back of your hand as two separate hands. Your whole body is another example. It is possible to think of your body as a collection of individual organs and mental processes yet who thinks of themselves in this way. When ask whom we are how many provide an itemized list of organs? All of these parts together are you and to separate them is nonsensical. It is this idea of oneness, that you and all things are an inseparable part of that whole that is the primary characteristic of the mystic mode of being.

Since all is One the idea of boundaries does not apply. Any separation of objects or events in space is wrong. All objects and events unite in a space-time continuum where there is no past or future. Within the seamless whole events do not happen, in fact, it cannot truthfully be said that there are any events at all. There is only the whole, eternal, changeless yet ever changing, illusion and material this is existence itself.

Everything being One all things can be thought of as flowing into one another. In fact, the mental images needed to think about unified reality are very similar to the ones physicists use to think about field theory. In modern physics, the true nature of the universe is more accurately described by fields of energy than by events or objects. It was for this reason that one of Dr. LeShan's alternative names for the mystical mode was the flow-process mode.

In such a world the idea of good and evil looses its meaning. To apply the terms good and evil to anything would be to separate it from the rest of reality, something that is not allowed. Good and evil then become just more concepts of the mind. They are part of the lines on the map not part of the underlying territory. Since only the whole exists to apply the terms good and evil to anything is to apply them to the whole and to call the universe good or bad is merely absurd.

The self is not separated from the whole and this is why the mystics do not recognize an 'I'. It follows from this that if union with the whole is desired then the self must be eliminated. To achieve this loss of ego is the goal of all the great schools of mysticism. Currently the Eastern schools are the ones most in vogue, particularly Yoga and Zen Buddhism. It should be noted, however, that Western civilization also has its traditions and schools of mystical thought, just as ancient and just as valid as those of the East.

All of the world's great religions have their outer and inner teachings. Rituals, rites, sacraments and beliefs form the outer teachings. This is the Church service every Sunday where the truths of religion are molded into a form of practical use in the daily lives of its members. These are the outer teachings used by people who lead busy lives and cannot spend 10 hours a day meditating. Religion also has its inner teachings, access to which requires more effort than just going to church on Sunday. This is the knowledge sought by the mystic. The mystics, then, are "channels through which a little knowledge of reality filters down into our human universe of ignorance and illusion." [6]

A by-product of experiencing reality as a unified whole is a tendency to begin to think of the physical world as an illusion. This is a view prevalent in Eastern philosophies. To the yoga, as long as the many forms of reality are confused with reality itself, one is laboring under the spell of maya. Maya is usually understood in the West as the belief that the world is an illusion. This subjectivist point of view is not confined to the East, however. Western philosophers as far back as Protogoras (c. 480-410 BC) have understood that the mind has a central role to play in establishing truth. This idea peaked in the work of

---

[6] Aldous Huxley

127

George Berkeley (1685-1753) who denied the reality of all matter and, indeed, of any extra-mental existence at all.

To be fair to the Hindu's they do not, strictly speaking, say that the world is an illusion in any Berkeleyian sense. To them maya is confusing the map with the territory. The Eastern sages are not saying that the world does not exist; the illusion lies in thinking of the things, events, forms and colors of the world around us as the territory and not as the map. In this we find more parallels to the thinking of the modern physicists than to that of Bishop Berkeley. The correspondence between the concept of maya and the world as envisioned by modern physics bears more than just a casual resemblance; they are in fact, two different cultural descriptions of the same thing.

Viewing the world as a seamless whole leads to some interesting ramifications. Extrasensory perception, the nature of God and death itself take on a new slant when viewed from the mystic mode. It is within the mystical mode of being that the concepts of God and of immortality have their origins and, like hitting the bull's-eye on our target, extrasensory perception, impossible in the sensory mode, is quite possible in the mystic mode.

To begin with it must be admitted that there has been a lot of nonsense written about ESP. The most common is the claim that psi phenomena occur outside of—or actually in defiance of—the laws of nature. The reasoning behind this idea goes something like this.

Someone suddenly awakens in the middle of the night with the terrible feeling that something has happened to Uncle Guido. A glance at the clock shows it to be 2:00 AM. They learn the next morning that Uncle Guido had died the night before at his home in Sicily. Making allowances for the time difference it was found to be exactly 2:00 AM when he died. It would seem that the knowledge of his death and the death itself occurred simultaneously and that this knowledge was gained in a manner that defies the laws of physics. But was it?

Assuming that this information traveled from Sicily to the receiver using ordinary electro-magnetic waves as carriers and also assuming that they followed the curvature of the earth and didn't pass straight through it the time needed to cover this distance at light speed would be something less than a tenth of a second. Leaving aside the problem of how one is to know at what instance the message was sent and when it was received, are the two clocks synchronized so exactly that they can detect a tenth of a second discrepancy. This type of fuzzy thinking is very common in the psi literature. When looked at with the least amount of rigor there is nothing in an ESP experience that requires a suspension of the laws of physics.

Remember that the second rule states that nothing is possible in one mode that will invalidate another mode. For extrasensory perception to defy the laws of physics would mean that the sensory mode is invalid and there is too much evidence to the contrary to accept this. No, the sensory mode is perfectly valid; it is just not the best mode to use in trying to understand psychic phenomena.

Does ESP even exist at all? If your criteria is the logic of the sensory mode then the answer must be no. Within the logic of science psi phenomena simply do not happen. However any parent who has ever awoke in the middle of the night with the horrible feeling that something has happened to one of their children only to find that the child has been in a car wreak is going to be hard to convince. Too many people have had these and similar experiences for the whole idea to simply be dismissed, as it stands extrasensory perceptions must be considered as a part of the human experience and as such they require an explanation.

By shifting our point of view from the sensory to the mystical mode of being a possible explanation now presents itself. Within the mystic mode there is no space to cross and no boundaries to overcome and so there are no barriers to knowledge. There is only the totality of One and this totality includes all knowledge. The problem then becomes not finding out something you do not know, but in consciously perceiving something you do know.

It has long been known that the mind has a filter that allows only a small fraction of the perceptions received into the conscious mind. This is necessary because sights, feelings, smells, noise and more noise all pour into the brain every minute of the ones life, without some kind of editing the mind would simply be overwhelmed by sensations and be unable to function. Yet all of this information is stored somewhere, ready to appear under the proper circumstances. Hypnosis can do it; under hypnosis knowledge you never knew was there can come out. The knowledge that becomes ESP is also taken in continually. Certain states of mind can allow the barriers to drop and portions of this knowledge into the conscious mind. Like balancing on a tightrope, the mind has to be in a delicately poised state for this to work. But given the right conditions it can work.

Knowledge gained in the mystical mode is reality as experienced by intuition alone. The role played by the speaking left-brain in realities formation now become clearer for a mystical experience is nothing else than a worldview not structured by language. Today's weltbild or world picture is then a product of the dichotomous nature of the human mind. Since human beings can acquire knowledge in only two ways, the weltbild is a blending of reason and intuition.

The reason that the mystic mode is associated with the non-speaking right-brain now becomes understandable and the reason that psi phenomena are associated with the mystic state also becomes understandable. Without language to break-up these perceptions all that is left is a united whole where there are no barriers to the acquisition of knowledge. Psychic phenomena remain as elusive as ever, but by shifting ones point of view what was unreal has become real and the ancient wisdom is shown to be right after all.

It is possible to bring the logic of the mystic mode to bear on more important questions than just to consider the origins of ESP. For example, what does the mystic mode tell us about the existence of God? Out of the depths of ecstasy the mystic speaks of a power or underlying essence that can—if one so chooses—be identified with God. Not all mystics call this essence by the same name, but they all agree on feeling its presence.

Within the Christian tradition, which is the one most familiar in Western society, this essence is called the Godhead. Since, in the mystic mode, all is One the Godhead cannot be separated from the universal being anymore than anything else can. God, as encountered here, is a pantheistic God not a personal God as personality implies separation. God is universal, combing within Himself all forces. God and His creation are One, Being itself. To the question of whether God exists the mystic would answer yes.

When the question of the existence of God is raised another follows close behind. Is there some portion of a human being, be it a soul or something else that survives death? Within the rationale of the sensory mode the answer must be no. Here a thing exists or it does not exist. Within the sensory mode life is defined by its attributes. Ask someone to define life and will get this list of attributes. A body is alive if it moves, breaths and radiated heat. When it ceases doing these things its dead, there is nothing else.

Not so in the mystic mode, this is a world without boundaries and the boundary of death is just as artificial as any other. Moreover, if the boundary separating death is not real then it follows that the boundary of birth is not real either. To the mystic there is no difference between life and death both are illusions.

A holy man is sitting deep in meditation when, suddenly he is struck by lighting. He is killed instantly. Was this the end or did some part of his being live on? Within the sensory mode where there is no such thing as a soul the answer must be no. The mystic mode is equally certain the holy man lives on. This is an inescapable outcome of the logic of the paradigm. To say that he no longer exists would be to create a boundary between life and death. What remains are two opposite answers to the same question. Common sense would indicate that one must be right and the other wrong, but it is common sense that is wrong. The relative nature of the universe has asserted itself again. Like the true age of the twins, both answers are true.

It must be admitted, however, that in the foregoing discussion the sensory mode is being pandered to. To say that someone is alive is no more meaningful than to say they are dead and this the mystic does not say. Like Schrödinger's cat a person can only be thought of as being, in some sense, alive and dead at the same time. What we have are two different lines of experience trying to describe the same aspect of reality. This being the case we can logically use the Schrödinger waves to think about the relationship between life and death.

The Buddha spoke the last word on this subject many centuries ago. On being asked by a pupil for clarification on this very question the Buddha made this reply:

Student: "Sir, do you hold the view that the soul of the saint survives death?"

Buddha: "No, to hold that the soul of the saint survive death would not be the case."

Student: "Then sir, do you hold the view that the soul of the saint does not survive death?"

Buddha: "No, to hold that the soul of the saint does not survive death would not be the case."

This answer is a paradox perfectly in keeping with the chimerical nature of reality as revealed by quantum theory.

The consensus of the mystics is that at the moment of death the soul merges back into the ocean of the Divine. Yet the question of which view is correct will not go away. It is easy enough to say that both views are correct and quite another to truly believe it. Yet this is a truth we must learn if salvation is to follow. For salvation is one thing that science cannot give you. It is a scary thought to realize that whether there is a life after death depends upon where one is standing on the boardwalk, but if the theory is correct the conclusion is inescapable.

This problem of whether a question can have more than one correct solution has been around at least since the middle ages. St. Thomas Aquinas and Siger of Brabant squared off over this very question. St. Thomas took the position that there can be only one correct solution to any problem and tried to prove it using Aristotelian logic with Siger of Brabant holding out on the side of multiple solutions. At the time St. Thomas was judged the winner. Modern physics has shown conclusively that he was wrong. It is possible to have more than one answer to given question and both answers can be equally correct. Siger of Brabant, wherever he is, must be smiling.

The Tree of Life

The mystic deep in a trance and the physicists studying the subatomic world have encountered the same truth. Both have passed beyond the range of what the senses can perceive and have entered a world where the ordinary rules of the Leberswelt do not apply. The encounter with those aspects of reality that exist beyond the bounds of the paradigm results in an experience that is also beyond words. Still if the contents of that experience are to be communicated to the non-mystic there is no choice but to try to put this experience into words.

Different mystical traditions have attached different terms to these ecstatic revelations. To the Hindu this super conscious union is called samadhi, in Zen Buddhism it becomes satori, Islam uses jama, the Christian pneuma, while in the Jewish tradition it is rauch. Giving something a name is a necessary first step to understanding, but it is only a first step.

To understand any idea it has to be amplified into a mental imagine compatible with the cultural understanding of the individual. In most cases this is accomplished by drawing on the imagery of whatever religious tradition the mystic is coming from. The Hindu expresses the triune base of reality as Brahma-Siva-Vishnu, while to the Christian this same concept becomes the Father, the Son and Holy Spirit. In today's world the most common source of terms and images for the mystical experience—for those who are not part of an established religious program—comes from yoga.

The problem that arises from this is that the Hindu faith—which forms the basis of yoga—is based upon a culture and a way of thought that is foreign to the Western mind. To give but one example in Christian thought time is linear, you live once, die and go to heaven, or not as the case may be. Hindu thinking views time as cyclic, you are born, die and are born again many times in your struggle to become One with Brahma. To make sense of what the yogis are saying Eastern thinking must be translated into Western thinking. This frequently results in considerable violence being done to Hindu tradition. What is needed then is a verbal explanation of mystical traditions, which has its roots in Western thought, and, fortunately, such a tradition is at hand.

The early Indic-speaking peoples of India can be said to have thought longer and deeper on life's deepest questions than have any others. Flowering into Hinduism, and its daughter Buddhism, the truths these early philosophers discovered now guide the lives of hundreds of millions of people. Moreover, what the Hindu sages are to the East the Jewish holy men are for the west. Western civilization traces its roots back through science, back through Christianity and Islam to these early Jewish thinkers.

What we have been referring to as Western civilization had its beginnings when the thinking of these Jewish holy men was wed to Greek thought. It was the prophets of Israel, looking deeply into the heart of reality, who have brought Western mysticism to its fullest flower. This has created a store of wisdom that we can mine without having to make sense of an alien culture at the same time.

In an attempt to systematize what their visions where revealing they created a diagram called the Tree of Life, the ultimate origins of which is unknown although it has been associated with the Cabala. This association has given the Tree a rather unsavory reputation. Developed in medieval Europe by some of the more mystically inclined of the rabbis the Cabala is a philosophy based upon a mystical interpretation of the Scriptures. In its highest form it is a means of probing the hidden secrets of the world and then using that knowledge to develop one's character into a superior person.

This is fine as long as the highest ideals and standards are adhered to. When, however, people of lesser character tried to utilize the Cabala in everyday life it tended to degenerate into magic. Too most people the Cabala brings to mind charms, spells and black magic. In this respect it bears a marked resemblance to Taoism. Taoism too has its higher philosophical teachings for the wise and a darker side of spells and enchantments for everyone else. It is this association with magic that gives the Cabala its shady reputation.

However applicable this may be when applied to the Cabala it is not at all applicable when applied to the Tree of Life. Whether the Tree is even a creation of the Cabalists is debatable for there is some evidence that it had an independent origin and was simply taken over by the Cabalists. Moreover, the Tree has been used by many others to shed light on their own understanding. Among these was Thomas Aquinas who tried to adapt the Tree to Christianity. As used here the Tree of Life will stand on its own independent of any other system of thought.

The Tree of Life, in the words of Z'eV ben Shimon Halevi (*An Introduction To The Cabala*, Samuel Weiser, Inc. 1980) is:

...an analogue of the Absolute, the Universe and Man. Its roots penetrate deep into the earth below and its top branches touch the uppermost heavens.

Man, meeting point between heaven and earth is an image of his Creator. A complete but unrealized Tree in miniature...

The Tree is a diagram of the relative universe and the principles that bring it about. This is a diagram of how the world of perception, what Kant called the "phenomena" comes into existence.

The mystics say that the Absolute can enter or exit the world through two poles. These two poles represent all and nothing with either pole being able to represent the other. "All else is, to the ultimate observer, illusion—a cosmic drama composed and dissolved in a cyclic round of plays within plays from the subtlest reverberations in the Highest world to the slowest movement and changes in coarsest Materiality."[7]

The Tree of Life has several different permutations. The form used here is the one I believe is best adapted to the current discussion. The Tree as constructed is composed of 10 spheres called Sephira. The Sephiroth are arranged in two columns with all the forces of nature coming together in the bottom Sephira of Malkut or the physical world. Of these two columns, the right hand one expresses the positive aspect of reality, while the left expresses the negative aspect. The positive right hand column is representative of the active, male, anabolic principle characterized by wisdom. The negative left hand column is the passive, female, catabolic principle characterized by understanding. Nothing can exist without these two principles.

Thus, we find the Tree beginning its description of the creation of the relative universe in the same place that all other mystical traditions begin. Whether called Yin and Yang, Abba and Ain or some other all mystical insight starts with a realization of the dichotomous nature of reality. Before anything can exist the unity of the One has to be broken and what breaks this unity is a thought.

In the unity of the Absolute there is no relativity, space-time knows no opposites. Nothing outside of our mind is good or bad, near or far, hot or cold, big or small; all of these are a product of thought. The idea of a single thought completely unconnected to any other thought is nonsensical. What the

---

[7] Z'eV ben Shimon Halevi

mystics are describing with their idea of a dichotomous universe is the dichotomy of the first thought that created it.

In trying to understand the Tree of Life, we will begin at the top and follow the lightning flash downward—as the Cabalists would say. As a template for reality, the Tree can be used to understand anything or any event in that reality. Here we will consider the Tree as analogous to man, as that will be the easiest to relate to for most people. To the occultist Man is a microcosm of the Universe who incorporates all of the forces of the universe in his person. Summed up in the occult statement "As above, so below" this is the same idea that the Hindus express with the concept of Atman.

Within Hinduism Brahma is the Absolute or Universal Soul. The Divine essence underlying all of reality Brahma is the principle of creation in the universe. If located in the body the same principle is called Atman, but in the end Brahma-Atman are just two different names for the same thing. Man and the universe are mirror images of each other and to understand the workings of one is to understand the workings of both.

As has been said of the Tao Te Ching, the study of the Tree of Life is a lifetime occupation. Within the space available we can do no more than to try to distill the essence into an understandable form. To do this we shall begin at the top with the Sephira of Kether or the Crown and work our way down to the Sephira of Malkut or the Kingdom. These two Sephiroth form the entrance and exit points for the Absolute. Either of these two poles can be thought of as the entrance or exit where, as sparks flash between the two electrodes of a Jacob's ladder, the relative universe comes into existence. Like a virtual particle in quantum mechanics, the relative universe appears out of the void, exists briefly, and disappears back into the unity of nothingness.

The Sephira Kether is the point where reality first begins to manifest out of the void. Kether is reality unified. This is the Absolute, the Godhead, Brahma, the Tao or space-time; this is the One from which the many form. However, before there can be any 'thing' the unity of Kether has to be broken. Somewhere in all the limitlessness of space-time there is a thought. And from this thought is born Hochma and Binah.

In Hochma and Binah the unity of the One divides into its positive and negative aspects, setting directly below Kether on the tree the three Sephiroth form a triad or trinity. This idea that reality has a three-point base is a very common one. The most famous is the Christian trinity of the Father-Son-and Holy Spirit. Hinduism also has its trinity of Brahman-Vishnu-Siva, although it never assumed the importance of the Christian trinity. Within Taoism the Yin and the Yang are sometimes understood in this way, while the first thing space-time does is to break into matter and energy.

The first Sephira on the right hand column Hochma or Wisdom is the positive principle. In the outer world Hochma is the active, creative, thrusting male aspect of reality. In man it is the inner intellect—the deepest part of the mind—where illumination occurs and the most profound ideas originate. Its irrational creative, intuitive, mute characteristics mark it off as a right-brain activity.

Binah or Intelligence is the negative principle. Setting at the head of the passive column Binah acts as a counter weight to the active Hochma. Outwardly, this is the material element, receptive and female. Binah resolves the active experiences of Hochma into understandable form. Moreover, since in man understanding is equated with language, what Binah is doing is trying to express all of these inner thoughts in words for only after an idea is put into words can it be understood. Its rational, verbal characteristics identify Binah as a left-brain activity.

Setting below Hochma and Binah Hesed and Gevura are the positive and negative aspects of reality made manifest. Hardly unique to the Cabalists this idea can be found in all mystical traditions, many philosophies and within the body of science. This insight usually expresses itself as the laws of creation and of destruction. These creative, destructive forces are Brahma-Siva in Hinduism and the Yin and the Yang of the Tao. In the body they take the forms of the anabolic-catabolic processes—to give them their scientific names. In Western religious tradition this idea appears as the mercy and judgment of God. All of which are different people's attempts to show the endless cycle of birth and death, creation and destruction, building up and tearing down that defines the world we live in.

Sitting on the right hand column Hesed or Love is the active, creative force. Identified with the Inner Emotions Hesed is also the constructive metabolism by which food changes into living tissue. It is from here that great art, devotion to one's family and to one's God, good works and the love our of fellow man issues. Synonymous with love this is more than just holding someone dear or ordinary sexual attraction. This is the "agape", the divine or spiritual love of St. Paul. Hesed is the driving force that carried the pioneers westward and carried their grandchildren to the moon.

Within Hesed are found the qualities of mercy and generosity, but left to itself Hesed can easily become unbalanced. Love can turn to jealousy. The job of preventing this falls to Gevura or Power. Gevura is the Outer Emotions, the power of reason. Here the passion of Hesed is brought under the discipline of reasoned judgment. Gevura is the loving mother controlling an unruly child. If it is Hesed that builds the fire Gevura sees that it doesn't burn down the house. However, an excess of Gevura leads to a milquetoast who has no ambitions and no accomplishments. A proper balance of Hesed and

Gevura are needed to produce a well-balanced, well-rounded person.

At the bottom of the Tree are the Triad of Hod, Netzah and Yesod. It is here that the workings of the mind most accessible to consciousness occur and it is here that the final distillation of the relative universe into Malkut takes place. Together with Tepheret—which sets in the center of the Tree and slightly above the Hod, Netzah, Yesod triad—these Sephiroth become synonymous with what we have been calling mind. The fact that all of the processes illustrated by the Tree have to pass through this triad shows that the Jewish mystics were perfectly well aware of the importance of the mind in the creation of reality.

The sephira Netzah or Lasting Endurance denotes the involuntary processes of the mind and as such is, more or less, synonymous with the subconscious mind. Netzah regulates breathing, heartbeat and all the other sympathetic and parasympathic workings necessary for the body to function. It is the storehouse of our most fundamental desires. Operating completely irrationally it incites or denies urges without any regard for realistic possibilities or moral acceptability. This is the realm of dreams. Sit quietly and feel yourself breath or listen for the sound of your own heart beating. This is Netzah.

While listening to your heart-beating raise and lower your right hand. You have just entered the Sephira of Hod or Majesty. Hod denotes the voluntary processes. Here logic holds sway and moral judgments do count. So does this mean that Hod is the conscious mind? Not at all, Hod is the subconscious mind. Now wait a minute, a short while ago you said that Netzah was the subconscious mind, right? Well not exactly, I chose my word carefully. What I said was the Netzah was, more or less, the subconscious. And this is true Netzah is the subconscious mind, it is just not the entire subconscious. The whole of the subconscious is Netzah and Hod combined.

Nevertheless, if Hod is associated with voluntary action how can it be part of the subconscious? As was shown in the Marbe experiment consciousness directs, but the subconscious carries the thought out. When you decide to raise your right hand you did not also give detailed instructions on how to accomplish this. The conscious mind gave the order, which the subconscious mind then executed. This part of the subconscious is Hod. In Netzah actions are undertaken without reference to the conscious mind, while Hod undertakes actions with reference to the conscious mind. The reflex actions we spoke of earlier originate in Netzah, but travel through Hod. Hod and Netzah then connect in the conscious mind, which is the Sephira Yesod.

Yesod or the Foundation of the World is the third member of this triad and referring to it as The Foundation of the World was no accident. Once again, sit quietly and close your eyes. Now without any effort watch yourself think. Crossing the 'screen' of the mind is a steady stream of words, images, concepts and descriptions. Every minute of everyday the mind is continually talking to itself. It describes, categorizes and fits into a coherent picture of the world everything it experiences. When Don Juan solemnly intoned that the world is "only a description" this is what he meant. This steady stream of internalized dialogue sustains and maintains the paradigm. Reality is created upon this foundation.

It is well to be clear about this. It is true enough that Yesod is the sphere were one is conscious of the stream of dialogue. However, Yesod does not create the paradigm the subconscious mind does that. The function of Yesod is to be aware of the stream and by concentrating it to focus the paradigm into a sharper, more sustainable image.

This stream of internal dialogue is what one tries to stop during meditation. With the cessation of this internal dialogue the concept of self disappears, as does a pluralistic world. Eliminate pluralism and what is left is monism. For most people stopping the inner dialogue is one of the hardest feats imaginable. Consciously willing the dialogue to stop and then holding this state for any length of time requires years of training and devotion.

And when you successfully stop the dialogue what happens? The everyday world you know so well collapses into the Oneness of the mystical experience. It is only when the dialogue is restarted that the middle dimension will reappear. Nowhere can you see the role Yesod plays in the formation of the middle dimension more clearly.

For a bunch of medieval rabbis, this is a pretty good description of the workings of the human mind. There is not really much here with which modern psychology can find fault. However, this still leaves one aspect of the workings of the mind unaccounted for. We have located the subconscious mind and the conscious mind, where then is the self-conscious mind?

Setting directly above Yesod on the center column of the Tree is the Sephira Tepheret or Beauty. Once again, set quietly and watch your internal dialogue. Now ask yourself who is doing the watching? The fact that you are 'watching' your mind work implies a separation between the observed and the observer. Moreover, a little reflection will show that this watcher is what you are identifying as self. The Sephira Tepheret is man conscious of himself. It is within this sphere that the concept of 'I' resides. This ability to think of oneself in the first person is the essence of what makes us human.

Setting squarely on the central column Tepheret has direct access to Kether through the invisible Sephira Daat or Knowledge. It is by using this sphere that unity with the one becomes possible. The mystic achieves the goal of experiencing non-experience in this sphere. Daat is the veil—"the world seen through a glass darkly"—that separated the Absolute from the relative universe.

All of the Sephiroth converge in the bottom Sephira of Malkut or the Kingdom. Malkut is the physical world of the Leberswelt. It is at this point that all the forces of all the Sephiroth unite to lift three-dimensional reality out of four-dimensional space-time. Look around you tap the couch you are sprawled on, this is reality, this is Malkut.

In their quest for knowledge the mystics have not stopped here, but have passed beyond the Sephira of Kether into a region they have described as the veils of negative existence. Within Jewish thought the Godhead exists outside of the relative universe. Between God and His creation are the veils of negative existence. These veils are the silence behind the music, the darkness behind the light or the canvas behind the painting. Thinking about anything can only be done in relation to something else and for existence this something else is nonexistence. This can be a very difficult idea to understand because nothing is not just the absence of something. Both are aspects of the Absolute or the Void and neither could exist without the other.

The closest modern physics has gotten to this concept of the Void is in the idea of the physical vacuum. Derived from field theory the physical vacuum is not just a state of nothingness, for within this nothingness lies the potential for all forms of particles and hence for the physical world. Here "form is emptiness and emptiness is indeed form."[8] Existing as it does between the Godhead and the relative universe it is the stillness before an action. It is nothing and yet without it nothing else could exist.

---

[8] Buddhist Sutra

The first veil encountered beyond Kether is Ain Soph Aur or Limitless Light. Often described by mystics as a blinding white light Ain Soph Aur is everywhere, permeating and supporting all of existence. Beyond Ain Soph Aur is Ain Soph—sometimes-spelled En Sof—the Limitless or "the hidden God." This is the point where being begins to form out of the void, while Ain, is the third veil from which the nothing is formed. And beyond this is the Godhead or the Absolute. Beyond eternity, it is timeless, without form, without even existence the Absolute is beyond the limits of human understanding.

This then is the universe of the mystic, flowing, timeless, without boundaries or limits. To be at One here is to know that you and the universe are One and that the One is good. Here nothing can ever harm you, here is freedom from want and fear, here is serenity, here is "the peace that passeth all understanding." It is little wonder that people throughout the ages have striven so mightily to get here.

The Eight Winds

With the mythic mode of being we encounter what is arguably the oldest of the paradigms. The dreamlike non-rational nature of the mythic mode marks it off as a right-brain creation. This is the realm of dreams and there were dreams long before there was language. The temptation is then to wonder if this was the original worldview of the human race. Was this the worldview until the "fortuitous mutation" made other paradigms possible? The answer is almost certainly yes. In a sense then this paradigm is the mother of all the rest.

Paradoxically—in spite of its long history—this is the least well understood of the lot. Born and bred in a society where the use of personality, powers and spirits to understand nature has been replaced by impersonal laws it is a mode to which most people find it impossible to relate. Since at least Greek times there has been a tendency to explain the mythic mode by translating it into whatever other mode is then in vogue. Today it is an embarrassment to be ignored if it cannot be suppressed. Nevertheless, the mythic mode is a valid mode in its own right and no theory that purports to explain reality can discount it.

The mythic mode gets its named because the currencies of its knowledge are myths. In this case myth is not being used in the modern sense of something fictitious or contrary to fact. Here it is used in its earlier meaning of a story, which metaphorically explains some of the phenomena of nature or of human origins. They are, in the words of Selustius (circa 4th century BC) "things which never happened, but always are." Myths are older than mathematics, older even than music and as such can be looked upon as humanity's first effort to understand the world they live in.

The primordial nature of myths shows up in the fact that the structure of myth and the structure of dreams are very similar. In fact, Joseph Campbell has called "myth a public dream and dreams a private myth." In dreams we find passions, longings, fears, anger and ritual. Less often seen is skeptical reasoning and rational thought. Although the details are culturally variable the basic structure and logic of dreaming is a universal of humankind. All of this applies equally well to myths. Myths are universals of time and space that flow from the deepest workings of the human mind. As such, the mythic mode can be looked upon as the easiest and most natural way for people to view the world.

The mythic mode—while having a profound influence on the other modes—can't be said to have ever been a dominant mode in any literate society in the sense that all the members of that society followed it. Instead, this was the worldview of our pre-literate hunter-gather ancestors. Where science typifies the sensory mode and religion typifies the transpsychic mode shamanism holds the same position in the mythic mode.

More a technique for organizing and handling the world than a religion shamanism today is down but not out. Called shaman (from the Tungus word samòn) in Siberia, medicine man in America and witch doctor in Africa all of these together are what I have been loosely—and rather inaccurately—calling magicians. I can get by with this because the underlying rationale for all these people is not mathematics, Aristotelian logic or religious thinking, but magic. The shamans deal with the spirits not God and their role is to mediate between that hidden spirit world and our own.

Even in today's media generated reality mythic insights still form the basis for much of our understanding of the world. The simple recognition that life is unpredictable and full of uncertainty was first delineated within the understanding of this mode. Moreover, the fact that today we ascribe all this to statistical factors rather than to fickle spirits has not changed this basic insight. That these myths were humanity's first efforts to understand reality means that all subsequent beliefs must, a prior, find their origins here. This is why even today the "archetypes"—to steal a phrase from Carl Jung— owe more to myths than to any other form of knowledge.

That these mythic thought patterns are still with us shows the prevalence of superstition. Living as we do in a literate, scientifically based society who among us is not aware that modern science has exposed all of the old superstitions for the ignorant nonsense that they always were. Yet how many computer wizards still throw a pinch of salt over their shoulder if they chance to spill some on the table? No, superstition has not vanished rather old ones have been exchanged for new ones. How many people, who have no fear at all of crossing the path of a black cat, pay out good money to get their lucky number to win the lottery?

No matter how advanced intellectually society becomes superstition will always be with us because superstition is more basic than the intellect. To hold a superstition is nothing more than to hold the shamanistic belief that we live in a mysterious world were the disruption of the spiritual realm produces problems in our own. Superstition follows naturally from a mythic view of reality.

As J.G. Frazer pointed out long ago, the underlying concepts of the mythic mode and of the sensory mode are identical. In both the universe is one of order where immutable laws form a succession of perfectly regulated events. With foresight and knowledge it is within ones power to influence the outcome of these events. Within this mode the proper actions produce the proper results as surely as mixing the proper chemicals produces a stipulated reaction. In both cases, the element of chance is eliminated and knowledge becomes power.

In the mythic mode subjective and objective are not differentiated. Things and events are related to and interact with each other based on the will. Here all events start with a specific act of will and are controlled by that same act of will. While under control of the will the mental image and the object can be thought of as a single system, which can be treated as a whole.

This being true any object or event can be connected to any other through on act of will. Once this connection has been made neither time nor space can break it. Joined by an act of will only an act of will can dissolve that connection.

Each part of an event or object is equal to the whole and can be treated as if it were the whole. This is true whether they are part of an intact whole or whether the whole has been broken into pieces. To control the part is to control the whole. This is why when a magician desires to do someone harm the first order of business is to secure some part of the person's body such as a strand of hair or nail clippings. Anything that was a part of the person would do for to control the part is to control the whole.

This equivalency also operates for symbols. The object, the mental image of that object, and the symbol describing it are all the same thing. There is no difference between what is 'in here' and what is 'out there'. It is for this reason that in some tribes a person's real name is a carefully guarded secret. A person's name is a symbol of that person and to possess it is to possess power over that person.

Space and time are creations of the mind. Connect two things within the mind and there is neither space nor time between them. If two things are unconnected in the mind the fact that they are in physical contact has no meaning. In the mythic mode the concept of space has its own structure and logic that has no connection with Euclidean geometry.

With all of this talk about reality conforming to the will of the magician perhaps we should pause and define just what this 'will' is. Will is a function of the mind that allows it to be firmly resolved or to be determined to complete an action. The will may then be thought of as self-control or self-discipline. This is the ability of the conscious mind to choose a deliberate course of action and then to see it through. And this is fine as far as it goes but in the mythic way of thinking there is a little more to will than just strong purpose.

All events start from a specific act of will that is itself inexplicable and needs no explanation. This concept of will presupposes the power to make it happen. Within shamanistic thinking power is an energy or force found throughout nature. This force underlies all things, permeates all things and radiates from all things. This 'energy' has been called many things. In the East it is Ki, Ch'i, or prana, while in the West it is pneuma, rauch, exhalations, serpent current or the Eight Winds. Very frequently it is associated with the breath. The accumulation of this power is the primary goal of the magician. Like a gun power itself is neither good nor evil, but only becomes so by how it is used. With enough personal power the wizard is no longer a reed bowing before the wind. Now the wind bows before him.

Within the mythic realm there is no such thing as an accident. Behind nature is power and all things move at the whim of power. It is universal and all pervasive and by it are all things governed. As Atman is Brahma within so the will is power within. Developed within the sensory mode it becomes the laws of nature, while in the transpsychic mode it becomes the Holy Spirit. Within the Holy Trinity there is the Father, the goal of which we seek, the Son to guide us to the goal and the Holy Spirit to give one the power to achieve the goal.

The shamanistic concept of power does in fact have many of the characteristics usually attributed to God within the transpsychic mode. Still, although the shaman may think of this power as being in some sense sentient, yet it is not God in the traditional sense. It is the way of the universe, the ordering principle behind all life, the rhythm of nature or the power to bring order out of chaos. As the ultimate way of reality power cannot be understood, it can only be used and it is the will that makes this possible.

The hunter-gatherers of 100,000 years ago lived in a world full of forces and dangers over which they had no understanding or control. Then, as now, when faced with a scary world people sought answers. Only then they were just beginning the attempt to unravel these mysteries. They had never heard of any of the basic precepts about how the world works, precepts so obvious that we take them for granted. And, the place where they seem to have started this search was with dreaming. For early man at the dawn of self-consciousness dreams must have seemed like a window into another world, different from ours but inextricable linked nevertheless.

As language developed people began trying to express what they were seeing in their dreams and so myths were born. "Myths are public dreams." With the creation of myths the patterns that governed the world began to appear. And what they saw was a world produced by spiritual force where all things have a soul.

In all times some people were more adept at making contact with their dreams than were others. Some people just have the necessary mental make-up to enter a trance and make direct contact with the spirit realm. Early humans called these people the chosen ones modern science calls them schizophrenics. By whatever name these are the people who became shamans. A shaman was the central figure in their society charged with maintaining the health and harmony of the tribe. Doctor, psychologist, historian, artist and college professor all rolled into one shaman's were the repositories of knowledge for the community.

The world of the shaman is not the world of 'in here' versus 'out there' that we see. For them everything, people, animals, plants, the rocks themselves, is infused with the spirit of the world, what occultists call the Anima Mundi. Where the sensory mode leads to a detachment from nature, the mythic mode leads to a unity with nature. For shamanistic societies the doings of man and doings of nature are inseparable. Everything is perceived as having its own consciousness —this Anima Mundi—so that the spiritual and the physical are the same thing. Man and nature are the same and as man controls himself so he controls nature. This is why in shamanistic thinking when things go wrong people do not blame chance or question what they have done wrong, but rather ask who has done this. What enemy has cast a spell on me? Divining from where the danger is coming and putting it right is the responsibility of the shaman.

This is the paradigm of the hunter-gatherer. For the greater bulk of mankind's sojourn on earth this was the way the world was beheld. The first traces of a fully developed human first appeared in the fossil record 50,000 years ago, while the transpsychic mode rose to prominence less than 10,000 years ago. The sensory mode, by contrast, has held sway for less than 500 years. For all of these thousands of generations it was within the mythic mode that life was lived.

The mythic mode today lives on around the edges of civilization in those areas that are so economically backward or so isolated as not to enjoy the full benefits of modern life. It lives on also in the realm of art, play and dreams and there will always be the individual who finds it the most natural way.

However, as the primary paradigm of a whole society uncontaminated by the influence of any other mode it can no longer be viewed as extant. What primitive people today are so isolated as not to have been exposed to the blessings of civilization?

OK, so the mythic mode isn't as prominent as it once was so why is this bad? Science has shown these ideas to be so much nonsense anyway right. Well maybe? Science has indeed proven to its own satisfaction that all this magic stuff is just so much irrational balderdash. However, herein lays a problem. Investigating the claims of magic science uses the rules and judgments of its own mode. Since the logic of the sensory mode is Aristotelian logic and since the logic of myth and magic is not it is no surprise that science finds magic invalid. It must come to this conclusion for to do otherwise would violate the primary rule, which says that each paradigm is the only valid way of looking at reality and that all others are illusions. The bottom line then is that science can have nothing to say about the validity of magic.

So then all one has to do to perform 'real' magic is to read a few books and really believe. Alas, it is not quite that simple. First off magic as it occurs in the mythic mode is not the same thing as magic as shown on television, which is the source of most people's knowledge of magic. Television magic is magic filtered through the sensory mode of being. The result, while entertaining, is not the world as seen by the shamans. Magic as presented on Bewitched or Harry Potter appears as it would if it obeyed the rules of the sensory mode.

In the end reality is a group enterprise. No single person can create a major paradigm; this is a function of many minds working together. The more people who live in a paradigm the more firmly its members will believe and the easier it will be to produce results. The lone magician surrounded by a sea of unbelievers is in an almost impossible situation. In today's world its shadow is the most we can hope to grasp of the mythic mode.

While discussing the ability of one mode to disprove another it must be remember that there is a difference between giving an alternative explanation for an event and disproving it. To see what this means let us look at the common tale of the voodoo witch doctor that kills his victim by sticking pins in a doll.

The witch doctor has taken great pains in the creation of the doll. If possible some physical part of the victim has been incorporated into this doll thus bringing the law of contacts into play. If the doll is made in the victim's likeness the law of similarity will come into play as well. The doll now becomes the symbol for the living man and since a symbol can substitute for that man the witch doctor now has power over him. Then, when all the rites and rituals have been satisfied the witch doctor pushes a pin through the doll. The victim, knowing what is happening and believing just as firmly as the witch doctor, dies. From the witch doctors point of view like has produced like just as it should

The scientific explanation differs. In this view all of the actions of the witch doctor were just so much mumbo jumbo. It was the mind of the victim through belief in magic and sheer terror that was the true cause of death. Although the question of how the power of suggestion can create the appropriate neurological processes necessary to override the instinct for survival and to cause the victim to, literally, commit suicide is not addressed.

Now think about what happened in terms of the mythic mode. Within the mind of both the witch doctor and the victim a connection with the doll has been made. There is no physical connection, but such a connection is not required. Here all connections are mental occurring at the will of the witch doctor. He willed an event using sympathetic magic and it occurred. The event has obeyed all the rules of the mythic mode.

By willing an event what the witch doctor has done is to create a mental picture of what is to happen. All of the rites and rituals serve the purpose of reinforcing this picture and hardening it from mere belief into an actual three-dimensional world picture. The same effect is had upon the victim. The witch doctor, by an act of will, creates a relative universe in which the victim dies. And the victim does die. When science says that the victim died of his own belief it is right. Belief altered the weltbild and the results followed. This is magic.

Now we have two alternate explanations for the same event with both being perfectly rational within the logic of their respective modes. And since there are no preferred modes one explanation cannot be said to be any truer that the other. Like the twin's paradox we have two alternate answers that are equally true. And, like all such answers, it was generated out of the relative nature of the perceiving mind. So if ask if there is such a thing, as magic the answer will have to be yes.

The fact that there is more than one valid answer to a question does not mean that all paradigms are equal in all situations. Pragmatism comes into play. Which mode is best adapted to any given question depends upon what one is trying to accomplish. If you wish to develop a new computer game you will find the task a lot simpler using the sensory mode rather than the mythic mode. At one time in Germany if a farmer's sheep broke its leg the farmer would put a splint on the leg of one of the kitchen chairs. According to sympathetic magic by binding the chair's leg he was fixing the sheep's leg as well. However effective this may have been, from our modern perspective it is hard not to believe that his time would have been better spent putting the splint on the sheep's leg.

To understand the mythic mode as the ancients did one would need to be born in it, raised in it, and know no other. To the 'savage' the world is conceived of as governed by supernatural agencies and beings with motive and impulses like our own. No distinction is made between the natural and the supernatural and where there are no natural laws there is no conception of a problem with breaking them.

Here the world is conceptualized as a person and not a thing. In a world so conceived the wants, fears and hopes that move people must also move the world. And herein is the explanation for the ancient belief that sacrifices, promises and threats can influence the course of nature for ones own benefit. Once the world is conceived of in this manner it is no great step for spirits to become gods and it is for this reason that it is not always easy to tell religion from magic.

How is one to know if they are dealing with the rites and ceremonies of magic as opposed to religion? J.G. Frazer in *The Golden Bough* (Collier Books, 1950) gives the following criteria:

1. No special class of persons is set aside for the performance of the ritual.

2. No special place is set aside for performance of the ritual.

3. Spirits, not gods, are recognized

4. The rites are magical rather than propitiatory.

Although one might quibble with him on some points this is a useful list. The question then arises as to what the difference is between a spirit and a god. Spirits, according to Frazer, have more limited power than gods have and are restricted to different departments of nature. Gods are not so restricted. Magic then becomes a personal interaction between the individual and the world.

Here life after death is possible. The soul exists although it is not confined to humans, but can be found in other animals, trees or inanimate objects. The belief that the soul can be found in all natural objects is called animism. In this realm, it is generally accepted that the soul does not cease to be at death. It lives on although ideas about where it goes are not uniform. The soul can transfer into another person, an animal, even a tree. It can just hang around the village causing mischief or it can go off to some version of the happy hunting grounds.

Since the mythic mode is the paradigm of the tribe and since the tribe tends to have a more parochial worldview than nations their ideas about the after life tend to be more limited as well. Because something can only be visualized based upon the images and concepts stored in the mind anyone's vision of heaven must reflect these images. It follows that the more rich and varied the images the more elaborate heaven will be. Living in a simpler less complicated world the 'primitive's' concept of the after life is likewise simpler.

Within the mythic mode life and death is just a change from one state of consciousness to another, like the difference between being awake and asleep. One does not gain entrance into the after life by good deeds or by propitiating a powerful god. It is gained be an act of will. What one needs is to know the proper rituals and recitations and to have the power to make them work. To borrow an image from Christianity, when you stand before those Pearly Gates St. Peter will open the door, not because you have lived a good life, but because you know the password.

This is why the acquisition of power is so vital. Since power underlies and directs all events it must underlie this too. The will, along with the rest of consciousness, is part of the soul not part of the physical body. Along with the soul it passes beyond the boundaries of death. There, as in life, it acts as a taskmaster pushing to completion those tasks assigned it. It is this unbroken flow of will through this life and beyond that determines your accomplishments, happiness and very existence.

To children playing this is the most natural mode in the world. However, to adults immersed in the sensory or transpsychic modes, it is much more difficult to understand. And the hardest part to accept is this idea that once two things are connected they become identifiable one with the other and can be treated as a single system. Here "things that were once together in an interaction remain in some sense part of a single system which responds together in future interactions."

Although a perfect description of one of the basic principles of the mythic mode of being, this statement was not made by a magician. It is a quotation of the physicist John Gribbin describing the interaction of particles on the quantum level. The only change made was to substitute the word "things" for the word "particles." Think back to the Einstein-Podlosky-Rosen thought experiment. Remember that the conclusion arrived at was that "the two particle system is an indivisible whole, even if the particles are separated by a great distance; the system cannot be analyzed in terms of independent parts."[9]

This idea, revolutionary at the time, has now been proven to almost everyone's satisfaction. Thus, it seems that the ideas of science and magic parallel each other in a most satisfying manner. Looked at in this way the idea begins to arise that the

---

[9] Niels Bohr

universe might not be so terribly complicated after all. Rather what this shows is that existence is based upon a basic set of premises that manifest themselves differently in different paradigms and on different levels.

There is one other point both cases have in common. Both are a little vague on exactly what the mechanism is that produces this bonding. Ask a magician and the answer is likely to be that it is just magic and, therefore, beyond our understanding. Ask a physicist and the answer is likely to be that the quantum realm does not obey the classic laws of nature and is, therefore, beyond our understanding. I submit that the mechanism at work in both cases is the same. Just as a physicist, by identifying the spin of one electron creates a universe where the spin of the other is known so a magician, by an act of will, creates a universe where a man and a doll are connected. In both cases the mechanism for the connection is the same, the workings of the human mind. The point has already been made, probably until you are tired of hearing it, that the mind creates reality. And the dynamics of how this created reality functions must express itself in some manner in all possible created pictures. The difference here is that the magician is not just observing but is actively trying to influence an event.

It must be admitted that time has passed the mythic mode by. While still showing up in play, art and superstition and still holding out in remote corners of jungle or steppe, as a dominant worldview it has been replace by other modes. Yet even today there are people who find that this mode of being offers a path towards the fulfillment of their needs that more popular modes leave untouched. Instead of trying to placate an unknowable god one tries to control ones own fate. Here one boldly tries to take ones own destiny into ones own hands and in so doing overcome fear, want and death itself. Such strivings survive today mainly on the fringes of society, within the occult sciences and in various New Age doctrines. It is not a path followed by many but for those who do it still has the power to guide one through "life's tangled web." Only today it will be a much lonelier journey.

Still, as long as there are children playing, as long as there are people who do not want to walk under a ladder the mythic mode will be with us. It is here that the flower of creativity blossoms into its fullest potential. Even the most recalcitrant of materialists draws on it for inspiration. As a way of life it may be gone, but as an undercurrent in today's society it is going to be with us for a long time.

The Double Truth

Lastly, we come to the Transpsychic Modes of Beings. Far from least this mode is the abode of religion, still the lens through which many millions of people view reality. Even in Western society where science is considered as the final arbitrator for all questions that "old time religion" still have many followers. Today we live in an outward facing world where the old idea that the world behaves more like a person than like a machine is passé. Rationalism reigns supreme bringing in its wake enormous technological achievements. And the price that has been paid for the highest standard of living in history is to make nonsense of the ancient teachings. Mankind today lives better but is more perplexed than ever before.

All of this is a direct result of the sensory modes proclivity for separating humanity from the rest of reality. The idea that before you can understand the world you must understand yourself has giving way to views that are more 'effective'. The observer has been separated from the observed and in so doing reduced a world designed by a living God to a series of impersonal laws of physics. In our rush for rationality a world that can yield to our hopes and desires has evaporated into quantum nothingness. "We do not explain the world, we explain it away."[10]

In today's world it is in the transpsychic mode that we seek this explanation. To the bulk of the world's poor and uneducated it is still their religious beliefs that are their guide through life. For these people science is a closed book and the sacred scriptures, myths, rituals, parables and legends form the common pool of ideas that set the pattern of family life and of society in general. Even among the over educated there are

---

[10] Sankara

many who find value and inspiration in their church on Sunday. In the current battle between science and theology, it is not yet a knockout for science.

The struggle between theology and science echoes the earlier strife between theology and magic. A long and sometimes bloody process the denunciation of the prophets against pagan rites, witchcraft and magic culminated in a win for religion. The dominant worldview changed from trying to bend the world to ones own will to submitting that will to the will of God.

Now the play repeats itself this time, mercifully, without as much bloodshed. In contemporary society religion has surrendered to science the sole authority to the final answer. With the sensory mode in the ascendancy archangels, angels, thrones, dominations, cherubim and seraphim become merely quaint. With the truths of religion being useful for those who wish to follow them, but irrelevant against hard science it has now come to such a pass that many theologians seem to feel the need to justify their religion to science as though scientific observations could actually threaten the truths of a spiritual revelation.

It was the belief of Sir J.G. Frazer that religion was a child of magic, although there is a school of thought that considers magic to be an outgrowth of religion. In the final analysis it is Frazer's view that seems the most likely, for when looked at dispassionately religion seems to require more sophisticated thought patterns than magic.

In *A Sense of the Cosmos* (Doubleday, 1975) Jacob Needleman says: " . . . by religion we mean an encompassing structure of publicly available ideas, patterns of family life, rituals, symbols and education that maintains the general stability of civilized life." Or as Paul Tillich said in the *Protestant Era* (Phoenix Books, 1966) "Religion is the substance of culture, culture is the expression of religion." Religion and civilized life would then appear to have originated together and to have walked hand in hand ever since. It is hard not to see some cause and effect here with religion supplying the rules of conduct that made civilization possible.

As previously mentioned the struggle between religion and magic can be witnessed in the early books of the Bible and as some of the earliest writings ever produced they may safely represent the dawn of history. What seems likely is that both civilization and religion are the outcome of an increasing population and a more complex society.

As society became more sophisticated, generating thinking that is more complex and an enlarged worldview, an all-powerful king replaced the chief who had guided the tribe by the wisdom of age. Government was born and the days when no man could, or would, tell another what to do ended. Class distinction was born with the common people now looking to the king in times of trouble. Thinking about the divine kept pace with a growing social order by becoming more elaborate and sophisticated.

The divine king—later split into king and priest—became the intermediary between this world and the next. Compared to tribal life the hustle and bustle of the city left less time available for learning and performing rites and this is where the priest came in. Only the priesthood, supported by the community, had the time to make a proper study of the rituals and to see that they were performed correctly. A priestly class had emerged that was the official intermediary between the gods and their people.

Magic had been transformed. A special class of people now performed specific rituals in specific places with the local spirits now becoming worldly gods whom it was necessary to supplicate by prayer and sacrifice. As the city-states grew into countries and countries into nations the simple ideas of animism grew into evermore-powerful gods encompassing greater and greater territory until finally forming one universal, omniscient God.

Despite many differences in religious beliefs worldwide, there is surprising agreement on many of the pivotal questions. All of the great religions unite in demanding the ethical life for example. By insisting upon morality harmony is achieved, which is the ethical base upon which civilization rests. Without these qualities of right and duty anarchy reigns and civilized society would be impossible. This is the role, in a secular sense that religion plays. It was the constraints imposed by religious belief that allowed large numbers of people to live together in a, more or less, harmonious state. Even today, when a scientist agonized over the ethics of his work the values of religion are what are spurring his conscious.

Religion is a much more personal experience than either science or philosophy. Within religious thought, prayer and meditation are the primary sources of knowledge with reason being used to supply theological insight to what prayer has revealed. The emphasis in religion is then upon the intuitive right brain with the left-brain in support. Used in this way an alternate worldview is created within which the mysteries of God and death becomes understandable. Still there is a tension between these two paths that is not easily reconciled.

Thomas Aquinas recognized this problem long ago. It was his conclusion that in the end reconciliation was not possible with reason and revelation constituting a "double truth." Opposing St. Thomas was the Arab philosopher Averroes who opted for a single truth. Interestingly one of Averroes most staunch supporters was St. Thomas' old adversary Siger of Brabant. So far, at least, the march of time seems to have given the victory to the Saint.

This double truth is expressed by the terms ecstasy and theology. According to Bertrand Russell, personal religion is derived from ecstasy, while theology has its roots in mathematics. This idea of personal religion comes from Rousseau who considered that "true religion comes from the heart." In this he agreed with the Buddha in believing that all theology is superfluous. Theology then becomes the logical left-brains attempt to express revelation in words. This rational process connects theology with formal logic. In contrast, personal revelation can convince the one having it, but cannot convince a third person in any empirical sense.

By saying this, we arrive at the same position as the mystic who claims that an ecstatic experience cannot be put into word. These ecstatic experiences, in either the mystic mode or the transpsychic mode, are both coming from the same place making it very easy to confuse the two. Writers of the highest caliber often fail to make this distinction resulting in something of a muddle. In spite of this, it should always be remembered that here are two separate paradigms that do not always lead to the same conclusions.

Within the transpsychic mode all is One just as in the mystic mode, yet here the One has parts. Each thing or event is a separate individual and yet it has no boundaries. Think of a wave in the ocean. A wave has form and independent existence but there is no boundary separating it from the rest of the ocean. The wave becomes a distinct entity by virtue of its shape and remains so as long as it retains that shape. "When the wave rises it is the water and when it falls it is the same water again. Tell me, Sir, where is the distinction? Because it has been named a wave shall it no longer be considered as water?" [11]

---

[11] Kabir

Like waves in the ocean, humans are continually forming and dissolving in an endless cycle of birth and death. While a wave holds its shape it exists, yet to try to characterize it and the underlying ocean as two separate things is meaningless. In just the same way a person forms out of the Godhead and merges back into the Godhead at life's end.

Just as the tremendous power of the ocean underlies each wave so tremendous forces underlie each of us. These forces, by an absolute single mindedness of purpose, can be brought to bear in time of need. It is as if a wave where to get into trouble and then, by intercessory prayer, summon all the power of the ocean to its aid. Such an occurrence is impossible in any other mode.

This help can manifest itself in one of two ways. It can be in the form of an impersonal power or it can manifest itself as a sentient being. How this is possible will be dealt with later. These 'beings' make their appearance in all religions. Christianity has its guardian angels and saints, Hinduism and Buddhism have their protectors and shamans have spirit helpers. All of these are different forms of spiritual entities that can render aid in times of dire need. Discounted out of hand by science angelic and demonic hosts are perfectly possible within the transpsychic mode.

Space and time exist, but are unimportant. Since all things are interconnected within the whole, there is no barrier between them. Good and evil also exist. An illusion in the mystic mode they are all too real in the transpsychic mode. If the universe is viewed as a whole of interconnected parts then whatever promotes harmony between those parts is desirable. To accomplish this people must be treated as subjects not as objects. Love, benevolence, generosity, understanding, patience even good manners all promote harmony and are considered virtues. All of these virtues work to eliminate self-centeredness, which is the beginning of all sin. It is no accident that the first deadly sin is pride.

A sin is then any action or feeling that caused disharmony. The idea of good and evil only makes sense in the presence of free will. Without it the very concept of good and evil, morals, ethics and character development loses all force. In a completely deterministic world human beings are nothing but a composite of all their experiences as created by physical laws. Only by allowing for the free use of ones will does the idea of responsibility, moral judgment and character growth regain there meaning.

Bertrand Russell has said that religion "seeks permanence in two forms, God and immortality." God is one of those ideas that need no explanation because, after all, everyone knows what God means. For most of us these ideas where formed in Sunday school and are what philosophers would call classical theism or supernaturalism. Heavily influenced by the thinking of St. Augustine (354-430 AD) God is understood as Supreme Being and creator. It is this conception of God that I have been routinely using here. Neither philosophers nor theologians have stopped here, however, and the ideas about the nature of God run the gamut from various forms of pantheism (Spinoza, Whitehead) through the limited God of Plato to the God is dead of radical theology (Altizer) ending with religious humanism and naturalism. Admitting no supernatural or personal deities' naturalism views religion as no more than the "quest for a more worthwhile life."

Do not let any of this scare you. Within all of this prolixity of theorizing the underlying concepts are actually fairly simple. Either God exists or He does not. And if God does exist either He is identical with nature or He is not. With their fussing the proponents of these last two ideas brings us right back to our discussion of paradigms. For the basis of the disagreement

169

between these two camps lies squarely in the fact that they are using two different worldviews to search for their answers.

God as encountered in the transpsychic mode is a living personal God very different from God as found in the mystic mode where God and nature is the same thing. There God is a pantheistic God, which some theologians feel is the same as no God at all. Judaism and its daughters, Christianity and Islam, have rejected pantheism and have made it clear that the Creator and His creation are two. In any case, this is by far the easiest way for most people to think about God. Even Buddhism—which technically does not even admit the existence of God—has succumbed by recognizing the Buddha as God.

This has been a point of contention from the beginning. In a nutshell the arguments of the two schools run something like this, in pantheism God is conceived as either identical with the natural world or that world "is predicated of Him as one of His modes."[12] Conceived in this way His thoughts must have the same starting point as our own. Under this scheme you are not so much created by God as you are an aspect of God Himself. This is the origin of the Hindu concept of Atman; roughly, equivalent to the soul Atman is Brahma within. This is the soul of the world, "That art thou." If God is identical with the world then any subsection you care to study must be as much a part of God as any other part. This idea leads to a non-personal God.

This is flatly contradicted in the Bible. Here God is seen as transcendent, outside of, and greater than, the universe He created. God so conceived is a God of attributes one of which is goodness. Although a good God is not the same as a good man for God is not good as judged by some independent standard nor is He good because He resists temptation. Rather He is good because He loves and because He forgives. Such a being is a

---

[12] Spinoza

personal God; sentient and all knowing who takes an active interest in the running of the universe.

The Church has recognized each of these views as being perfectly correct. In Western religious traditions these two points of view take the form of the via enimantiae and the via negationis. The former is an all-knowing God interested in and caring for His children. Here the Divine has attributes, which may include a form—usually a human one. God, then, becomes a sort of super king setting on His throne in heaven while dispensing justice and giving succor to the needy.

The latter is the negative way, God without attributes. Here the Divine Godhead can only be described by negative predicates. Making any positive statement about the Godhead is to place limits upon It and that is an error. The Godhead is beyond all language and is, therefore, beyond all understanding. As so often before the Hindu's have a saying that sums this up nicely, "some contemplate the Formless, and others meditate on Form, but the wise man knows that Brahma is beyond both."

For those who meditate on Form the desire arises to prove their beliefs. Long and hard has been the effort and yet to date no one can be said to have been successful. These proofs have taken many forms, but in keeping with the double truth they divide into those based upon reason and those based upon intuition.

Their are some theologians who don't feel any obligation to prove God's existence at all, while others feel that the very idea of perfection itself implies the existence of God. After all, if He did not encompass the attribute of existence He would not be perfect. William James took another track, for him the unseen realm of the Divine produces effects in this world. As we have seen in science, something must be considered as real if it produces effects that require us to postulate its existence. Since

Dr. James believed that God fulfilled this requirement God must, therefore, exist.

The philosophical arguments on this question tend to fall into three classes: ontological arguments, cosmological (or caused) arguments and teleological arguments. The idea that God must exist otherwise He would not be perfect is an ontological argument. What it is saying is that God must exist a priori, that is the very idea of God implies His existence. God is then "that than which nothing greater can be conceived."

The other two classes fall under the heading of explanatory arguments. That is they start from the idea that the universe requires an explanation. Cosmological arguments attempt to do this by showing cause. Since every effect must have a cause ultimately there must be a Prime Mover as First Cause. We have encountered this idea already as a sensory mode explanation. Teleology, on the other hand, argues from design. The idea being that the universe is to perfect in the harmony of its complexity to have simply coalesced out of chaos.

Imagine a Cro-Magnon man walking along the beach and finding a watch that some time traveler has dropped. This is an object completely beyond his experience. What is he to make of it? Now imagine that while he is fumbling around with it he manages to get it open and looks inside. He has never seen metal and has no idea what a gear is yet he feels intuitively that what he is holding in his hand is not natural like a rock. Such an object could not have occurred by mere chance. A watch implies the existence of a watchmaker. He may conceive of this watchmaker as another person or as a god, but no matter. The point is he realizes that some thing must have created the watch. In just the same way the universe, by the harmonious beauty of its existence, implies the presence of a creator.

On the other side of the question is intuition. Here the reality of the Divine is established by direct encounter. While the above arguments take there stand in logic and are, therefore, vulnerable to logical objections personal encounters are not so burdened. The basis of all religion, a mystical union of the soul with the Divine seems irrefutable to the person having it, but can never constitute sufficient proof to force anyone else to change his mind. Other people may choose to believe, but if they do not there is no logical way to compel them to do so.

All of these approaches to the question of Gods existence have one thing in common. They have all failed in their goal of proving God's existence in any empirical sense. Each has its own set of objections but in the end they all fail for the same reason. And in this failure something is revealed about God's true nature. If God were real in the same way a rock is real His existence would hardly be in doubt. God, therefore, cannot be real in any objective sense. If, then, God does exist He must exist subjectively.

These two traits—a lack of empirical evidence coupled with a feeling of certitude—are the hallmarks of a subjective being. The nature and characteristics of a subjective being can prove to be very subtle. So much so, that considerable space will be devoted to it later on. For now, it is enough to say that while a subjective entity is not real in any objective sense it is not an illusion either.

God so conceived is a transcendent God who must exist outside of and is greater than any paradigm. Only a subjective being can do this. By showing God's subjective nature we come back to Rousseau's belief that it is only in ones personal experience that God can be found. Simple logic shows that he is right. Rousseau's belief is based upon reality as experienced in a subjective manner and since God cannot be experienced objectively He fits this definition by default. The question of whether God exists then becomes a personal question. If you have ever experienced God's presence in church, in prayer or in meditation then for you God exists and you need no further proof. When you have said this you have said all that can be said.

Mr. Russell's other way in which religion seeks permanence is in immortality. The belief in and the desire for an after life seem to be universal and yet our own mortality is something most of us would prefer not to think about. The root of this fear is that death cannot be faced in our ordinary state of consciousness. Neither science nor the sensory mode in general can offer any understanding or hope for what is to them essentially a non-issue. Only by entering an altered state of consciousness with a different worldview can hope be found.

If the question of God's existence is ask within the rules of the transpsychic mode the answer must be yes. If the question of life after death is asked the answer must again be yes. Within the transpsychic mode, the idea that some part of the individual survives death is just as inexorable as the sensory modes conclusion that it does not. What it is that survives death has been called by many names. For Catholics and Protestants it is the soul, while Quakers speak of the inner light. Jewish tradition speaks of the divine spark; Hindus call it atman, which in Buddhism becomes Buddha nature. Call it what you will, each of these terms represent different peoples attempts to express in words the intuitive knowledge that yes there is something more.

Just as God can be thought of as having form or as being formless so can immortality. A formless afterlife leads to a formless immersion with the One, what the Buddhist's call nirvana, while an after life with form leads to heaven, a blissful union with God where the personality is retained. Under Jewish, Christian and Islamic doctrines heaven is not metaphysically different from the ordinary world of life. Most people find the idea of heaven a more pleasant concept than formless immersion. Again from India: "I wish to taste sugar, I don't want to be sugar."

All this talk of immortality and alternative realities is interesting, but in the end it is just wishful thinking based on the instinct for survival, right? When all is said and done it is still just a matter of faith. And this is true, where there is no basis upon which to calculate odds faith is all that is left. Still it would be nice if there were at least a glimmer of evidence in its support that is more than just sophistic statements and ghost stories. Strangely enough such evidence does exist, sort of.

This evidence lies within the so-called near-death experience (NDE), a term coined by Dr. Raymond Moody. Someone dies, is pronounced clinically dead, and is then revived. Afterward it is not uncommon for these people to speak of having had some sort of vision while they were 'dead'. Although what is described is not uniform for all they do have a certain similarity. The NDE's of Indian swamis have been found not to differ in any essential way from those reported in the West.

Typically, at the moment of death a feeling of overwhelming peace is reported. The deceased watch as they float above their bodies in an experience that bears more than a little resemblance to an out-of-body experience. They travel thru some form of tunnel with a light at the end and waiting at the other end to welcome them to a world of great beauty and eternal happiness is Christ, their parents or some other benign being. Carl Sagen has pointed out the great similarity of these accounts to what the birth experience must have been like. Could this vision be a repetition at life's end of the experience that began it?

It is possible and, for our purposes here, quite irrelevant. This is because we have no interest in the contents of the experience. The fact that these experiences vary between different people is of no importance. What is important is that they occur at all. That this is such a common experience with people who have died and come back—and presumable with those who did not come back—can only mean that it is wired into the brain and, like language, is innate in all human beings, although the exact form may have to be learned. If this is true then the question arises as to what purpose, in a biological sense, is being served that would have caused it to evolve?

Evolution is not haphazard; it does not waste time selecting for functions of no value. According to present understanding evolution works by selecting for those traits that enhance ones chances of survival and eliminating those that are detrimental. This can be likened to a process of feedback that operates across generations. In electronics feedback is the feeding back of part of the output into the input. In biology mutations can be looked upon as the output with natural selection working to feed those new traits that give an advantage back into the input to strengthen the signal. Any function so universal and complex can only be the result of such a process.

Admit this and right away we are faced with a problem. How can such a function evolve at all, for if when you die your dead that would seem to be the place where feedback stops? How can oblivion be a positive trait? And the image all of this brings to mind is that of the computer. When it comes time to shut down a computer there are two choices, a hard shutdown or a soft shutdown. In a hard shutdown the power is turned off and the computer ceases to function. Like death within the sensory mode one moment it is working and next it is not. However, at the moment of death this does not seem to be what happens.

Instead, an extensive procedure is gone through roughly analogous to a soft shutdown. And a soft shutdown is done with the expectation that the computer will be used again. If at the moment of death life goes out like a light bulb then it becomes difficult to imagine what purpose a NDE is serving. The only way a near-death experience makes any kind of sense is to think of it as a transition between one state and another. How else could it have evolved in the first place? Grant this and the conclusion follows; death is not the end.

In Western religious tradition the afterlife is visualized as having form, St. Peter standing at the Pearly Gates. But if the idea that the contents of a NDE are learned is correct this leads to another conclusion. If the life one is living is culturally determined and the NDE is culturally determined maybe the architecture of heaven arises from the same source. The most obvious retort to this is that our picture of heaven is indeed created culturally in the sense that it has arisen as an elucidation of an experience ultimately beyond all experience. This picture of heaven is then equivalent to "the forms of the phenomena" of everyday experience and does not differ in any material way from reality as we live it now.

Grant heaven actual existence and the possibility becomes real of an after life having its mental component as well. If survival of consciousness is postulated this is not unreasonable since without this mental component consciousness cannot be said to be present at all. This does not mean that individuals go to a heaven unique to themselves. What his means is that the next life holds different forms based upon ones cultural beliefs in a manner analogous to the way this life forms.

If the survival of death means the survival of ones conscious essence as the transpsychic mode implies then this must be so. The personal consciousness of the individual survives 'on the other side' and interacts with whatever it is confronted with. Not to do so would mean that we are not talking about consciousness at all. And since relativity is that aspect of reality that allows consciousness to work in the first place it must exist wherever consciousness does.

The conclusion then follows that life after death requires the proper state of consciousness. Children seem to enter the proper state quite naturally, but adults, carrying a life's worth of baggage, find this more difficult. The emphases that all major religions place on ones last moments now begin to make sense. All have specific prayers, rituals and last rites designed to help the dying person 'cross over'. This proper state of mind is one in which one knows with absolute certainty that you are the wave and God is the ocean.

Religion, then, is right when it says that the soul's entry into heaven is not automatic. To prepare ones mind for that moment is what all the liturgies, sacraments, rituals, hymns, good works and prayers are designed to do. By creating, guiding and strengthening belief the Church attempts to instill the ability to enter the proper state of mind. The Church tries to expose its members to the proper state of consciousness and then to nurture and strengthen that other way of looking at the world until it becomes so commonplace that one will naturally fall into it in ones last moments. For only in this way can survival be assured.

If ones state of consciousness at the instant of death is as important as all of the religious formalities would indicate surely this has something to say about the nature of death. The common practice when thinking about death is to create a picture of someone else dying. Picturing a death scene with you as the dying person is not something most people find very enchanting. The result of this is a tendency to look at someone's final moments from our own vantage point rather than from theirs. From our point of view the dying person's last thoughts come and are gone. Instead of viewing the dying persons last thoughts from our point of view lets try looking at them from their point of view.

Within the understanding of the sensory mode someone's last thoughts have a finite existence they come and are gone. None of the other modes of being requires this. Within the sensory mode time is all-important along with space as the background against which all things are measured. The transpsychic mode acknowledges the existence of time but here it is a more pragmatic device that can be disregarded if the need arises. From the vantage point of the transpsychic it is not necessary to think of these last thoughts as even being in time. In an ordinary ecstatic experience—this is probably as close to a simile as we can come—time loses its meaning.

This feeling of timelessness disappears with the disappearance of the altered state of consciousness. However, a dying person never does return to a normal state of consciousness. Within the mind of the dying person these thoughts may be thought of as eternal. But, of course, whatever your state of mind, however timeless they seem, they will still stop when your brain ceases to function, there is no getting around that, right? Wrong, there is no getting around it in the sensory mode that is true enough, but to use this argument is to presuppose the answer. For that is only a valid argument if death is the end, grant the transpsychic's conclusion that death is not the end and such a state of timelessness could indeed be looked upon as being immortal.

All of this, in turn, raises some interesting questions about the true nature of God. Within the boundaries of this discussion we have been looking at God from our own point of view. Rather than seeing God as Prime Mover sufficient unto Himself the impression has been given that God is somehow a creation of our own minds. When looked at in this light God begins to take on the characteristics of a functional entity. This is something we have touched on briefly; for now, it is enough to remember that the mind creates a functional entity to perform a specific function and that it has no independent reality outside of that function.

The fact that an omnipotent, personal God exists only in the transpsychic mode does suggest that we are dealing with a property of mind. This then is why all efforts to prove God's existence have failed. God has the same properties as consciousness because both are mental concepts. You can only know your conscious mind by direct experience just as you can only know God exists by direct experience.

Someone once said that if God did not exist mankind would have been forced to invent Him. It can be argued that this line of reasoning points to that very thing. The early books of the Bible are then a history of the invention of God rather than the discovery of God. What the prophets of Israel did by endowing God with the very noblest attributes of the human character, which were the highest ideal they were capable of conceiving, was to create a God worthy of being worshipped.

There is, however, a subtle point here that should not be overlooked. God as just described has the characteristics of a functional entity. And the primary feature of a functional entity is that it must perform the function it was created to perform. This is what makes it 'real'. And one of the functions assigned to God is creator of the universe; another (scary when you think about it) is to render judgment. So where does this leave us? We are left with a relative universe in which the human mind created the God who created the humans who created God. Here is relativity at its most paradoxical. What we have found is a circle without beginning or end and what comes first depends upon how one chooses to look at it.

So which is right? Is God a functional entity created out of the human minds need to worship something greater than itself or is God Ain Soph Aur personified. Serious philosophers have expounded both. And, of course, in a relative universe both views must be considered equally valid. To do otherwise is to dismiss arbitrarily whichever line of thought you do not like. Either way demonstrates the existence of God.

In a relative universe different modes yield different results. If the sensory mode prolongs life and brings material comfort the transpsychic mode gives hope. Here you can come into direct contact with the Supreme Ruler of the universe. Here also is somewhere to turn when life has gotten you down. Cut off from each other by the primary rule each paradigm is capable of nourishing only certain aspects of ones needs. A life lived within the confines of only one paradigm is at best a shallow one.

The remedy for this is to understand the paradoxical nature of reality. The mystic mode gives the reasons for living, the sensory mode the techniques, while creativity flows from the mythic. The transpsychic mode gives the moral imperatives that guide us through life. Only by moving between paradigms as needed can our full potential as humans be realized, understanding the relative nature of reality then becomes our first task as human beings.

The Damned Facts

An adult human brain weighs less than three pounds and looks rather like an oversize gray walnut. It operates by an electro-chemical process that is not well understood to maintain and regulate bodily functions, to receive and process information and to generate cognition. As a physical object obeying physical laws it follows that the brain can only acquire information by means of the physical senses. Attaining information by any other means is clearly impossible.

It is, however, the collective judgment of the human race that the mind can acquire knowledge by means other than the five senses and that it possess abilities that go beyond what physics can account for. Folk wisdom in all times and all cultures tells stories of precognition, telepathy, psychokinesis, faith healing, dozing and many others. Occurrences of these kinds create what Charles Fort called "the damned facts"; things that cannot be, but are.

The fashion now is not to consider all of these abilities as separate phenomena, but to think of them as different manifestations of the same phenomenon. Within the last century these phenomena have been christened with many names. These include parapsychology, the paranormal, psychic ability, psi phenomena and extra-sensory perception, better known as ESP. Dr. J.B. Rhine, then head of the Parapsychology Department at Duke University, coined this last phrase. It was he who made the first serious effort to investigate psychic claims in a scientific manner and by so doing legitimized the paranormal as a field of study.

A little thought will show that paranormal abilities naturally fall into more than one class. Four of these classes are recognized: 1) Life-after death experiences; 2) Mind over matter or psychokinesis (PK); 3) Information talents; and 4)

Time anomalies. Of these four classes category three, which includes telepathy and clairvoyance, has already been touched on during our discussion of the mystic mode of being. What we saw was that since this mode possesses no barriers to knowledge, the logical conundrums posed by the classical view of the world do not apply and the direct acquisition of knowledge is possible. We will have more to say on this shortly.

The time anomalies class, which includes precognition and prophecy, is amendable to a similar explanation. Life-after death experiences, which include reincarnation, spiritualism, ghosts and others, will be dealt with later and for now, we will concentrate on the mind over matter class. Within this class can be found those types of psi events where some sort of physical action takes place. This ability to cause a physical object to change its position, alter its shape or change its constituents without the application of any discernible force is called psychokinesis. Grouped together under this class are various forms of magic, poltergeists, inexplicable energy, transportation, bilocation and faith and/or divine healing.

For our type specimen here, we are going to concentrate on faith healing since I believe that this offers more opportunities to explore the implications of this phenomenon. PK of the ordinary spoon bender variety is such a favorite of charlatans that it is more difficult to find valid evidence. Faith healing has it share of chicanery too, of course, but the volume of evidence is much greater giving a broader area in which to search for relevant illustrations.

Examples of these types of phenomena can be found within all mystical, religious and occult traditions. Here we are going to rely heavily on examples from the Catholic tradition. The reason for this is that of all traditions the Catholic Church has the most stringent and well-defined rules for accepting any such claims as authentic. Before any Saint is accepted or any miracle certified a whole quasi-judicial proceedings, involving testimony under oath by witnesses and thorough investigation by disinterested parties, is gone through. By the time any miracle is certified it is as fraud free as it is possible to get under these circumstances.

In our everyday lives, we all function based upon a set of assumptions of how the world works. We know that this picture is sound because we operate far too efficiently in our daily lives for these assumptions to be false. If these ideas are correct then disbelief in the paranormal should be too. Yet for thousands of people the world over "the damned facts" keep happening.

No society right up to the present has ever doubted the validity of paranormal happenings. In this respect, we today with our rational skepticism are the anomaly. Earlier cultures have viewed psi events as an intrinsic part of life not very different from any other part. Telepathy, clairvoyance, ghosts and goblins might exist on the fringe of normalcy, but no one doubted that existence. Even in today's rationalistic world the old views have not so much disappeared as gone underground.

Belief in the paranormal is a subject that has not changed a bit throughout all of recorded history. You either believe in it or you do not and no amount of rational argument has been able to change this. The problem the rationalists find so hard to accept is that the PK type of psi events bears more than a little resemblance to magic, which seems to reinforce the ancient idea that thoughts have power. The very essence of magic this idea is enough to make disbelievers of many.

To counter the arguments of the unbelievers the believers turn to personal anecdotes. Unfortunately, for reasons we will get to later, individually these stories are almost completely worthless as evidence. Believers counter this by pointing to the sheer number of such stories. If, they claim, in all these stories there is only one that is true then the pro side is proven. And to believe that so many people over so many years from so many cultures could all be mistaken would seem to be and impossibility in its own right.

To see what kind of gut reaction confrontation with the paranormal can generate—even by otherwise sober scientists—take a look at an article published in 1955 in the journal <u>Science</u> entitled "Science and the Supernatural." Written by the chemist George R. Price the article is a virulent attack upon the field of psychic research. Price, who did not question the statistical methods used by the various researchers so far forgot himself as to commit a mortal sin of science, resorting to personal attacks. His arguments boiled down to the following that since "the results are incompatible with modern science, and since some men lie, the alternative is clear."

"The choice" according to Dr. Price, "is between believing in something 'truly revolutionary' and 'radically contradictory to contemporary thought' and believing in the occurrence of fraud and self-delusion. What is more reasonable?" He followed up this diatribe with the statement that he would not accept the evidence if there were "1,000 experiments with 10 million trials and by 100 separate investigators giving odds of 10^{1000} to one." It is hard to know how to answer such reasoning, although equal intransigents can be found on the believers' side. In fairness to Dr. Price, it should be noted that in later life he so far mellowed as to allow that the whole subject might not be total bung. A wise answer, we will adopt it.

Nevertheless, if it isn't total bung what then can it be? For Dr. Price is right, within the laws of classical physics the paranormal is an utter impossibility. Several explanations have been proposed. On the believers side various powers and energies—the exact nature of which is not always made clear—have been postulated. Science too has weighed in with its own solutions that mostly rely on the power of statistics. In looking at the scientific (or any other) explanation, however, one must always be careful not confuse a hypothesis with a fact. Showing a reasonable alternative and proving it is not the same thing.

To explore this idea lets look at sciences most commonly given explanation; that psychic phenomena are explainable by statistics. The idea is that the reason paranormal events seem to occur is that most people simple do not understand the nature of odds. Flip a coin. As everyone knows, when a coin is tossed the chances of it coming up heads is exactly fifty-fifty. Now suppose that a sequence of tosses comes up heads five times in a row. If ask to bet on the outcome of the sixth toss the tendency would be to bet on tails. The reasoning is that since the odds against getting five heads in a row are very large then the odds of the sixth flip being another head must be great as well. Not so, the odds of the sixth flip being heads are exactly fifty-fifty. The proceeding tosses have no effect on the outcome of the sixth toss whatsoever.

How many people have suddenly thought of someone they have not seen in years only to run into that person shortly thereafter? How many people have had a bad feeling and so didn't take that flight that crashed? The odds against these events being coincidence would seem to be very large, but are they? With billions of people on the planet, the number of thoughts generated in one day must be astronomical. It is probable that over time almost any thought imaginable will be had be someone. With the number of events occurring in the world at the same time also in the astronomical category coincidence becomes not just possible, but an absolute certainty. With billions of thoughts and events mingling each minute coincidence must occur on a regular basis.

In *The Psychology of the Psychic* (Promethean Books, 1980), the psychologists David Marks and Richard Kamman explain it this way:

> *Let's say that in an ordinary day a person can recall 100 distinct events. The total number of pairings of these events for a single person in a single day is thus 4,950 (99+98+97+ . . . 3+2+1). Over a period of 10 years (or about 3,650 days), 1,000 people are thus expected to generate 18 billion pairs (4,950 x 3,650 x 1,000 = 18,067,500,000). Out of so many pairs of events, it's likely that some of those 1,000 people will experience some weird, incredible pairings.*

This is a good idea and we will concede its main points. There is nothing implausible about this idea at all.

This is a very attractive hypothesis but understand that it is still only a hypothesis. Before it can be considered as proven, it will be necessary to demonstrate that the number of coincidences does not exceed what has been statistically predicted. One cannot help believing that this will prove a daunting task. It is surely going to be no easy thing to even know the thoughts of billions of people let alone correlate them against events.

The only way to tackle the problem would be to use a representative sample and extrapolate the results. Even here, problems arise. Is thinking culturally inspired? Do a Harvard graduate student and a Myanmar hill tribesman recall the same number and type of events per day? Given both the indefinite state of knowledge about the workings of the mind and the difficulty in gathering and correlating thoughts and events it is no easy thing to imagine the definitive study being made. In the end what we have is a fine sounding hypothesis—very scientific—but from the standpoint of proof it is no more true that the idea of astral vibrations. It just sounds more reasonable because it was generated within the approved paradigm.

It will be noticed that while this hypothesis is a valiant attempt to account for clairvoyance, telepathy, precognition and the like it does not say anything about the mind over matter problem. When it comes to PK, poltergeists and faith healing statistics do not seem a viable answer. The only statistics that would be applicable would be quantum statistics where it is mathematically possible—given enough time—for your car to materialize outside of your garage without going through the door, possible, but not very helpful here. Nor does it help just to say that the whole thing simple falls outside the laws of nature. To admit this is to violate the rule that one paradigm cannot disprove another.

The laws of nature are the sensory modes interpretation of certain aspects of reality. The views of other paradigms may give different interpretations but relativity dictates that they cannot be disproved or as St. Augustine once said: "A miracle is not contrary to nature, but contrary to our knowledge of nature." For these things to disprove the laws of nature it would be necessary for them to exist outside of reality itself, which is indeed impossible.

All of the mental side of reality has its roots in the brain. No brain no mind. This is true whether the brain is thought of a generating mind or tapping into a universal mind like a television receiver. All of those TV signals flying around only have meaning; they only become a picture, when a television set processes them. Either way requires a sufficiently complex brain to generate a coherent picture.

Before any psi ability can manifest it must be latent at the physiological level. This must be true because it is with physiology that reality has its beginnings. What all disciplines clearly demonstrate is that 'thing' we call reality is a mind-generated phenomenon. Reality has its base in the workings of the brain. And since faith healing exists within the framework of that generated reality it too must have a physiological base.

Until quite recently, medical science has taken a rather Gnostic approach to the mind-body problem regarding them as two separate—and in some sense unrelated—systems. What modern psychology has discovered is the separating the psyche and soma is more difficult than Descartes imagined. We know now, for instance, that it is possible for the conscious mind to influence the workings of the autonomic nervous system. The yogis accomplish this through meditative practices, doctors use biofeedback techniques.

Biofeedback is a procedure whereby the patient is hooked up to a device that produces some kind of visual, auditory or other signal in response to specific physiological changes. This allows those changes to be brought under the direct control of the conscious mind. By using these techniques, volunteers have learned to control their heartbeat, raise and lower their blood pressure and to relax. In biofeedback experiments rats—although not volunteers—have learned to blush in one ear and to slow down their heartbeat, in some cases until they died of heart failure.

Meditation can accomplish these same things. When modern medicine began to take an interest in meditative practices it found that the altered states of consciousness the mystics spoke of were associated with a change of brainwaves. The brainwave pattern found during meditation is the famous alpha state.

In the 1920's, a German psychiatrist named Hans Berger got the idea of attaching some electrodes to a patients head and studying the electrical wave patterns generated. The device he was using was not very sophisticated, but it did pick up two distinct cycles. What he discovered was that mental activity in a normal waking state produced a pattern of fourteen cycles per second or higher. Dr. Berger called this the beta state. He also found another pattern roughly between eight and thirteen cycles per second that seemed to be associated with drowsiness, meditation and revelation. He dubbed this the alpha state.

Over the years, as the machines became more sensitive, other cycles were found. Below beta waves in a pattern of four to seven cycles per second is a cycle called theta, which appeared when the subjects were at their most creative. Lower still, at one-half to three and a half cycles per second, is a pattern associated with degeneration, disease and death. This was called the delta cycle. Seen in sleep these waves seem to indicate some sort of a pathological condition, such as a tumor. With this discovery, a direct correlation between one's mental state and various emotional and physical states was established.

When science began to study the actions of the brain, the natural reaction was to study it as a physical organ. Pluralistically the brain was then divided into parts such as the cerebellum, cerebrum and medulla on down to neurons, axions and synapses. The mind has proven a more difficult nut to crack. As of now just to be able to identify the area of the brain where some mental activity occurs is considered a major achievement. This is a long way from understanding how all of those neurons and synapses interact to produce a thought.

While categorizing the physical structure of the brain tends to liberate thinking about these structures categorizing mental activity leads to more limited results. This is because the mind the brain generated—in spite of its physical base—is an abstract entity whose abilities cannot always be directly correlated to physiology. This idea rubs many the wrong ways. For them the mind is a straightforward consequence of the physiology of the brain and nothing more.

However, the idea that nothing can be greater than the sum of its parts is one of those ideas that sounds very logical and just is not so. Take ordinary water for example, there is nothing in the physical nature of either hydrogen or oxygen atoms that would predict the quality of wetness. Hydrogen is not wet, oxygen is not wet, but attach one oxygen atom to two atoms of hydrogen and wetness appears. Such a feature is an "emergent property." In just the same way the mind is an emergent property whose abilities cannot always be predicted from its underlying physical base.

This brings us back to those "damned facts" and to faith healing. The physiological changes produced by the meditative state give us a place to start. It is now known that the habit of regular meditation reduces blood pressure, improves memory, increases sensory acuity, shortens reaction time and reduces the level of lactate in the blood. This last is a substance linked to symptoms of anxiety. All of which is showing that there is a direct link between the state of the mind and the state of the body.

The mind may be greater than its physiology can explain but it still has its beginnings at the physical level. Moreover, since the physical is the province of science, let us begin by looking at what science has to say about the mind and bodies relation to disease.

Once science decided that a mind-body connection existed with relation to illness its first instinct was to classify. The resulting types fall generally into four classes. First, there is ordinary sickness in which the body comes under attack by some kind of infectious agent. This type of illness is considered to have a straightforward organic cause and an equally straightforward cure.

Next is an illness that is the result of one or more of the body's organs malfunctioning that throws the whole system out of whack. Next, there is mental illness, which results in personality disorders such as schizophrenia. Lastly, there are purely psychosomatic illnesses that are genuine bodily disorders, which have their cause in the workings of the mind. Hysteria, which is a psychiatric disorder, characterized by excitability, sensory and motor disturbances and the simulation of organic diseases is such a disorder. Hysteria can mimic almost any disease imaginable.

Science has identified the agents of disease as bacteria, viruses, rickettsia, and now "stressors." The last stems from a realization that a great many illnesses result from stress. This can be pollution that stresses the body or adverse emotions that stress the mind. A mind under stress is like an automobile engine that is out of tune. What will happen is that the whole engine is affected until finally the weakest component fails.

This can answer many questions. If the wrong or garbled signals get out through fear, anxiety, depression or whatever there will be a corresponding foul-up in bodily functions. If we correct these mental problems, through medicine, meditation, psychiatry or belief and the corresponding physical problem will clear up. This seems straightforward enough and is, of course, the principle behind treating psychosomatic disorders. The problem that arises, however, is that some of the cures claimed by faith healers seem to go beyond what this explanation can account for.

Faith Healing

All of the illnesses we have talked about so far fall within the province of the psychosomatic. They are disorders with their roots in the psychic that can be cured by methods understandable to medical science. There are claims from the faith healers, however, that go beyond what this explanation can account for. Some of these claims can best be described as miraculous. Repeatedly there have been reports of cures that would seem to require actual cellular reorganization. In some cases, these cures take place faster than one would think that cells could undergo mitosis.

Consider the case of Gerard Baille. Born in France in 1941 at an early age his sight began to fail. Diagnosed with bilateral chorioretinitis and double optic atrophy the doctors could offer no hope. By the time he was seven he was totally—and incurable—blind. In desperation, his mother took him to the shrine at Lourdes. By the second day, he began to see shapes and by the time he went home he could see. Taken back to the doctor tests revealed that, while his vision was not completely restored, he could see well enough to lead a normal life. And all of this was in spite of the fact that the same tests that verified that he could see also revealed that his bilateral chorioretinitis and double optic atrophy had not improved. He lived the rest of his life seeing the world through optic nerves that were completely atrophied.

Impossible! Gerard Baille's illness and subsequent healing was verified by the Catholic Church using the judicial procedures already alluded to. Gerard Baille's experience is as well documented as anything of this kind can be. Like Mike the Headless Chicken what we have here is an event that cannot be, but is.

There is more going on here than biofeedback, psychosomatic illness or hysteria can explain. If someone cannot see with normally functioning, optic nerves and then regains their sight at Lourdes that is hysteria. If someone regains their sight by the optic nerves healing themselves that is the mind-body connection. If that same person can now see without optic nerves that is a miracle.

The reality of life is greater than science has yet encompassed. Consider stigmata, which is a disorder—some would say psychological disorder—where the sufferer manifests bodily changes in such a way so as to mimic the wounds of Christ. If medical science is right and this is of psychological rather than of divine origin then something interesting has been learned. For the only way this could be possible would be for the mind to have the power to alter the cellular structure of the body in such a way so as to make wounds appear. The mind then has the ability to institute rapid cellular changes in the body.

When a wart appears because you have handled a toad and then disappears when washed with stump water collected at the full of the moon we see this mechanism in operation. Beliefs have manifested themselves in the physical realm. If there is a mechanism present that can cause wounds to appear it does not stretch credulity to far to suppose that this self same mechanism could cause wounds to heal. What stigmata do is to give faith healing a physiological base.

Once again, the trigger is belief. Most stigmatics, for instance, are deeply religious people who feel empathy for the suffering of Christ and firmly believe that God visits their affliction upon them. An even more common example of the power of belief can be found in the actions of placebos. A placebo—Latin for I shall be pleasing—is any inert substance taken in the belief that it is medicine with the classic placebo being the sugar pill. That belief is at the bottom of the actions of placebos is shown by the simple observation that if it is known that the pill being taken is a sugar pill it does not work. People have a preconceived cultural bias about how a medicine should work. Studies have shown that the closer these ideals are approached the more effective the pills are. For starters, they should taste bad, because everyone knows that medicine tastes bad.

This may be more than simple cultural bias, however. Studies of chimpanzees and other primates have shown that they use select plants as medicines to treat themselves for various diseases. These plants tend to be loaded with chemicals giving them a bitter, unpleasant taste as opposed to the 'good' tasting things they normally eat. This predilection for bad tasting medicine can then be understood as a survival technique that dates back to Proconsul.

The better placebos conform to the minds preconceived picture of how a medicine behaves the better they work. In fact, they work so well that all new drugs are routinely tested against them in what is know as a double-blind experiment where neither the patient nor the doctor administrating the pills knows which is which. This is necessary because even if the doctor has the stoicism of an Iroquois warrior it is still possible for the patient to pick up subliminal clues. Properly tendered placebos have been proven to be almost 50 percent as effective as many medicines, 54 percent as effective as aspirin, for example.

Placebos are not better than real medicine, if you have a bacterial infection go with the penicillin. The question is not, however, why placebos do not work better than they do, the question is how can they work at all? How can a belief that one is being helped cause a physical ailment to go away? However, work they do and in so doing our subject is validated for getting better after taking a placebo is nothing less than an act of faith healing.

That placebos effectiveness resides in the power of belief and not in the pill, itself is shown by the fact that the placebo itself is not even necessary. Just going to your doctor and having a name put to your misery is enough to make many people feel better. In fact, you do not even have to see the doctor at all; those sitting in the waiting room are feeling better already, while just making the appointment is enough for some. In short, if you take an action that you believe will help you many times it does help you.

Experiments have shown that when a faith healer attempts to help someone without their knowledge no effect is seen. Only if the patient is told that a faith healer is trying to help them— whether one is or not— will there be any improvement. When faced with a sick person Jesus would ask; "Do you believe?" When answered in the affirmative He would reply; "Your faith has made you whole."

Belief as used here is usually regarded as a positive thing used to help a variety of ailments. Nevertheless, it should always be remembered that belief is a two edged sword no better or worse than the way it is used. Put to constructive use it can have a positive effect on high blood pressure, reduce stress and even cause a woman's breast size to increase, still any ailments that can be cured by positive beliefs where almost certainly caused by negative beliefs to begin with. The power of belief—for good or ill—can be seen in the fact that in our example of the voodoo witchdoctor it was almost certainly this very power that killed. How many modern patients have obeyed their doctor's predictions and dutifully died.

As old as humankind faith healing can trace its roots back to the earliest of the hunter-gatherer societies. Every tribe had a central figure charged with healing the sick and maintaining balance and harmony with nature. Although called by many names no society has been without one since. In today's pluralistic world of the expert, the duties of the shaman have been split up as well. Today instead of one shaman, we have the doctor, the therapist and the psychologist. All of which can trace their roots right back to the "mog-ur."

Of course, many of the cures produced by these early medicine men have their origins in the placebo effect. It can—and has—been argued that modern doctors are as reliant on the power of belief as any shaman. Besides, to characterize the shamans as being ignorant is unfair. Many of them combined extensive knowledge of herbal medicine with an advanced understanding of psychology that was certainly more effective than the eye-of-newt and blood-of-frog prescriptions of the physicians of the middle ages.

In all ages, there have been reports of healers with the ability to heal the sick with the most famous of these miracle workers being Jesus. Even today, when most people think of faith healers they think of holy shrines, Catholic saints, Pentecostalism, revivalism and popular evangelists typified by such people as Aimee Semple McPherson and Granville Oral Roberts. It is people like this—some of the highest character and some not—who keep the tradition alive.

With the heavy emphasis on healing in the religious tradition, it is easy to identify such people as being in some sense holy. Sanctity, however, is not a prerequisite. To cite only one example, right up into the eighteenth century the Kings of England, few of whom where noted for their piety, were thought capable of curing a disease called scrofula. By simply touching the sick person, the "king's evil" was dispelled and the person healed. Even today, the laying on of hands is a common practice among faith healers.

. For science faith healing—if it occurs at all—must have a physical explanation. Briefly, this explanation runs something like this. The brain maintains control of the body by producing neurotransmitters and neurochemicals. It is now known that different areas of the brain are responsible for different functions. To do this each of these areas produces an assortment of chemicals. In a sense then each of these areas can be looked upon as individual glands that work together to regulate and maintain health.

All of which is coordinated by the minds assumptions of how the real world, i.e. the paradigm, works. What we are seeing is an illustration of the idea that the world we live in is constructed of what we believe to be true. Bad assumptions will activate, deactivate or alter the functioning of these individual glands, which, in turn, alters the chemical make-up of the body in deleterious ways. Now our simile of an out of tune engine comes into its own.

Throw the 'timing' of the brain out of sync and stress is the result. Stress being here defined as any attitude or belief that created mental tension or strain leading to a mind-body disharmony. If the list of placebo treatable and psychosomatic ailments is gone over, it will be found that stress is implicated in most of them. Relieve this stress and the problem is cured. This then is the foundation for the rational explanation of faith healing. The patient's belief in the healer's ability relieves the stress and affects the cure.

As might be expected the explanation of the faith healers themselves differs. Those explanations divide into three groups the first of who believe that their work is accomplished through the power of prayer. Through prayer, God intervenes in the affair and affects a cure. This differs from the passive placebo style of healing in that succor is actively sought from a higher power. By intercessory or petitionary prayer, such aid is possible and can result in cures that are inconceivable under ordinary circumstances.

Prayer has been shown to have positive effects on blood cell counts, blood pressure and even to reduce post myocardial infarction complications. All of which are understandable as placebo effects. Prayer does not stop here, however, but goes on to bring about effects beyond anything that placebos can account for. These range from the simple—if still unexplainable—such as causing seeds to sprout faster and grow quicker to remission of cancer and the instantaneous healing of wounds.

The second group believes that "spirits" are producing these healing. Here disincarnate spirits either intervene directly or supply the healer with the necessary knowledge to affect a cure. While the third group believes, they are acting as some sort of transmitter or originator for a special 'energy' or 'power' that produces the cure. In the end, all unite in saying that there is something outside and greater than man that can be brought to bear in times of need.

This is an idea we have encountered before in our discussion of the transpsychic mode. When Lawrence LeShan began his search for an understanding of the paranormal, he first asked the mediums involved to describe what the world looked like at the moment they were receiving psychic knowledge. They were uniform in describing the world as seen while in an altered state of consciousness. As noted the power of prayer can also produce such an altered state. Alter one's mental state so as to enter fully into the transpsychic mode and such beliefs will no longer seem outrageous.

This raises the question of why an advanced faith healing is so difficult to initiate. This extreme difficulty bears more of the characteristics of a psi event than of an automatic bodily function. A purely physiological response should function as reliably as blood clotting. The solution to this can only be that any such healing has its roots in the mental side of reality.

That this phenomenon is not purely mental, however, is shown by the fact that in faith healing not all things are possible. Faith healers have been credited with a rather wide range of cures including ailments that science knows to be caused by germs. However, no healer has ever regenerated a missing limb or even re-grown hair. Not even Jesus accomplished this. It is for this reason that George Bernard Shaw called the shrine at Lourdes the most blasphemous place he had ever seen. His objection was that while there are tons of discarded crutches, braces and wheelchairs there are no prosthetic devices of any kind. To his mind, this implied a limitation of the power of God, hence the blasphemy.

There have been cases of cuts healing themselves before the eyes of witnesses and yet no amount of belief will regenerate a lost limb. How can this be? One would seem no more miraculous than the other. Amphibians can regenerate a lost body part but no amount of faith will cause a human to do so. This can only confirm the idea that faith healing is a mixture of the mental and the physical. The amphibians have a mechanism that allows a limb to regenerate. Humans do not and no amount of believing will change this.

Belief can manipulate and magnify abilities the body already possesses, but it cannot create abilities that are not there. It follows from this that if the physical side is unchangeable then the healings must be generated on the mental side. That some of these healing can be thought of as miraculous shows just how powerful the mental side can be.

We begin to get some idea of where the line between the noumena and mind is drawn by looking at what faith healing can and cannot do. Think of illness as points on a line between x and y where x = the noumena and y = the mind. X then becomes a purely physical ailment that no amount of belief will effect while y is a purely mental problem that meditation alone may cure with most ailments falling somewhere in between. The closer x is approached the more difficult it becomes to produce results. Because faith healing is not an isolated phenomenon distinct from the rest of reality, this construction can also be thought of as reflecting the make-up of life in general.

When speaking about the participator mind creating reality we must realize that, this includes the body itself. The human body is part of the 'out there' that the mind creates not part of the 'in here' doing the creating. The impression is of a solid body with the mind contributing details of interpretation. Faith healings show this idea to be false. The minds contribution to the reality that is you is more than just a veneer. A greater part of this 'real' body is mentally produced with the unconditional thing-in-itself buried much deeper than usually supposed.

The picture that the mind produces of the world is the real world there is nothing else. This is why the observer and the observed are not separable and this is why a placebo works. Within the subconscious mind, there is an expectation of what an illness should be like and how it can be cured. If you become sick, (by whatever means) the mind automatically alters the chemical workings of the brain in accordance with the mental picture being used as a template. The state of the body and the picture of the body are inseparable, once the subconscious mind begins to create the proper picture all bodily physiology realigns ands you begin to feel better.

No clearer illustration of the power of the mind-body connection can be found than in those people with multiple personalities. Multiple personalities are a psychiatric condition where the same person will exhibit two or more—sometimes many more—distinct personalities, Dr. Jekyll and Mr. Hyde.

The relevance lies in the fact that not only can a person's personality change but in some cases, their physical body can too. Just like in stigmata, a mental state has produced a physical effect.

Each subpersonality has its own personal paradigm or template from which it creates its own personal hologram, although the same body each personality can have their own individual heart rate, blood pressure, allergies and reactions to drugs. Scars, birthmarks and cysts can all change. One personality may be right-handed the other left-handed one may be color-blind while another is not, even eye color may change. Women with several personalities may have several menstrual periods in the same month. Nothing can more clearly show the role of the mind in the physical processes.

No one does anything as well as they are able. No one walks, talks, writes or fights at 100 percent efficiency. In no one is the mind's full potential, either quantitatively or qualitatively, utilized. It may not be irrelevant that one of the most common methods to try to maximize these abilities involves altering the picture in your mind. This idea is neither esoteric nor new. It is the basis for many of the self-help programs available today.

What these programs have in common is that they use some variation of visualization techniques as the basis for their training. It is claimed that by creating a mental image of something you desire and believing it to be true you will cause it to become true. Techniques of visualization have been practiced since ancient times based upon the philosophy that "as man pictures in his mind and in his heart—so he is."[13] The picture creates reality not reality the picture. Of course, in actual practice, it is not so easy or we would all have hit the lottery by now.

---

[13] Harold Sherman

For those who are unfamiliar with visualization practices a generic version of how it works goes something like this. You create a mental picture of whatever you wish to have or to achieve. The more vivid and detailed the picture the better. This picture is not a wish for something to come, but a picture of something that has already arrived. The goal is to believe the picture to be true. To do this it must be held in your mind with the faith of the heart not just the belief of reason. Now comes the hard part; you have to let it go. Knowing that it is true you dismiss it from your mind without fear or worry. For, like all psi events, the harder you try the less likely it is to happen.

Notice how similar all this is to hypnosis. Some of the uses visualization practices have been put to is to try to use the power of suggestion to alter some physical problems such as relieving stress or learning to relax. Hypnosis can affect these things too. And like multiple personality, hypnosis has the ability to produce physiological changes. Alterations of blood pressure and heart rate have been achieved has have changes in allergic reactions and in far and near-sightedness.

The difference between visualization and hypnosis is that under hypnosis mental control is transferred to another person who then tries to effect change by implanting the proper suggestion; whereas in visualization you try to implant the suggestion yourself. Hypnosis works because, just as your teenager will tend to behave better around strangers than around you, your subconscious mind will more easily except a suggestion from someone else than it will from it's own consciousness. As you may have noticed, visualization is very similar to something else we have already looked at.

The whole thing is very reminiscent of the techniques our voodoo witch doctor used to cast his spell with the dolls and pins. In both cases, a mental image is created in an attempt to create a particular event in the real world. The whole effect of all the rituals is to increase the realism of the images being created to the point where the objective mind steps aside and lets the subconscious do its thing. Many practitioners of self-help visualization programs would be horrified at the thought that they are performing an act of magic, but that is essentially what they are doing.

There is an old saying that in the realm of the mind "like attracts like." This is no more than an ancient understanding that the picture of the world in your mind and the world itself are the same thing. Let the subconscious mind accept that good things are coming and events so arrange themselves that good thing do come your way. Having a positive mental attitude has long been accepted as the single most important thing that can be done to insure a quality life.

Let us try to frame this in a way that makes sense in today's Leberswelt. To begin it must be realized that the brain must possess whatever latent abilities are needed to produce these phenomenon. To understand what this means let us return to our analogy of the computer. All computers have latent abilities in excess of those being used with what the hardware can accomplish being governed by the software. For example, any computer has the latent ability to solve a mathematical equation. Nevertheless, it can only do so if it has the proper program

There is no single program capable of utilizing all of the capabilities build into the computer. To access different areas of interest, it is necessary to switch programs. Each program is designed to meet a specific need and in fulfilling that need there are things it can do and things it cannot do. In this, a computer program is analogous to a paradigm.

As it is with a computer, so it is with the human mind. There is no single paradigm that allows the mind to utilize its full potential. To employ all of this potential it is necessary to switch to the paradigm best suited to solving the problem in question. Only in this way, can the unused powers of the mind be brought to bear and, just occasionally, created the miraculous.

So what is this power that is being utilized? As already noted faith healing is more of an event than a thing and as such bears a strong resemblance to a psi event. Moreover, since this ability is able to manipulate matter—witness stigmata—this indicates some form of psychokinesis. Whether this is PK itself or some closely related ability is not so easy to say. Whichever it is it has the ability—as we will see later—to manifest as either a personal or impersonal power. In its personal form it is perfectly consistent with the idea of 'spirits' as being the causative agent. Couple this with the power of belief and we have an agent quite capable of producing all of the phenomena observed.

This is all well and good but how does all of this explain Gerard Baille? If all of faith healing has a base in the physical how can he see without optic nerves? The theory as stated would have predicted that for a cure to be effected the optic nerves should have healed themselves, but this did not happen. To save the theory a mechanism is needed that can produce this result even without the basic physiology being present. Surprisingly, we have already encountered such a mechanism. For Gerard Baille's experience of 'seeing' without the use of his eyes is no different than 'seeing' in an out-of-body experience. Because Gerard was conscious, no problem arose from projecting what was seen in the normal manner. The only extraordinary thing about his experience was the fact that he could sustain it indefinitely; perhaps this is were divine help came in.

Unusual, but not unheard of, other people have also had the ability to 'see' without the use of their eyes. People have been credited with being able to read with the tips of their fingers, the end of their nose, the lobe of their ear, even with their armpits. The similarity between 'seeing' in this manner and 'seeing' in an OBE is great enough to suspect a common origin. Once again, this common ground is the mind and its ability to use incoming sensory data to generate a picture.

Within this hypothesis, faith healing becomes understandable within the boundaries of known mental abilities. All that is needed is the proper belief to alter the programs in such a way so as to activate them. And while learning something about how faith healing works we have also learned something about the nature of reality. That not all things are possible confirms the judgment of the Copenhagen Interpretation that reality is neither completely material nor complete illusion. Bishop Berkeley was wrong and Immanuel Kant was right, the world is the noumena plus the mental. What it also shows is that things normally thought of as materially real are actually products of the mind. Grant these as true and even stranger conclusions follow which lead us straight into the realm of Forteana.

Forteana

So far all of the anomalies that we have looked at are, so to say, within the mind or rather the mind-body. For none of these phenomena make any claims to being autonomous. Whatever position may be taken as to their validity no claims are made for an independent existence. There are, however, types of anomalous phenomena that do claim such independence. As with psi phenomena, the evidence for the existence of these 'things' is ambiguous with many people simply dismissing the subject out of hand. Again, this attitude does not do much to advance the cause of knowledge. For the phenomenon— whatever it is—undeniably occurs and therefore requires an explanation.

What we shall look at now is a class of what might be called immaterial, material beings. Within this group are found such entities as Unidentified Flying Objects, Bigfoot, Yetis, the Loch Ness Monster, Sea Serpents, Mermaids, Goblins, Fairies, Leprechauns, Spirits, Spirit-Controls, Ghosts and many others. Also, found here are things now out of fashion such as Giants, Cyclops, Pegasus the Winged Horse, Unicorns and Black Lions.

Whether these 'things' exist in the real world or not they certainly do in the minds of millions of people. The presence of such far-fetched beings in the weltbild of all peoples, both ancient and modern, is an undeniable fact that has to be fitted into any overall picture of reality. Explanations for these things are many and varied. They are real but undiscovered. They are phantasmagoria, products of whimsy and an overwrought imagination or again they are modern manifestations of ancient myths and collective memories.

When looked at coolly, without any preconceived theories to advance, a case can be made for the idea that we are dealing here not with dozens of different phenomena, but only one.

Others have made this suggestion and been roundly vilified for their trouble. A dispassionate review of the evidence, however, leads to no other conclusion. Realizing that all of these beings are really only different manifestations of the same phenomenon is the first step towards understanding what they are.

Trying to think factually about a fantasy is no easy task nor can it be denied that this is a subject that is considered to be supremely illogical. As John Napier has noted in his book *Bigfoot* (E.P. Dutton & Co., 1973) the rules of formal logic "forbids the drawing of inferences from hypothesis, but this is the currency the monster establishment commonly deals in." This hypothetically constructed world of the monster community Dr. Napier (borrowing from Basil F. Kirtley) called the Goblin Universe.

As used here the Goblin Universe is roughly equivalent to the field of Forteana. This is the field of study dealing with odd occurrences seemingly outside the boundaries of science. Within Fortean literature the equivalent term for the Goblin Universe is the Fortean Universe. The Fortean Universe gets its name from Charles Fort, of the "damned facts" fame, who was one of the pioneers of the field. Mr. Fort spent many years researching and writing about these shadowland events and in so doing helped popularize—if he didn't actually invent—the entire field. We are not going to split any hairs and here the Goblin Universe and the Fortean Universe will be used interchangeably.

Whatever else these things may be, they are certainly universals of time and space. There is no society known that does not have tales of some elusive creatures or supernatural beings existing just outside the norm of everyday life. So pervasive are these stories that one is forced to the conclusion that this need for the mysterious and unexplained has a biological origin. Somehow, the possession of these stories gives an edge in the fight for survival to the groups that have them.

At first glance UFO's, Bigfoot, the Loch Ness Monster, Sea Serpents, Leprechauns, Goblins, Fairies, Brownies, Angels, Demons and Ghosts do not appear to have very much in common. If, however, instead of concentrating on what the objects are we concentrate on how they are perceived the similarities begin to stand out. As John Napier pointed out Unidentified Flying Objects and Pegasus the Winged Horse may look very different, but they fly out of the same stable. In today's rationalistic world, nobody believes in flying horses, but they have no problem with UFO's routinely defying the laws of physics.

I am afraid I must begin this look at Fortean events by disagreeing with some of Dr. Napier's reasoning. I dislike doing this as I consider his handling of the Bigfoot issue to be one of the most intelligent treatments of the subject ever written. Still he was perfectly correct in stating that no one can draw conclusions from hypothesis. Where I differ is in saying that the subject is an illogical one. There is only the appearance of illogic because the data is being twisted to fit the theory rather than the theory to fit the data. If all of these hypothesis and theories are set aside and we stick to demonstrable facts then the logic of the problem is really rather simple.

So what are these facts? One we have already mentioned is the universal nature of the phenomena. There are two others that, taken together, points—like a good birddog—straight at the quarry. The first is the fact that all of the denizens of the Goblin Universe have resisted all efforts to prove their physical reality. And the second is that all of these beings find their basis in the eyewitness account. There will be hundreds—if not thousands—of reports from people who claim to have seen the thing with their own eyes. The numbers are so great that on probability alone it would seem impossible for all of them to be mistaken. Standing opposite each other the eyewitness account and the lack of physical evidence form the two pillars upon which a Fortean event rests.

When dealing with Forteana most authors begin by presenting a whole series of these eyewitness accounts with the object, seemingly, of demonstrating reality by sheer repetition. At first glance, the weight of all this testimony seems overwhelming. A second look will reveal more thunder than lightning. "Seeing is believing," they say, but the problem with any eyewitness account is that in the end that account is a memory.

We have already encountered the problems that arise when trying to prove a memory. Stop the first police officer you see and ask her about what happens when different people describe the same accident. In all probability, there will be as many versions as there are witnesses. And since the accident cannot be repeated what physical evidence is present must be used to determine whose version is most accurate. Without any objective evidence, it is just one persons word against another.

To look at the implications of this we will begin by giving an example of an eyewitness account. Rehashing dozens of such accounts will accomplish nothing so we will confine ourselves to a single account, which I believe is typical. This eyewitness account is a UFO story and it was chosen because I am the witness.

As a young lad, I grew up on a farm in rural America. Early one morning I set off for the barn to check a Morgan mare that was ready to foal. It was that time of the morning when it had just become light enough for the stars to disappear and, as the barn was north of the house that was the direction I was facing. As I walked down the lane I noticed a very intense white light coming from the east on a flight path that would cause it to pass directly in front of me. My first thought was that it was the landing lights of a plane and my second was to be surprised at how fast it was moving. It was then that it dawned on me that it was not making any sound.

The object itself appeared to be an intensely white circular disc that looked to be about the size of a quarter held at arms length. I realize now—with the benefits of higher education—that it could not possibly have been that large, but that is what I thought at the time. By now it was light enough that any solid body this light was attached to should have been visible, but there was nothing. As it passed directly in front of me it suddenly began to bounce up and down like "follow the bouncing ball" in the old sing-a-long cartoons. It then faded away, brightened back up to its full intensity, continued on for a short distance, bounced up and down once more and was gone. Just like turning off a light bulb, the light was there and then it wasn't. And after it was gone, there was no sign of a solid body anywhere.

When I got back to the house, I found that my mother had been looking out of the kitchen window and had also seen it. Within the conventions of a UFO investigation this is significant for any UFO sighting witnessed by more than one person is assigned a higher degree of importance than the same event with only a single witness. As to my experience, not much came of it. I told some friends at school and then pretty much forgot the whole thing.

So what was it? It was not a conventional aircraft and since it was moving against the wind, it was not a weather balloon or swamp gas. Ball lightning? Well maybe, I know very little about ball lightning so I cannot categorically rule it out. Still the very existence of ball lightning is controversial enough that it does not raise much above the level of a Fortean event itself.

And since meteors don't bounce what are we left with? In the end, and after all these years, the most I can say is that I saw something that I was never able to identify.

So, if I actually saw this with my own eyes how can I say that it did not have physical existence? I can't and this is one of the main characteristics of the eyewitness account. Just as very few people who have ever had a mystical union with the One ever doubt its validity, so few people who have ever witnessed a Fortean event ever doubt that it is real. This is a common feature of all such experiences whether it is meeting a ghost in a dark hallway, seeing a manlike creature in the headlights of your car, or a leprechaun hiding in the grass. They all have the power to convince the person seeing them of their reality. What is lacking is any form of physical evidence that would compel a doubter to believe.

As the skeptics pointed out long ago proving the truth of anything is not so easy. Add to the stubborn capacity of people to see things differently the fact that it can never be known under what conditions of drink, drugs, stress or fatigue the sightings were made and the problem becomes even more acute. Most sightings are, no doubt, straightforward misidentifications, some are hallucinations, some are outright lies and some are the unvarnished truth. The question then becomes how to determine which is which? The reputation of the witness ultimately counts for nothing because pillars of the community have been caught lying just too many times. The same goes for statements taken under oath. On probability alone, some of these witnesses must be sane, sober and truthful, but which ones are they?

Consider a man sitting peacefully on his own front porch completely alone. As he sits ruminating, he sees an ultra-light plane fly by. Later he recounts what he saw to some of his friends and since they are all familiar with ultra-light planes, no one doubts his word. Suppose, however, they did doubt his word? Suppose they called him a liar and said, he could not possibly have seen what he claimed to have seen. How is he to prove himself right? Photographs, he didn't have his camera with him and even if he had the state of the art of today's special effects would make the them suspect. Even if he were to go out and buy an ultra-light and show his friends that still does not prove he saw one when he claimed he did.

Science has taken a bad beating over its perceived disinterest in this whole field. This is frequently put down to some dark conspiracy to protect some cherished belief. This is so silly an idea as to hardly be worth refuting. For scientists are human beings and if there is money to be made, fame to be won or careers to be advanced someone would have broken ranks by now. No, science as a body has no interest in investigating Fortean events because when your evidence consists of eyewitness accounts there is really nothing to investigate.

It is this total lack of confirming evidence that is the second major feature of a Fortean event. For no matter how real the event is to the witness circumstances will always arrange themselves so that definitive proof is lacking. Many footprints of Bigfoot have been found, photos have been taken of UFO's and Nessie has been tracked on sonar, but who's to say they're not fakes. The brutal fact is that in spite of years of effort by many people there is not one single piece of hard evidence that would compel the average scientist to give the matter a second thought. Couple this lack of hard evidence with the eyewitness accounts and it leads to what is the dominant characteristic of a Fortean being. This is that, when all is said and done, it is not possible to either prove or disprove their existence.

This sounds like one of those cute little play on words used in relativity that really doesn't have any meaning; but here, as there, it is the crux of the matter. To see why this is let me tell you the story of my brother George. Imagine that you and I are aboard a spaceship in interstellar space. We are as alone as it is possible for two people to be. One day, to your amazement, I walk up and introduce you to my brother George who has just popped in for a visit. Not seeing George, you conclude that all this solitude has affected my mind. For my part, I am equally surprised. I do not understand how you can claim you do not see George since he is standing right next to me. Now it is my turn to doubt your sanity. OK, you say, if George is real prove it, have him say something. But, unfortunately, George is a sensitive soul who takes offense at your lack of belief and leaves in a huff.

Now was George there or not? The normal procedure in a case like this would be to submit the question to other people. If they see George then you are crazy, if they do not see George then I am crazy. But here there are no other people. It may be possible for one side to convince the other by sheer eloquence, but in the absence of hard evidence, neither side's opinion can be more than a belief. Just like any good Fortean event the question of whether George really exists cannot be answered. Now let us name this spaceship Earth. I am the half that believes in UFO's and you are the half who does not. So do UFO's exist? Just as with George, this is a question that cannot be answered.

All of this is aggravated by the fact that all of this eyewitness testimony, that looks so substantial, has yet another weakness. The authors of books dealing with one or another of our entities will take a large body of testimony and use it to create a sort of identikit profile of the entity in question. Each author will give the material their own slant emphasizing the things they belief to be important. In the absence of evidence, this is all they can do. Other authors will do the same with all of these versions congealing into a standard picture. Once this happens, all later authors will tend to follow its lead and the parameters of the phenomenon have been set.

Take Bigfoot, for example. The picture that emerges is of a 6-14 ft. tall human-like creature covered in a short brownish hair. This creature walks upright like a man on rather enormous feet, hence the name. It has practically no neck, is not very intelligent and has a serious BO problem. What is not generally realized is that in arriving at his description a very extensive literature has been culled.

Distributed throughout the many sightings are ones that simply do not fit the established pattern. There are sightings of Bigfoot that were white. There are reports of footprints that are wedge shaped or only have three toes. Yet others look more ape-like than human. Of course, serious Bigfoot hunters discount all of this aberrant evidence as false since it fails to conform to the ideal. Still to select ones data to support a preconceived idea is a cardinal sin of science and does not do anything to aid believability here.

Now wait a minute, any good researcher has to sift through the available evidence and discard the part that is junk. Anyone so credulous as to accept all evidence unquestioningly will never make any advances. And this is true, but to sift this evidence in a meaningful manner requires some physical evidence on which to base judgments. This is exactly what is missing here. Without physical evidence to back it up accepting or rejecting, any single piece of evidence amounts to no more than personal opinion. In the case of Bigfoot's footprints, for instance, sifting through all the various types of prints that have been found is an arbitrary act founded upon our daily experience of what a footprint should look like. This is the most natural act in the world for if we accept all evidence unjudgmentally you will have allowed for the existence of the Devonshire Devil.

On the evening of February 7, 1855, it snowed in Devonshire in England. Sometime during the night the snow stopped. The next morning February 8 when the locals awoke, it was found that sometime during the night something had come walking through the Shire. What was found was a line of tiny hoof-shaped tracks exactly eight inches apart extending through no less than 18 towns and villages in Devon. Whatever it was, it was no respecter of obstacles. Tracks were found on footpaths, on roofs, in walled gardens and in open fields. They stopped at the Exe estuary near Powerham Castle only to reappear on the other side eventually ending at Totnes. From one end to the other, the tracks formed a trail over 100 miles in length.

The London newspapers had a field day with many columns devoted to speculating on what the "beast" might have been. The answers that were offered, that they were the marks of kangaroos, birds, a wolf or even a meteor shower really do not impress. Of the explanation of the local villagers, the Times wrote, "The superstitious go so far as to believe that they are the marks of Satan himself," and I really have no better explanation to offer. The point of it all is that the tracks in Devonshire and Bigfoot tracks in California are exactly analogous, if you accept one you must accept both for there is no logical way to exclude either.

Much has been made of the fact that some large animals have only been discovered within the last century. The mountain gorilla and the okapi are frequently mentioned with a new species of peccary having been discovered in South America within the last 20 years and a new monkey species just last year. As with eyewitness accounts, the significance of these discoveries are more apparent than real. First off when an animal is undiscovered what this means is that it is unknown to Europeans. They are officially discovered when a European— preferably an Englishman—finds them. Let us not forget that while European scientists may have been in doubt about the mountain gorilla's existence the local natives had no such problems. But, of course, none of them were members of the Royal Society. The reason that the gorilla, okapi and all the rest went undiscovered for so long was basically because no one was looking for them. When science finally began to take an interest the animal was discovered within just a few years.

To be believable even a phantasmagoric being needs a history. After all one of the properties of any physical being is it's history and any object professing to be real must have one. To speak of the Yeti or the Loch Ness Monster is immediately to label it a myth. No flesh and blood entity is so simple. In the case of an animal, for instance, it must be biologically functional as well. The Cyclops has fallen from favor precisely because no one believes that such a being could exist. Once biological reality is conceded, it frequently happens that a whole Systema Naturae will develop. Again, let us look at Bigfoot.

Far from being one kind, Bigfoot is part of a rich folklore that is worldwide. In North America alone, there have been sightings in every state with the possible exception of Hawaii. Worldwide there are so many types that they have been divided into three classes. The first class contains what are essentially wild men. Not that different from us they are basically humans that have gone to seed. The Alma's of central Asia are an example of this type. Next are the small pygmy types. Mostly human with animal characteristics this class of beings bears more than a little resemblance to Fauns, Earth Spirits and other minor deities. Last, but not least, there are the giants. Conceived of as almost wholly animal it is into this class that Bigfoot falls.

Reports of these beings have a worldwide distribution. From the high montane forest to the temperate forests of N. America, Europe and Asia, throughout the tropical rain forests of S. America, Africa and the Orient and all points in between. Throughout this enormous range there are reports from eyewitnesses of Bigfoot, Saquatch, Yetis, Satyr, Silvetres, Wodehouse, Orang-pendek, Sedapa, Nittawo, Kriffi, O-mace, Duendis, Kaptar, Almas, Abbasti, Gool, Sesqac, Cyat-Ko and Zamedwas to name a few. For such a plethora of creatures to exist as flesh and blood animals over such a range and to be unknown to science is a flat out impossibility that not all the ingenuity in the world will change.

The sad truth is that these stories bear more of a resemblance to myth and legend than to any living creature. As Michael E. Bell (*Food For The Dead*, Carroll & Graf Pub., 2001) puts it: "The shadowy region between the possible and the impossible, the known and the unknown, the natural and the supernatural is precisely the domain of legend." This also seems to be the domain of all of these manlike creatures. They abduct women for immoral purposes, walk with their feet on backwards, have long hair that falls over their eyes and obstructs their vision when they run down hill, the females have such pendulous breasts that they have to throw them over their shoulders or they have a terrible stench. All of these things occur repeatedly in the wild man stories and all are classical myth motifs.

A myth is an explanation of an otherwise unexplainable phenomenon of nature. This explanation serves as a guide for our conduct and is an explanation of life's mysteries without having to be true in a scientific sense. Even today, these motifs continue to function in molding the world we live in, although, if you wish to get technical, Fortean events bear more of a resemblance to legend than they do to myth. For example, none of these eyewitness accounts has a story line. There is no triumph of good over evil, no guidelines for living ones life, no moral whatever. They sound like straightforward observations of nature and this is what gives them their power. What we begin to see in all of this is an entity that bears a strong resemblance to a subjective being.

We have touched on this subject before. Basically, a subjective being is an entity that has subjective existence so that you cannot say definitely whether it exists or not. In fact, the mental concepts needed to understand a subjective being are very similar to the ones needed to understand Schrödinger's cat. A subjective being can only be thought of as, in some sense, existing and not existing at the same time. What is needed then is a being that has these properties and is, as it were, available for study. If such an entity could be found it would give us a base from which to draw conclusions.

Experience has shown that Fortean events cannot be explained in terms of the physically real. Whatever these things are, they are not flesh and blood in the ordinary meaning of the word. If it is impossible to understand a Fortean entity in terms of what it is, perhaps they can be understood in terms of what they do. To accomplish this it will be necessary to stop thinking of these things as objects and to begin to think of them as a process. We will pursue this line of inquiry by starting with a simple such entity and then working up to full-blown Fortean event. And the best place to begin to look for these proto-Fortean entities is in the modern phenomenon of channeling.

To call channeling modern is to begin with a misrepresentation. It is the term channeling that is modern; the phenomenon itself is as old as the hills. Channeling is the obtaining of knowledge from a source outside of the ordinary everyday world. Channelers—or mediums as they were once called—are people who, by going into a trance, are able to make contact with disincarnate spirits. Called spirit-controls or just controls they are thought of as being from another plane or dimension. The entire field of channeling is broader than just speaking with controls, but since it is the controls we are interested in we will confine ourselves to them.

Known by many names the idea that the living can communicate with the dead has been taken for granted by virtually every society right down to modern times. This spirit or soul was considered the true essence of a person with the physical body being only a shell. This nonphysical essence survived death and, on rare occasions, could communicate with the living. Channelers claim to be able to make this communication possible. Only with the rise of rationalism did the existence of the soul come into question.

So who or what are these messengers from the beyond? Among channelers themselves, the most common explanation is that these entities are the disincarnate spirits of those who have passed on. Historically many other theories have been offered. For some it is God Himself speaking, while for others it is only His angels. Demons, divas, elements, animals, even plants have all had their followings. In our more enlightened age, we have outgrown these simple beliefs. It is now thought more likely that they are Extraterrestrials, the Higher Self, Group Beings, the Universal Mind or the Collective Unconscious. For most of the medical profession, they are hallucinatory delusions, multiple personalities or plain frauds. When speaking of these controls the Harvard University theologian Harvey Cox has said, "They're so cuddly and friendly. They seem to be yuppified versions of the demons and spirits of another time." And this was very perceptive of Dr. Cox because that is exactly what they are.

The major characteristic of a Fortean entity is that independent existence is impossible to prove. The gorilla was discovered because it was a noumena base. Without this component, physical reality can never be proven. And since Fortean entities have shown themselves to be incapable of being objectively proven they must lack this element. This is why the ingenuity of countless people—scientist and nonprofessional alike—has failed to produce any physical proof. No one has been able to find any physical evidence because there is no physical evidence to find. Fortean events are only subjectively real which makes them strictly a mental process. This is not the same thing, however as being a hallucination.

Having said this we must immediately back off. The mental mechanism that creates hallucinations almost certainly has a role to play here. Only what is being produced is more than simply seeing spiders and pink elephants. No, what we are seeing here is the same thing we saw with faith healing; which is, that some parts of the world we normally consider as physical are really constructs of the mind.

A Fortean being has the appearance of being real, it has length, breadth and height; all the concepts used to structure reality are present. Note that once these constructed beings have been projected into the hologram they not only look real, but produce the appropriate physical actions as well. So far, we have concentrated our discussion upon sight; but of course, all of the senses can be hallucinated. After the mind creates reality, these constructs are, for all practical purposes, real.

This is all very interesting but somewhere we have lost track of channelers and their controls. It is time to go back to them. Using these controls as our base, we shall set ourselves the task of explaining how all this is possible using only such abilities as the mind is known to possess without invoking any supernatural aid whatever.

In fine, what a spirit-control does is generate information, usually in response to specific questions. To accomplish these one or more physical effects may be manifested. These can include not only speaking through channelers, but raps, bangs, thumps and the movement of physical objects with all of this being used to convey some message. The value perceived in these messages varies depending upon who is asking. Some find them quite profound and have their lives altered. Others find them useless drivel.

If channeler's produce the disincarnate spirits they are called spirit-controls. If they appear on their own, they are called ghosts or poltergeists. Poltergeists or "noisy spirits" are spirit-controls untamed relatives. At one time or another, they have produced all of the different phenomena encountered with spirit-controls. From medieval times, onward poltergeists have been associated with strange and eerie happenings.

Traditionally these happenings begin with raps, thumps or other noises and proceed to the movement of physical objects. The only thing they do not do is speak through channelers. In olden times such goings on where attributed to mischievous spirits. Today's explanation is that it is some form of psychokinesis produced by someone, usually a teenager, in the house. Of course, this is no more understood than noisy spirits, but at least you do not have to use the word ghost. All of which leads us to a fascinating gentleman named Philip.

Philip

Philip was the brainchild of a group of researchers at the Society of Psychical Research in Toronto, Canada. The Society had been engaged in standard psychic research when the question arose as to whether the spirits they were in contact with were independent beings or some form of group hallucination. An experiment was devised to find out. To carry out this experiment a group was formed that eventually consisted of eight people, five women and three men. The stated goal of this group was to consciously produce their own 'ghost'.

All spirit-controls have a history as befits an independent being. This history is usually a dramatic one that explains how the control got to be a spirit. Therefore, the first order of business was to create a suitable story for their 'ghost' whom they named Philip. The story decided upon was that Philip had been an aristocratic English gentleman living in the 1600's at the time of Oliver Cromwell. He had married a girl named Dorothea who, although beautiful, was frigid making his home life far from happy. Surrounded by unhappiness in his marriage he eventually found happiness outside of it in the arms of a gypsy girl named Margo.

Dorothea was not the continental freethinking type and when she learned of the affair she had Margo charged with witchcraft. Bringing her influence to bear she saw to it that Margo was condemned and burned at the stake. Philip was not a strong personality and he was too frightened of losing his reputation and possessions to offer any protest at the trial. Finally, overcome with remorse and self-loathing for his weakness, he threw himself from the battlements of his home.

Dr. Iris M. Owen was called in as technical advisor and the experiment began. The group started holding regular séances in which a deliberate attempt was made to contact Philip with the

225

first results of all this effort being exactly nothing. Fortunately they endeavored to persevere and finally, after many months, where rewarded with a rap. From this beginning, they proceeded to get the entire story from their new friend.

During the course of the experiment, Philip developed a distinct personality that included a repertoire of raps, rumbles and scratches. In the later stages of the experiment, the group succeeded in getting Philip to levitate the table, although they failed in their attempts to materialize him. After Philip became well established, it was found that the presence of any four members was enough to produce a visit. Following on this success a separate group at the Society created and made contact with the spirit of a French resistance fighter named Lilith. And a still later group was able to establish direct contact with Santa Claus.

So far, everything had gone as planned. Philip had been created as the theory predicted and once created had told his story exactly as it had been concocted. It would seem that the hypothesis that this phenomenon was some sort of group hallucination had been proven. Then a strange thing began to happen, every once in a while Philip would contradict the group's story. Not only that, but on other occasions he seemed to have genuine knowledge of the period that the group lacked.

Within the premise of the story, it had been established that Philip's love for Margo created the remorse that led to his suicide. When first ask if he loved Margo he dutifully responded with a yes. Later, however, when ask directly, "Did you love Margo very much?" he responded with a definite no. This answer produced some puzzled people. If Philip was nothing but "a personal creation of their own minds" how could he vary the story?

On other occasions, Philip showed himself more familiar with Cromwellian England than his creators. None of the members of the group or their advisors were historians. The details of the era were familiar to them only in a general way but since the story was fictitious anyway fine points of detail were deemed unimportant. In the creation of the story, it had been asserted that Prince Rupert was Elizabeth the Winter Queens brother-in-law, both Rupert and Elizabeth being real people of the period. When ask about this Philip said no Prince Rupert was not Elizabeth's brother-in-law. When Dr. Own researched the matter, it was discovered that Philip was right and the group was wrong.

The implications of these answers are rather startling. It seems to show that more was going on than the theory could account for. If Philip is nothing more than the hallucinatory product of the groups collective mind then for him to give an original answer is a little like a cartoon character ad-libbing its lines. Nevertheless, if Philip is not a hallucination he cannot be a traditional spirit either. So what is he?

As we have seen, a thing is considered real if it possesses a physical presence or if it produces an effect that can only be accounted for by assuming its existence. It is this second category that is of interest here. In this second category, you can never know what a thing is you can only know what it does. What this leaves us with is an entity whose chief characteristic is function.

Within science itself, the most hardheaded of mathematicians use these nonexistent entities on a routine basis with the classic example of such a thing being the square root of negative one. Used daily in many branches of science modern mathematics would look quite different without it. Yet it cannot be proven mathematically that the $\sqrt{-1}$ exists at all.

A square root is "the quantity which when squared produces a given quantity." Three x 3 = 9 so 3 is the square root of nine. Now try and find a number that will give -1 as the product when multiplied by itself. Multiply 1 x 1 and you get one, multiply -1 x -1 and you get one. Within the formal rules of mathematics, there is no such thing as the √-1. Scientists get around this by simply using it without trying to assign it existence, a useful idea.

You may already have recognized this as our old friend a functional entity. The term itself is the one opted for by Lawrence LeShan although other names have been used. Hans Vairhainger has called these artificial creations "fictions", while Zolar used "thought-forms" or "pseudo-ghosts." Fictions have too many negative connotations and pseudo-ghosts smacks of the paranormal. Thought-forms we will come back to, but for now, we will stick with functional entity as a good, solid, neutral term. In fairness to Dr. LeShan, it should be noted that our definition of the term might not be exactly the same as his.

The traditional definition of a functional entity is an entity that exists to fulfill a particular purpose. It exists when, and only when, it is being used. A functional entity does not require any of the physical properties usually associated with a physical being. It cannot be said that it does not exist nor can it be said that it does exist. Once it has been created, it will function consistently with the way it was conceptualized. Such an entity will be self-consistent and logical unto itself. Moreover, like any other created being, there will be things it can do and things it cannot do.

For instance, if its description permits a functional entity may be able to travel faster than the speed of light. If you look at the North Star through a telescope, the point of focus in space may be considered as a functional entity. Now swing the telescope across the night sky and focus on the star Regulus. As you moved the telescope, the point of focus crossed many light years of space in just a few seconds. It moves from one star to the other at a speed greater than light's. This is possible because the ability is built into its description. Once a functional entity has been created that description and, therefore, its properties cannot be changed at will. Once created a functional entity begins to take on a life of its own.

Moreover, this is not just a figure of speech. Once a functional entity has been created, it behaves 'as if' it where real and in so doing it becomes real. This is what happened to Philip, once created he has an existence that is independent of the group that created him. He still does not exist between the times he is being questioned; he still must conform to the rules of a functional entity, but within those rules, he is real. And therein lays the secret of Philip's independent answers. He has the memories of a 17th century Englishman because he is a 17th century Englishman. Philip was less than a physical human being, but he was more than a hallucination.

It does not require much of a stretch to see the similarities between Philip and a Fortean event. Like any good functional entity Fortean beings cannot be shown to exist between events. Unlike Philip, these entities appear to possess a body. I say appear for without any supporting evidence they may be no more real than the pink elephants you see after a weekend bender. Still people have touched UFO's, smelled Bigfoot and had their boats tossed about by the ripples produced by Nessie. Photographs have been taken of all of them and the velocity of UFO's has been clocked on radar. Things like this are what allow these beings to fulfill their function of appearing real.

Philip, as created, had all of the characteristics of a functional entity. He had those traits needed to fulfill his function and no others. If the group had succeeded in their efforts to materialize Philip, he would have had an even greater resemblance to a Fortean being. They never succeeded, but other spirits have been materialized during ordinary séances.

Actually seeing a spirit is common enough in both séances and hauntings for this to be a not unreasonable goal.

A spirit-control is what might be called a domesticated ghost, a spirit that has been tamed and put to use. Philip, as created, had all of the characteristics of a ghost. Everything that Philip did, from start to finish, finds its counterpart in the literature of haunting. There is more than one tale from this same literature where someone has meant a ghost so real they were unaware it was a ghost. Ghosts have not only been seen, they have been heard, they have been touched, and they have moved objects and left footprints in old English mansions. In fact, they have been credited with producing every physical manifestation needed to create a Fortean being. If we admit the validity of the Philip experiment then the existence of ghosts must be considered as proven.

The Society of Psychical Research's experiment was a milestone in the field of paranormal research. In their cool headed and scientific approach, they scored a first in the annuals of psychic research and in the process gave us one firm fact to get hold of. Yet what they did was really nothing new. For in the end Philip is nothing but a "yuppified" witches familiar.

Aliester Crowly, in his book on magic, devotes considerable space to the art of raising demons, while Carlos Castaneda spends an equal amount of time learning to acquire an ally. Of course, not all people will consider either Aliester Crowly or Carlos Castaneda as sterling examples, but the plain fact is that the beings they describe have exactly the same characteristics as Philip. If the Philip experiment is valid—and it has been confirmed more than once—then such things are possible. You cannot pick and choose the ones you like. If Philip is real then all the other denizens within this class of beings must be considered equally real.

What it all boils down to is that a functional entity is a creation of the human mind that fulfills some conscious or unconscious need. What it can or cannot do is build into its description. The eerie ethereal quality of ghosts and haunting are part of their description, while the solid material appearance of UFO's and Bigfoot are part of theirs. Once created it will be real while it is functioning, while it is not functioning, it will not exist. All questions about whether it really exists will be impossible for anyone to answer; except perhaps for my brother George, if you can find him.

If we grant all of the above then the term functional entity begins to look to limited. While expressing the idea it does not convey the full range of possibilities. What is needed is a term that covers a materialized functional entity. Now the term "thought-forms" begins to have its attractions. Zolar conceived of thought-forms "as having an objective thought transient reality . . . creatures of the mind of man being highly concentrated masses of thought-forms with no energy other than that given by their creators." And this is a convenient way of conceptualizing something that is very difficult to think about otherwise. Thought-forms, then, are a metaphor and metaphors are the common coin used in understanding the Fortean Universe. For in the absence of any physical evidence any name applied to a Fortean being can be considered as no more than a metaphor with the idea that flying saucers are extraterrestrial spacecraft being the classic metaphor.

I hope I did not short out anyone's pacemaker, but the belief that UFO's are spacecraft from another planet is just as much a metaphor as any other. Looked at coldly the idea that UFO's must be space vehicles, because, hey, what else could they be, is not founded upon very strong logic. For one thing, the technology used by the aliens always seems to be just ahead of current technology here on earth. There are reports from an earlier time of Unidentified Flying Objects with sails. This is beside the problem of how they got here in the first place in defiance of the speed of light limit.

The usual explanation for this is that aliens are highly intelligent with an advance technology that has overcome this problem. Well maybe, but the fact remains that according to our present understanding the laws of physics are built into the fabric of the universe and cannot be overcome. However, since our science may not be the last word we will grant the possibility that they have found a wormhole or some other esoteric feature of space and have made the journey from their world to ours.

Here a technically advanced civilization has, through a vast expenditure of resources, managed to reach our planet. If they really wanted to learn about us, the simplest way would be to make contact. Why spend all this time flitting about. And if they do not want their presence known, they certainly have not been hiding it in a very intelligent manner. Faced with the same problem we would solve it by using satellite technology; but, of course, when UFO's were first reported satellite technology had not yet been invented.

This cannot be pushed to far as the motives; actions and thought processes of an alien race need not conform to any pattern with which we are familiar. We are still left with the fact that the encounters of people with these objects just as easily fit into our functional entity scenario as into the other. The idea that UFO's are of extraterrestrial origin was arrived at more by default than by any more solid evidence. For, once again, solid evidence is lacking. As it now stands, the probability is that the intelligence behind a UFO is right here on earth. This is true for all of Forteana. The names of all Fortean beings may be thought of as metaphors, which like myth give understanding without necessarily giving truth.

The universality of Fortean events leads to the conclusion that some basic property of the mind is involved. The Philip experiment has shown that a group of people has the ability to consciously create an entity indistinguishable from a Fortean being. In this experiment a group did the deed, but in ordinary séances a single medium has achieved the same result, which points clearly to a latent ability within the mind that some people possess to a greater degree than others. Its simplest and most common manifestation is an ordinary hallucination. It can also be seen at work in those persons with paranoid delusions. In other words, the mechanism needed to create a Fortean event is an ordinary feature of the human mind, which only requires the proper trigger to set it off. The question then arises; if this group could create this being by a conscious effort can others be created by an unconscious effort? The answer is almost certainly yes.

When searching for a mechanism by which this phenomenon could be possible we are drawn irresistibly to the idea of the collective unconscious. The collective unconscious is the great Swiss psychologist Carl Jung's term to describe that vast, unexplained region of accrued archetypes and shared memories that form the link between the mind and nature.

Its contents are not personal but collective; that is, they do not belong to one individual alone but to a whole group of individuals and generally to a whole nation, or even the whole of mankind. These contents are not acquired during the individuals lifetime, but are products of innate forms and instincts . . .the primordial image which always has basis of mans thinking--- the treasure house of mythological motifs.

For Jung aspects of truth where revealed to man in one of three ways. These were scientific experimentation, rational analysis and through the creativity of the arts and literature. The latter has revealed universally recurring themes and motifs, which each generation has expressed in their own way. The results range from the primitive myths of Stone Age peoples to dreams of a technologically better future expressed today in books and movies.

Jung thought of this collective unconscious as representing mental processes common to all humanity and, seemingly, did not think of this process as being linked into one collective unconscious capable of functioning as a sort of super mind. His training as a doctor would have grounded him firmly in the sensory mode and would have made this view inevitable. Viewed from the sensory point of view the idea of portions of the unconscious of all people being connected into a single functioning unconscious mind lacks logical cohesion. It is for this reason that the idea is usually meant with either yawns or ridicule when it has been trotted out. The transpsychic mode, however, not only allows but also requires such a connection.

Within the boundaries of the transpsychic mode of being it is permissible to think of the subconscious of all people as linked into one continuous living mind. The image that forms is one of a continuous mental sheath enveloping the world. In fact, if we take the idea of the collective unconscious from Jung and couple it with the transpsychic modes interconnection requirements what we end up with is strangely reminiscent of Pierre Teilhard De Chardin's idea of the noosphere.

Teilhard De Chardin was a scientifically trained Jesuit priest with a penetrating mind and a keen interest in the natural world. He used that mind to try to reconcile what science was teaching him with what the Church had taught. What this amounted to was the reinterpretation of Christianity in the light of evolution. Over the years, this self-imposed task was to produce a body of philosophical writings that many in his Order found less than congenial.

The portion of these writings of interest here is what he termed the "Noosphere." This is most easily visualized as the thinking layer of the earth. Pierre De Chardin regarded this thinking envelope as a biosphere—a sheath of consciousness if you will—encircling the world. In this vision the ordinary zoological depiction of life as a branching tree is replaced by a series of spheres resembling nothing so much as the electron shells enclosing the nucleus of an atom.

A sort of halo of psychic energy the human sphere—above the animal sphere and below the Theo sphere—was "the sphere of reflexion (sic), of conscious inventions, of the conscious unity of the souls." Like Carl Jung De Chardin never seems to have actually taken the final step and unified this enveloping halo into a single consciousness, but he came perilously close. This halo has been continually gaining psychic energy since its creation. Today "it has appeared as a possible element in a sort of higher organism which might for itself, one from all, by constipation. This would indeed be a "unity of the souls."

As a Jesuit trained cleric Pierre Teilhard De Chardin would have been deeply rooted in the transpsychic ways of thinking and so his failure to take this last step is faintly surprising. Still he gives us what I am sure he never intended, a useful metaphor to use in trying to understand the origin of the Fortean Universe.

Even without allowing for any direct psychic connections between minds, it can still be argued that the Noosphere is only the interaction of the minds of the Philip experimenters' writ large. Since the group succeeded some mechanism must be present that makes this possible. Wheather one allows for an interconection of these minds or not the dynamics of the mental process needed to create a Fortean being is exposed.

If Fortean beings can be looked upon as thought-forms created by the unconscious mind of mankind suddenly they become explainable. If thought-forms have no reality outside of their function then it becomes clear why no physical evidence has been, or ever will be, found. Yet by performing their function, it is equally impossible to say that they do not exist. All that can ever be known about a thought-form is what it does. Bigfoot leaves giant footprints on dusty California roads because he is a ten foot tall bipedal humanoid with big feet. And, the reason no one has been able to find him is that he does not exist.

Explanations for Fortean beings—we will continue with Bigfoot as our type specimen—fall into two categories, those that attempt to utilize the rules of science and those that do not. For some all of these sightings, footprints and even scats belong in the world of the occult. Bigfoot, and by implication all Fortean events, become then a paranormal phenomenon. This rather loose grouping includes beings from another dimension, space aliens and apparitions from 'time warps.'

The reaction of most people to these outlandish and far-fetched theories is just to throw up their hands in disgust. Even to admit the possibility of a paranormal explanation is, in their view, to abandon reason and any hope of a scientific explanation. After all, if there is ever to be any hope of finding the truth one must keep their feet firmly on the ground and stick to the facts.

This has led to a situation where those working on the problem cannot see the forest for the trees. For the one principle overriding fact about Fortean events is that there are no facts. There is not one single piece of undisputed evidence that you can hold in your hand and say this is a piece of leprechaun gold, this fell off a UFO, this is the scalp of a yeti. Without this evidences all of this hardheaded, rational thinking leads only to nonsense. For without data conclusions are being drawn from hypothesis and data is being manipulated to fit the theory making this logical approach anything but.

There is a population of 300 Sasquatch living unknown to science in the Lower Peninsula of Michigan. There is a population of air-breathing creatures only slightly smaller than a gray whale scattered in lakes and lochs throughout the arboreal regions of the northern hemisphere. To ridiculous to be believed, this is the inevitable outcome of trying to use logic in the absence of facts. That I saw an Unidentified Flying Object is a fact. What it was is conjecture? Garbage in, garbage out. Such reasoning only leads to chasing your own tail.

However, if the scientific approach is eliminated that just leaves the paranormal. Surely though if science has no data the paranormal has even less. But, strange to say, this is not so for the paranormal has the Philip experiment. This experiment was conducted with due regard to the scientific method and its findings have been verified by independent researchers. It is, therefore, repeatable. Its findings must be considered as factual. And what did this experiment show? That it is possible for a group of people to consciously and deliberately create an entity indistinguishable from a classical spirit. Moreover, since these spirits—or ghosts if you prefer—are paranormal events Philip must be considered a paranormal being.

Major premise: Philip is a paranormal being.

Minor premise: Fortean beings have the same characteristics as Philip.

Conclusion: Fortean beings are paranormal.

See, I told you it was simple. That Philip is a consciously produced event is a fact. Grant this and it leads to a conclusion that conforms to the rules of logic. This will be a very unwelcome conclusion for many; but it has what the 'rational' explanations lack, the ability to explain the data. So am I saying that Bigfoot, UFO's, Nessie and the rest are ghosts? Yes, more or less. Although technically what we have here is a broad-spectrum phenomenon in which ghosts are only one of many possible manifestations. Ghosts are then no more fundamental or basic than any of the others.

This idea has been made before and is then rejected because everyone knows that ghosts are eerie, ethereal beings of dark hallways and empty houses, while monsters are corporeal beings of open spaces. Yet even a cursory reading of the haunting literature will reveal stories of ghosts having been seen in bodily form in broad daylight, ghosts that make noise, emit odors, move objects and leave footprints. The parallel is exact. There is no single fact that forbids the inclusion of Fortean beings within the paranormal.

This can be done with something like a sigh of relief for if these things are creations of the "participator" mind all the logical conundrums disappear. The reason that these stories have so many mythic qualities is now perfectly clear. They appear to be modern manifestations of classical motifs because that is what they are. The reason that the evidence consists mainly of eyewitness accounts with the intrinsic evidence being so slight the even Ivan T. Sanderson called it "to paltry to be of use" is also made clear. For a mind created paranormal being is a subjective being and this is exactly the characteristic a subjective being has.

Fortean beings are not beings from another dimension, they are not projections by the crews of UFO's and they are not time travelers. They are—for all practical purposes—ghosts. The same property of the human mind that produced Philip is also at work here. Moreover, its basis can be none other than the ability to have a good, old-fashioned hallucination. Grant this as possible, grant that any of the senses can be hallucinated and the rest follows. The difference is only one of degree.

Anima Mundi

If we are to look at Fortean beings in the process of forming, we must begin by taking a closer look at hallucinations. In *Journey To Ixtlan* (Pocket Books, 1972), Carlos Castaneda tells of an experience he had while wandering the desert with don Juan:

"There!" he said in a whisper and pointed to an object on the ground.

I strained my eyes to see. There is something on the ground, perhaps twenty feet away. It was light brown and as I look at it, it shivered. I focus all of my attention on it. The object was almost round and seemed to be curled; in fact it looked like a curled up dog... The animal shivered again and then I noticed that it was alive. . . A new jolt moved the animal's body and I could see its head. . . Judging by its body the animal was obviously a mammal, yet it had a beak like a bird. I stared at it in complete and absolute horror. My mind refused to believe it . . . and then something in me arranged the world and I knew at once what the animal was. I walked over to it and picked it up. It was a large branch of a bush. It had been burnt, and possibly the wind had thrown some burnt debris which got caught in the dry branch and thus gave the appearance of a large bulging round animal . . .I laughed at my idiocy . . .

Dr. Kenneth Wylie, in his book *Bigfoot* (The Viking Press, 1980), tells a similar story. While hiking alone in a remote section of Olympic National Park:

Suddenly, in a momentary flash of half-conscious apprehension and expectation, there stood a huge creature, hulking, dark, enormous. It seemed to glower at me from beyond the inner ring of trees its body like a tree trunk, its vast arms reaching to the earth, into the ground. The deep shadows moved very little as the wind stirred, moaning through the towering top of the conifers hundreds of feet above. My instant recognition passed, and all I could see was a lightning splintered tree, truncated to about ten or twelve feet above the ground . . . Though enormously relieved at my delusion, I was also secretly disappointed.

In telling of his experience, Dr. Wylie refers to the apparition, he saw as a delusion. It might be more accurate to refer to it as a hallucination. A hallucination involves the apparent perception of sights, sounds or an actual physical presence. What it does not entail is any firmly held belief in its reality. If contrary evidence is present or it conflicts with the established paradigm, it will be abandoned. There is nothing strange or unworldly about the ability to hallucinate. This is a perfectly normal attribute of the human mental make-up, which any ordinary person is capable of experiencing under the proper circumstances.

Still hallucinations have a bad rep. Hallucinations are usually thought of as the product of a mind, temporarily at least, off its stride. This can be due to mental fatigue or illness, stress, anxiety, drugs or drink. This idea is wrong. Hallucinations occur across the entire spectrum of the human race from the sanest to the most whacked out. To see how prevalent and natural all of this is it has only to be realized that the most natural hallucinators in the world are children. How many children have worried their long-suffering parents by talking to their imaginary friends? Most grow out of this but it does illustrate the inborn nature of the ability.

While most normal people are capable of hallucinating the ability can be increased with appropriate training. Hypnosis is one way to do this. While under hypnosis, people have been made to perceive objects that are not there and to fail to see something that is there. They have also been induced into perceiving things that are there in a radically different way than they would normally appear. These hallucinations can appear so real as to be indistinguishable from waking state perceptions. Studies have shown that when a hallucination is in progress the eye movements of the subject are such as would be present if there were a real object present.

The psychiatrist Dr. Morton Schatzman wrote a most revealing book on this very topic called *The Story of Ruth* (Putnam, 1980). At the time, he began treatment Ruth was a twenty-five year old American living in England with her husband and children. It did not take Dr. Schatzman long to identify the root of Ruth's problem as lying in her relationship with her father. As a child, her father had both mentally and physically abused her culminating in an attempted rape. An alcoholic her father had been a regular inmate of various prisons and mental institutions.

Ruth's mental disturbances took the form of hallucinations. She would hallucinate an apparition of her father (who was alive and living in America) that was real in every way. She could walk around him, carry on a conversation with him, and even smell him. In the absence of any other people, there would have been no way she could have determined whether her father was there or not.

Eventually, with the good doctor's help, she learned to control these hallucinations. She was even able to establish control over her hallucinations and to turn them on and off at will. She could conjure up the image of her father or anyone else upon demand. At one point—while on a trip —she even had a satisfying evening of sex with her hallucinated husband.

Remember that while Ruth was having these hallucinations her father was alive and living in America. In fact hallucinating people who are still alive is not at all uncommon. As far as the mechanics of such a hallucinatory event is concerned they seem to be the same for either a living or deceased person. This argues against the idea that a ghost is a disincarnate spirit and for the idea that it is a purely mental phenomenon.

Such a being does not differ in any substantial way from a materialized Philip. Eileen Garret, the most intellectually gifted of the 20th Century mediums thought long and hard about the question of whether her spirit guides had any separate reality. In her autobiography, *Many Voices* (G.P Putnam's Sons, 1968) she had this to say about her guides, "I have maintained a respectful attitude towards them, I have never been able wholly to accept them as spirit dwellers on the threshold which they seem to believe they are." Pressed on the question of whether her controls where spirits or fragments of her own mind she gave the following answer (as quoted by Lawrence LeShan):

I have to answer you in a way that seems light and frivolous, but it's really very serious. It's sort of as if on Monday, Wednesday, and Friday I think that maybe they're spirits as they claim to be. And it's sort of as if on Tuesday, Thursday, and Saturday I think that they are multiple personality split offs of my own mind that I have devised to make my life easier. And it's sort of as if on Sunday I try not to think very much about it.

Couple this ability to hallucinate with psychokinetic abilities as displayed in poltergeist events and there is nothing any Fortean does, be it ghost, Sasquatch, UFO or forest sprite that cannot be covered by the theory. While the ability of the mind to hallucinate is real in the sense that the medical profession accepts it, PK abilities are another matter. Falling under the mantle of the paranormal its reality is more problematical. Still the movement of objects is well attested to and if we are not to invoke spirits, some mental ability of this kind must be admitted.

Fortunately, there is a little more than belief to back this up. In October of 1961, Professor John G. Neihardt formed the Society for Research into Rapport and Telekinesis. The model for the Philip experiment the Society began holding meetings with the goal of producing PK phenomena. As with the Philip group a decade later, their initial success was nil. With perseverance, however, they eventually succeeded in getting raps, moving a deck of cards inside a sealed box and levitating a small table.

Several conclusions follow from this. In combination with the Philip experiment, it shows that PK abilities can manifest themselves with or without an accompanying entity, while showing that PK is a normal ability of the mind that everyone has to some degree, however slight. It also shows what mystics have always said, that certain states of mind aid in the process. A "good, jovial state of mind" along with a firm conviction of the reality of PK worked best and it is probably not without significance that when the first group began to achieve success many members of that group thought they where dealing with an actual spirit or entity.

The PK element is necessary because a Fortean being as we have conceived it is slightly more than just a hallucination. This raises the suspicion—to use the language of science—that more energy has gone into its formation than goes into a hallucination. It therefore becomes unlikely that any single individual could muster the energy needed. A Fortean being seems to go beyond what even a group the size of the ones in the two experiments could achieve. This can only mean that it is the product of a much larger group. This brings us back to the idea of the collective unconscious.

The simplest way is to think of this phenomenon as the product of an interconnected collection of minds. When we do, we end up with an entity that, during the performance of its function, is indistinguishable from an ordinary being. And in so doing yet another facet of the participator mind reveals itself.

When Dr. Wylie saw his monster, was it a tree or Bigfoot? A no brainer right, but is it? When you say that the tree was the true reality what you are really saying is that the tree is the approved form of conceptualization within the current paradigm. However, just for those few seconds, Dr. Wylie's mind conceptualized the world in a different way. And in a relative universe to give preference to one view over the other is not allowed.

When we talk about the minds role in creating reality the presumption is that the 3-D image within the mind is connected to the unconditional in such a way as to produce a more or less accurate representation. However, as Kant pointed out long ago there is no necessity for this. Beginning life with a blank mind, we all have to learn to conceptualize the world in the approved fashion. Creating the proper image of the unconditional thing-in-itself we call tree is a skill that has to be learned. Only when we can do this, only when we can conceptualize the world in the approved fashion do we become fully functioning members of society.

The assumption this is challenging is the idea that when an image forms in the mind it must be in response to a distal stimulus. What hallucinations show is that this is not the case. The mind can form its holographic images even without any underlying stimuli. Moreover, the most interesting thing revealed by this whole hallucination business is that some of the things usually associated with the physically real thing-in-itself are really products of the mind.

We saw this before with faith healing. And just as the mind can create a reality, where your cancer goes into remission so it can create a reality where you see hairy humanoids. When the mind creates reality, it creates all of reality. When the research group in Toronto created Philip, they created all of him. They created a 17th century Englishman, one part of such a person is a mind, and that mind had the memories of an English aristocrat. That is how he knew things the group did not. Just as measuring ten years to pass creates a universe that ages ten years so it is here. Time is what you measure with a clock and a thought-form is what you experience it to be.

Reality is then a cultural interpretation. To say that the animal with hoof and beak disease that Carlos Castaneda saw or the Sasquatch Dr. Wylie saw where not real while they were being experienced is to say that my paradigm is better than your paradigm. Since reality is what you experience, for that brief instant they were real. To try to say more, to try and settle the question academically is to go back into the same quagmire we just waded out of.

Of course experiencing one anomalous event is not enough to reshape a paradigm. Deeply ingrained childhood beliefs are not banished that easily. Learned in childhood these beliefs are not based upon logic or evidence. What they do is form the base of the communal mind of society. Think of one's perceptions as pieces in a jigsaw puzzle. Your task as a child is to learn to conceptualize each piece correctly and then fit it together into a united picture. One errant piece from a different puzzle is not going to fit and will be discarded. Anyone who continues to try to force such a piece to fit where it does not belong is going to have their sanity questioned.

Still a perfectly functional paradigm could be constructed where the piece does fit. Learning to conceptualize the world in a different way and knowing that it is real was the very thing don Juan was trying to teach Carlos Castaneda. A Fortean event can be thought of as one of these errant pieces.

It is well enough to say that Fortean beings have a sort of pseudo reality as thought-forms that bear a striking resemblance to Philip. Phillip, however, was created by a conscious effort. To see how this might be accomplished unconsciously begin by granting that most sightings are misidentifications of know objects, exaggerations, or outright fraud. Add to this man's penchant for telling stories. Tell a 'fish story' often enough and eventually someone will believe it. Take all of this, mix it up with the knowledge and beliefs of the prevailing culture and what you get is a UFO, Sasquatch, Leprechauns, Agogwes or Satyrs.

Still there are plenty of strange ideas floating about that never are raised to the level of thought-forms. Santa Claus is the classic example of this. Thought-forms begin as bizarre ideas on the fringe of knowledge. Rooted in the archetypes these ideas are expressed though the milieu of culture to produce a swirling mass of folktales, legends, ballads and myths. In a pre-rationalist society, these are believed without question. Even today those beliefs are stronger than most people would admit.

Think of these beliefs as waves permeating the ocean of life. Sometimes the waves and troughs will intersect and cancel each other out, sometimes the crests will intersect, and they will reinforce each other. And just occasionally, some combination of events will result in a tidal wave. The actual mental gymnastics that sets this in motion bears a close relationship to superstition as both may be held without regard to, or in actual defiance of, logic. We have already seen that suggestion can produce changes of behavior. Initiated by suggestions behavior changes, which in turn, reinforce the belief of others. As decades pass and belief becomes stronger, more people will belief, which will pull in yet more people creating an upward spiral until finally you see George.

A functional entity has been created. Whether it has independent existence or is a hallucinatory impression imposed on some known object is irrelevant. Having such a nature also explains why no knowledge has ever been gained from spirit-controls, extraterrestrials or any other source greater than the level of knowledge of the times. One hundred years ago spirit-controls spoke of universal love and planes of existence, but it was Albert Einstein who came up with $E = mc^2$.

Carl Jung, himself, recognized the archetypical and mythic elements inherent in UFO sightings. It was he who first proposed that flying saucers, and by extension all Forteans, find their base in the collective unconscious of the human race.

Although Jung did not couple this with the idea of a hologram, others have noted this idea. The French astrophysicist and UFO researcher Jacques Vallee was remarking on this very quality in UFO sightings when he stated, "It is the behavior of an image or a projection." These are sentiments echoed by the philosopher Michael Grosso when discussing apparitions of the Virgin Mary. Combining Jung and Vallee he makes a case for these appearances as being holographic projections of the collective human unconscious.

This idea of a separate or higher dimensional plane that is populated by angels, archangels, spiritual teachers and other assorted beings is very common in most major religions. When Thomas Aquinas tried to adapt Christianity to the Tree of Life, he was trying to account for these planes of existence. Called "the country of the hidden Imam" in Islam this dimension is thought of as being inhabited by imaginary entities that still have their own corporeal reality. Henry Corbin, late professor of Islamic religion at the Sorbonne, called this hidden realm the "imaginal." Created by the collective imagination of the human race they lack physical presences yet are no less real than physical reality.

Robert Graves echoes this in saying, "ghosts seem to be events rather than things" and this describes Fortean phenomena beautifully. It is only of subjective beings that this can be said.

The mental aspect of the whole phenomenon is associated with altered states of consciousness. What the Philip experiment and Forteans in general suggest is that while in an altered state of consciousness we can evoke personalities whether spirits, deities or demons from the depths of our minds.

Impossible in the sensory mode this phenomenon becomes perfectly possible in either the transpsychic or mythic modes. Grant the interconnectedness of the transpsychic and what the Toronto group did consciously a larger group could do unconsciously. Allow the unconscious to interconnect and it does become collective in a way that is very similar to the occult concept of Anima Mundi, the Soul of the World. This, in its turn, bears more than a little resemblance to the idea of a Noosphere, a sheath of consciousness enveloping the world. Functioning unconsciously, in just the same way as the Toronto group did consciously a Fortean being is born. Amplify it by a greater number of minds, reinforce it by a continual renewal through personal anecdote—the eyewitness accounts—and you have the full-blown Fortean Universe.

Take ghosts, spirits and all the phenomena associated with haunting. Once the human mind had evolved enough to conceive of a soul and an after-life the idea of a ghost would follow quite naturally. Once the idea formed confirming stories would, just as naturally arise. The whole mechanism of misidentification and fraud would come into play. As more and more stories are told, the number of people who believe go up until someone sees a ghost.

Fortean beings are paranormal events and the paranormal is just as much a part of life as anything else. Ghost sightings are events at the edge of normality that are associated with a particular emotion. In the case of ghosts, that emotion is fear. The ghostly realm is one of the monstrous and inconceivable, inhabited by unspeakable horrors of the darkness ready to pounce on the unwary. In a hunter-gather past, the survival value of this belief is easily seen. In a world inhabited by saber-tooth tigers, cave bears and dire wolves, no one who wandered about alone in the dark contributed very much to the gene pool.

Whatever other emotion a Fortean event may provoke one emotion they all evoke is exhilaration. This feeling has been called "legend tripping." Legend tripping is essentially the same thrill one gets riding the roller coaster. Someone experiences a creepy feeling in a weird setting, hears a strange noise or sees something they cannot explain. Their first reaction is to awe their friends with their experience. The interpretation of what this experience means now becomes a social event.

The conclusion, which will tend to incorporate any local legends that seem applicable, will owe more to titillation than to reasoned argument. The avowed reason for all of this interest is to solve the puzzle, but the result is to perpetuate the thrill. With legend tripping a story becomes an event.

Today's Forteans are the modern equivalent of good old fashion monsters sanitized and civilized to bring them into line with today's ideals and morals. In ancient Greece, the Cyclops sat in his cave and dined on passing sailors. Fire breathing dragons wiped out whole villages while capturing fair maidens. Yet murder and mayhem are not conspicuous features of Fortean events today. Whatever their function it is being arrived at within the accepted mores of society.

It might not be without relevance to take note of the fact that those cultures and paradigms within which many of these phenomena originated and developed were not our paradigms. Earlier societies did not feel our need to find answers devoid of metaphysical paradox. Primitive peoples inhabited a world where man and nature or man and monsters were different expressions of the same thing. To the native there is no distinction between the 'real' world out there and the 'real' world of their religious beliefs. Still if we are to make any sense of all of this, it must be related to our own time.

In today's language, Fortean beings can be thought of as conferring some sort of survival advantage. Some of the possibilities we have already looked at. In the absence of scientific knowledge myths, legends and folklore were what gave life its structure, coherence and meaning. Common beliefs and common understanding were what held the group together and made them stronger in adversity. In human societies, where oral traditions have replaced ritual grooming, anything that reinforces the truth of those beliefs would lead to greater cohesion and a better chance of survival.

Times of adversity are also times of stress, the two being inseparable. If there is any validity to this idea that Fortean phenomena help in overcoming adversity then they should be more prominent during times of stress. In fact it would not be stretching the idea to far to wonder if stress was the trigger. Take poltergeist activity for example, when investigated it has been found that in the majority of cases there is a teenager in the house undergoing some sort of stress. In many cases, this is brought about by the onset of puberty. This is so common that it is considered a diagnostic feature of poltergeist outbreaks. According to modern thinking, repressed emotions are released as psychokinetic events with stress being the causative agent.

Stress is also implicated in UFO reports. Sightings of strange things in the sky have been around since Greek times; but these reports were, at best, sporadic with UFO's, as a cultural phenomenon, really only coming into their own in the late 1940's. It was during the 1950's, when the implications of nuclear weapons where beginning to be understood, that the first major flaps occurred. And since many people find the idea of being incinerated in a nuclear holocaust distressing, the cold war can fairly be thought of as a time of stress.

From then on sightings waxed and waned more or less in step with US-Soviet relations. With the collapse of the Soviet Union and a decade of economic prosperity these reports dropped off so sharply that some of the leading investigating organizations closed their doors. Since 9-11, however, reports of strange happenings have begun to pick up again. And what is true for UFO's is true for the others as well.

The Philip experiment has shown that a being with the qualities of a Fortean entity is possible. These beings, on the edge of reality, can be viewed as forming smooth progression from someone using a oujia board to Bigfoot looking in your bathroom window. And the nice thing is it does not require hypothesizing any astral planes or mental powers beyond those humans are known to have. The whole phenomenon can be explained by extrapolating these powers. The world, then, is not divided into the normal and the paranormal it is divided into the objective and the subjective, which make it much simpler to understand.

We will now leave such ordinary things as Fortean beings, faith healing and the paranormal and strike out into the truly metaphysical. Early on I invited you come with me and joust with the jabberwocky. It is time now to don your amour and mount up.

The Eternal Present

There has been a lot of talk about how strange and incomprehensible is the world as revealed by modern physics. What science had done, however, is not to discover basic truths unknown to philosophy or magic. What it has done is to give these insights a mathematical base. For what is the uncertainty principle but the quantum level expression of skepticism? By showing that entangled particles can be thought of as one system what was learned that a shaman did not know? The world is a strange place to be sure, but as John Wheeler has said, "We will only understand how strange the universe is when we realize how simple it is."

Wise men throughout history have tried and failed to produce a theory that will account for the whole of reality. In a relative universe this is not surprising, although none of this has stemmed the tide. Here we will look at some modern attempts to understand current findings and add a couple cents worth ourselves.

If there is a common hub out of which western understanding of reality radiates it is the theological explanation. Western thinking may use the logic of the Greeks, but its ultimate base is Judaic thinking. Carried forward by Christianity and Islam, this thinking shapes the beliefs of many millions of people. As revealed by the Book of Genesis the world was created by an all-powerful God who looked upon His creation "and saw that it was good."

Within this account can be found the premise of objectivity upon which Western thinking rests. Opposing the Eastern view of maya Western tradition postulates a world that is physically real regardless of whether there are people in it or not. We live in this objectively real world because the ancient Hebrews lived in it. God created humanity in His own image and since God is separate from the physical world humanity must be as well. This world was created for the benefit of humankind to be used as they see fit. God has given humanity a code to live by and the circumstances of everyone's life are dependent upon how well they follow this code. This is the origin of the idea of sin and it is also here that the emphasis upon cause and effect had its beginnings.

When science advanced beyond the clockwork universe of classical physics it found itself confronted with numerous contradictions, paradoxes and anomalies. Here we will look at a few of the ideas that have been proposed to try to make sense of it all. What these theories are is an attempt to translate into words what the mathematics is saying.

There are many schools of thought on what this is. Here we will take a brief look at the Matter/Mind School, hidden variables, many universes, quantum logic, holography and our old friend the Copenhagen Interpretation. We will begin with a more mainstream idea that is hot at the moment, which is string theory. String theory— and now M-theory —grew out of efforts to unite the four primary forces (electromagnetic, the strong and weak interactions and gravity) at the atomic level into a Grand Unification Theory. This theory is the first viable candidate for a unified quantum field theory of all the elementary particles and their interactions. The part of it we are interested in is the idea that the universe is multi-dimensional.

The idea that the universe might be composed of more than one dimension dates back to the 1920's when Theodor Kaluza and Oscar Klein proposed a unification theory to unite gravity and electromagnetism that required one extra dimension. From these humble beginnings, successive theories have added dimensions until today it is up to eleven or so with no end in sight. As understood the whole of the everyday three-dimensional universe can be thought of as a patch on the fabric of the super universe. Since no quantum level particle or any electromagnetic phenomenon can spread into these other dimensions (only gravity can do this), the world is the same 'as if' it were three-dimensional.

This idea, that reality is composed of layered dimensions, is a common enough motif in descriptions of reality outside of the scientific ones. Various religions and many esoteric schools postulate other planes of existence inhabited by assorted powers, spirits, angels and archangels. All of which is dismissed out of hand by the scientific community as without relevance to any of its own theories. Within these scientific theories, extra dimensions are described by mathematical equations that make no mention of any extra dimensional beings.

Of course, these equations are describing the house and not its contents. The mathematics describing the three-dimensional world does not reveal any beings here either. Such beings in fact may not exist, but our present level of knowledge does not allow that determination to be made. In the final analysis, science can have nothing to say on the subject. What may or may not exist in any extra or parallel dimensions must always remain a matter of speculation.

One of the more popular of today's theories is the Many Universes or Many Worlds Theory. Different physicists have given this theory a slightly different slant with some speaking of "Many Worlds" while others speak of "Many Histories." Setting aside the fine points what the theory says is that all the possibilities contained in the Schrödinger wave functions do occur only they occur in different branches of the universe. The cat is alive in one branch and dead in the other.

Imagine a universe that, when a choice is made, splits along the lines of choice. That is whenever a choice is encountered the universe splits in two so that both outcomes are equally real. Faced with two doors you have a choice. You can go thru the right door or the left door. You choose the right door. According to the theory at the moment of choice, the universe splits into two universes. In one, you go thru the right door and in the other you go thru the left. Moreover, this happens every time a choice is made whether it is you choosing doors or subatomic particles choosing a pathway. Infinity of choices creates an infinite number of universes where every possible combination of events has occurred. No contradiction arises from this since there is no communication between these universes.

What we now have is an infinite number of worlds where each must differ from all others in at least one respect. If the history of each world is thought of as a graph this means that point x on one graph need not correspond exactly with point x on another graph. Consider your birth, out there somewhere is a universe where you were born one second earlier than in this one. In yet another universe, you were born one second earlier still and so on throughout the past. Moreover, what is true of the past is equally true of the future. Since what is true of your birth is also true of your death, you can be thought of as existing throughout time. With every possible lifeline for every person, spread throughout this super universe the distinction between individuals begins to blur.

Somewhere out there is a universe where you were president during the Civil War and somewhere else is one were you had an affair with Marilyn Monroe (a pity you guys can't remember that one). Now consider, if all possible choices are actualized within this super universe then that is the same as no choices at all. Remember the subatomic particle used in the example, if it splits in the absence of an observer there is no question of a choice. It simply fills all available niches. Everything that can happen has happened and we are left with a super universe very reminiscent of the unified whole of mystical revelation.

If we can be thought of as being—so to say—spread throughout this super universe so must our consciousness. Yet if this were so it could not rightly be said that there was any consciousness present at all. For consciousness is nothing but the ability to make choices and where there is no choice, there is no mind. Your individual lifeline then represents a thread (one is tempted to say string) of awareness. Again, we find the mind creating reality for without the mind to make choices there are no choices. No one goes through either door. Reality then becomes an infinitely tangled ball of twine with each thread representing a single thread of awareness.

A variant that, perhaps, illustrates this better is what has been called the Cubbyhole Theory. Think of ultimate reality as an infinite number of enclosed spaces like the cubbyholes once used by hotels to hold messages. Each of these cubbyholes represents one dot in a picture containing all possible happenings. When someone looks in a cubbyhole, what it contains is illuminated. As ones gaze flicks across the cubbyholes a sequence of events is generated which the mind interprets as the real world. If this sounds familiar, it is because this is the very scheme we have been using here with a DVD disc substituting for the cubbyholes. Consider that laser scanning the disc as one string in the ball of twine and you have the many worlds model.

There are many who are uncomfortable with these and other ideas posed by quantum mechanics, which they try to solve by using a system of thought called Quantum Logic. The proponents of this method say that the reason quantum events seem so weird are that we are looking at them in the wrong way. As exponents of this system see it, the problem is that the quantum realm simply cannot be understood using ordinary everyday reasoning. If the quantum world can only be considered as being understood when it fits the mode of daily logic then it will never be understood. Any weirdness perceived is a result of thinking about this event in an inappropriate manner.

There is more than one system of reasoning used to try to understand the universe with Euclidian logic being the most familiar. The mathematical system used to comprehend everyday existence is called Boolean logic. Within Boolean logic such words as 'and', 'either' and 'or' are encountered. These words reflect the specific order or relationship of events and are, in fact, the logical basis for the minds construction of reality. Within Quantum Logic, the order and relationship of events need no longer be as predicted by Boolean logic.

Since Boolean algebra cannot be used to understand the subatomic realm and since Quantum Logic cannot be used to balance your checkbook, some scientists look upon this as a cop out. For them non- Boolean logic is a parlor trick that puts quantum weirdness in the mind of the observer instead of in the physical world where they feel it properly belongs. Instead of one system that covers all of reality there are two systems, for which empirical necessity dictates, which is used.

Using non-Boolean logic to grapple with the quantum realm leaves us with two alternatives. We can retain the idea that the world has an objective reality and use Quantum Logic to think about it. Alternatively, we can abandon any idea of the world having an independent existence in the absence of an observer. Quantum Logic is the counter from scientists who simply cannot accept the Copenhagen Interpretation of the non-objective nature of reality. Still it is this weird idea that the world only exists when being observed that is the most popular today.

Another solution proffered is the concept of Local Reality. This idea challenges the implications of the principle of local causality, which says that any physical event must find its cause in adjacent physical events. No events in the far reaches of the galaxy can have an instantaneous effect on events here. To do so would violate the rule that no information can be exchanged faster than the speed of light. Still, in the end, the concept of Local Reality is just Quantum Logic wearing a different hat.

Another idea offered in this same spirit is the Hidden Variables Theory. Like Quantum Logic and Local Causality, it tries to win the game by changing the rules. In this case, it says that the collapse of the wave packet is not random but occurs for a reason that the particle 'knows' but the observer does not. Most advocates of this idea consider these hidden variables to be non-local.

Another idea attracting interest is that of the holographic brain. The Holographic Theory was developed by combining the work of the neuroscientist Karl Pribram of Stanford University with that of David Bohm of the University of London. Flying in the face of more conventional ideas about how the brain works this idea was and remains controversial. The idea of the hologram has been used steadily throughout this work, but its use here and this theory are two distinct understandings of how all of this applies to the mind.

To understand this theory it is first necessary to understand holography. Holography is a method of lensless photography that produces a three-dimensional image of the object being photographed. To produce a hologram a laser beam is split in two. The first beam bounces off the object being photographed while the second beam collides with the first to create an interference pattern. Drop two stones into a lake and watch the resulting ripples interact this is interference. And it is this interference pattern that is recorded on a piece of film. This pattern looks nothing whatsoever like the original object. Place this film back in a single laser bean and a 3-D image appears. And, be it noted, any piece of the holographic plate can reconstruct the entire image.

According to the formal holographic theory, this is how the universe is. Our brains then construct reality—by mathematical means in this theory—by converting this meaningless pattern into the everyday world of time and space. We might also notice how similar this idea is to the Tree of Life where each sephira is considered to contain a complete miniature of the Tree.

This idea that the brain is a hologram within a hologram has provoked much resistance. One of the first problems to present itself is that our current understanding of holography is capable of producing only static pictures while the universe is full of movement. It is for this reason that David Bohm used the term holomovement to try to capture this dynamic quality of reality. Many of these problems disappear if all literal understandings are abandoned and it is used as a metaphor. For in the end this theory is just another way of trying to put the experience of the Absolute into words. Describing it as nonlinear rather than linear is just an attempt to make "all is One" sound scientific.

Lastly, there are the matter/mind connection theories. Taking many different forms what this idea says is that it is the act of taking a measurement that collapses a probability wave into an event. Consciousness is, therefore, that property that created reality. The introduction of the conscious mind into physics has been codified into the Copenhagen Interpretation. However, as mentioned earlier, the Copenhagen Interpretation has more than one interpretation.

In the first interpretation, it is maintained that the collapse of the wave packet is purely random. Like power in the mythic mode, it has no need of an explanation, it just is. This being true there is no need to postulate the presence of a watcher; probabilities are all you can ever know.

Introduce the idea of the importance of the observer and many physicists will immediately disassociate themselves from the theory. Now, instead of calling it the Copenhagen Interpretation, it is called the Matter/Mind Connection. However, this is just a rose by another name. David Bohm, himself, contents that this idea that nothing ever happens in the absence of a watcher must be wrong because there are many physical processes that occur without any observer present, with the workings of a distant star being used as an example.

Unfortunately, for all those aligned with this school of thought philosophy has shown this idea to be wrong for the only way to know anything about a distant star is to observe it. What it was doing when it was not being observed is, and can only be, an assumption. We have seen what happens when one tries to reach a logical conclusion based upon an assumption. No, if the strict rules of logic are followed then the matter/mind connection must be considered as established.

A fact has been established; the "participator" mind exists. The reason that human beings have so much trouble struggling to prove objective reality now becomes clear. There is only reality as created by the participator mind. What we consider as 'real' is the noumena of space-time as interpreted by the mind. Fail to understand this and you have committed the mistake of maya, you have confused the map with the territory. Correct this and the world becomes a much more understandable place. John Wheeler is right; the world is a lot simpler than it appears at first sight.

The burden of this message is that nothing can be said to exist when it is not being observed and when it does exist it only does so in relation to something else. Common sense rebels as this. It is OK to say that everything is relative, but there is still a gut feeling that somewhere there must be a beginning. It was this idea that relativity must begin somewhere that the medieval philosophers were trying to express with the idea of "First Cause." Somewhere there must be a foundation upon which all else rests.

Such a foundation described mathematically would be a constant. In mathematics, a constant is a factor that never varies. Moreover, since nothing that varies can be the unchanging base of reality it is among constants that we must look for this foundation. Among constants, the big three are Planck's constant, Newton's gravitation constant and the speed of light, usually designated by the symbol c. These constants form the basis of quantum mechanics and relativity theory respectively. It is upon these constants that our modern understanding of reality rests.

All arithmetic numbers are constants in the sense that they do not change in value. A constant is a little more than this representing some unchanging principle of reality. Constants, therefore, represent a limit to our understanding of reality. Like the Big Bang to try to pass the limits delineated by these constants is to pass outside of the universe itself. Constants can then be looked upon as a boundary where the universe stops. Or where it begins, whichever you prefer. Between Planck's constant, Newton's gravity and c, we will concentrate on the speed of light as being—if not more basic—more useful in trying to understand how the relative universe comes into existence.

If we are going to use the speed of light as our exemplar, it might be as well to clarify how this is understood. Everyone knows that the speed of light is a constant in all circumstances; but, like everything else, it is a little more complicated than that. For there are things that can go faster than light and, in certain situations, light can slow down. To begin to comprehend how this can be it must first be understood that the term "the speed of light" has two distinct meanings. The first is "the speed at which light travels" and the second is "the speed of light in a vacuum."

The speed at which light travels can indeed vary depending upon the medium through which it passes. Within this meaning light travels fastest in a vacuum, a bit slower in air, about 75% for water and 66% for glass. In fact there have been experiments performed that claim to have brought light to a complete standstill, something about sodium clouds and laser beams. However, if the speed at which light travels can vary, where the idea that light speed is a constant come from?

This universal constant idea derives from light speeds second meaning "the speed of light in a vacuum." It is this second meaning that —as an absolute invariable—is symbolized be c. So far, the speed of light in a vacuum has been rather laxly defined as approximately 186, 000 mile/second but, for the purist among you, the exact figure is 299,792,458 meters/sec. Whenever the speed of light is mentioned, it is this speed, symbolized by c, which is meant. So important is this limit that some physicists are in favor of changing the designation c to Einstein's constant.

To be precise, Einstein's constant does not claim that nothing can go faster than light. What it says is that no material object—i.e. no object possessing mass—can accelerate to, nor can any information be exchanged faster than, c. Take the beam of a searchlight sweeping back and forth across the sky. As the end of the beam extends further and further outward it will move faster and faster in its sweeps. When the distance becomes great enough c will be exceeded and the end of the beam will actually be moving faster than the speed of light.

A pair of scissors can produce the same effect. As the blades of the scissors close, the notch between them moves outward with a velocity that becomes infinite at the moment of closure. Like the searchlight beam, the velocity of the notch can exceed c if the blades are of sufficient length. The scissor blades have mass so they can never exceed c, but the notch itself is massless. You can prove this yourself; all you needed is a pair of scissors with long enough blades for the tips to reach the orbit of the moon.

If all of this seems familiar it is because each of these examples in none other than a functional entity. The focus point of the telescope seen earlier is analogous to the points of the searchlight used here. And since a functional entity does not exist in the classical sense, the laws of that existence do not bind it. Instead of the laws of physics, functional entities obey the rules of their description. Still, no matter what its description, no functional entity can ever convey any information at a speed greater then c.

The question then arises as to why light speed is the speed it is and no other? Why is it that no physical object can ever reach light speed and why is it that light coming out of a rocket traveling at 1,000 mph isn't c + 1,000. Ask a physicist and she will probably begin by explaining that as the speed of a material object increases its mass will also increase; the greater the acceleration the greater the mass, which requires even more energy to continue the process. At light speed such an objects mass would be infinite requiring infinite energy to push it, and impossibility.

But, someone may point out; there are things that are already traveling at the speed of light, light for instance. So why isn't a beam of light from a rocket ship moving at light speed plus the velocity of the rocket? Your physicist friend will then patiently explain that the speed of light is not additive. It is not like the addition of numbers, but rather like the degrees of a circle. A circle has 360° and no matter how it is added up, it will never equal more than 360°. But, you say, this may be a perfect description of what is observed but it does not answer the question of why c is what it is.

The answer lies in Special Relativity Theory's most famous consequence, the discovery that time is not changeless, but varies in proportion to speed. Time, in fact, slows down until it stops completely. And in this stoppage of time lies the answer of why the value of c is what it is. "Time is what you measure with a clock" and when the clock stops there is no way of measuring any faster speeds. This is also the reason that the speed of light cannot be added.

I am sure that by now someone has his hand in the air. If nothing can go faster than light what about tachyons? Ask your physicist and she will tell you that relativity theory does not forbid faster than light travel. What it does say is that no material object can ever reach, let alone cross, the light barrier. There is no reason why supraliminal bodies cannot exist provided that they have always been supraliminal. They cannot cross the light barrier either. These supraliminal particles are called tachyons. Such particles would seem an embarrassment to any theory that claims that nothing can go faster than light. But, of course, it all depends upon how you look at it.

To begin with, the evidence for the existence of tachyons is equivocal. There is some experimental evidence for their existence but not all physicists would accept it as valid. We will give them the benefit of the doubt and grant them their existence. Grant this and the conclusion follows that if these particles are truly going faster than light then they also must be going backward in time.

If it is true that time slows down as speed increases, then it must also be true that as speed decreases time will speed up. Follow this line of reasoning to its conclusion and you end up with a mirror image of the light barrier. Eventually a point will be reached where all motion will cease and time will have nothing to measure. It is motion then that creates both space and time. This mirror image of the light barrier also constitutes a boundary to reality.

Now, just for the purpose of this discussion, let us designate the point where all motion ceases and time is (so to speak) absolute as the lower limit of the universe. The point c—where speed is maximized and time stops—becomes the upper limit of the universe. Both are barriers created by one aspect of reality reaching its limit. The relative universe exists between these two boundaries.

If tachyons exist, they must do so within this universe. This is a given for there is no other 'place' for them to exist. Since everything that exists must do so within the confines of this universe it follows that, they must obey the laws of this universe. As conceived tachyons are supraliminal objects that must forever go faster than light. Just as ordinary particles—called tardons—can only slow down as they move away from the light barrier so a tachyon must speed up. And since a tachyon is already beyond the light barrier there would seem to be no limit to how fast it can go.

So how fast can a tachyon go? Just as the light barrier represents the fastest possible speed for a tardon, this same barrier will represent the slowest possible speed for a tachyon. From a tachyons point of view c represents absolute motionlessness. The light barrier as viewed by an intelligent tachyon would look exactly the same as the lower limit of our world would look to an intelligent tardon. All motion would have ceased and time is absolute.

Since this supraliminal particle must be subject to the same laws of physics as tardons, it can only alter a state of motionlessness by speeding up. Moreover, since the same mathematical equations describe both tardons and tachyons a supraliminal tachyon can, starting from zero motion relative to itself, speed up until it reaches 186,000 miles/sec. as measured by its own clock. At that point, it will be going as fast as it can possibly go. From our point of view, it is going faster than light and backwards in time. From its own viewpoint, everything is perfectly normal and the tardons are going faster than light and backwards in time. If, by some miracle, someone could be transported across the light barrier they would never know it. Everything would look just the same. Nothing can go faster than light.

It is said that, as a teenager, Albert Einstein began to think about the problems that led to the theory of relativity by imaging what he would see if he could ride on a beam of light. Let us change that slightly and ask what an intelligent photon would see at the speed of light.

First off as time has stopped such a photon would have no concept of time at all. From its own perspective, it would travel from point A to point B instantly. Since time and space are only two different forms of the same thing for time to stop means that space does too. Differentiating point A from point B then loses its meaning. From our viewpoint, this photon is moving at light speed, from its own perspective it is not moving at all. From its own point of view, it will exist instantaneously wherever it is possible for it to exist.

So what would this photon see while traveling at the speed of light? It would not see anything at all. Since all light is moving at the same speed there is no way that any other light waves or any of the information they are carrying can reach it. From a photons point of view it is not really correct to even speak of it existing at all for it is only where motion exists that experiences are possible and with it existence. This is why the relative universe can only exist between the upper and lower limits of motionlessness.

The Leberswelt moves at normal speeds. Kids on bicycles, planes flying or babies crawling are speeds with which we are familiar. Even astronauts travel at only a tiny fraction of the speed of light. In the anthropic realm of the middle dimension, light speed is completely beyond our experience. Yet between the light barrier and motionlessness is a smooth graph with no one region being more normal than any other.

From the everyday viewpoint, relativity has revealed a world that appears layered. Above the classical world of the conventional is a world of ultra-high speeds and relativistic events. Reach the speed of light and any reality we can know ends. In addition, if it is true that this is the place where reality stops it is equally correct to think of this same place as where reality begins. Think of the world as forming at light speed and slowing down to us.

To us a beam of light comes on with the flick of a switch and it is gone with another flick. To us that beam exists in time. To light itself there is no time. From its own perspective, it is eternal, everlasting, unmoving, unlimited and unchanging. We have seen these words before; the mystics used them to describe the Absolute, which, of course, is just another name for God. So am I saying that the light barrier is God? No, I am saying that the speed of light is Kether, the point where reality begins to form out of the void.

Kether is the Crown, the first Sephira of the Tree of Life. It is here that the relative universe begins to form out of the veils of negative existence. All schools of mystical thought agree that the relative universe first splits into divisions called the father and the mother, the Yin and Yang, Hochma and Binah or light and dark. By whatever name the idea is that the Crown divides into a dynamic positive element and a passive, negative element. What was one is now two.

One of the great finds of quantum mechanics was the discovery of the dual nature of light. The wave nature of light can be thought of as the dynamic active principle corresponding to Hochma, while the particle nature of light corresponds to the inert, passive principle of Binah. This duality of energy and matter is the basis for the modern understanding of reality.

Is it only a coincidence that the first thing we encountered at the light barrier has a dual nature? All mystical traditions report a duality as the first phase of an emerging reality and here we have one. The light barrier is a limit; a point where experience begins and what is found there can be viewed as having a positive and negative nature. What physicists have found is precisely what the mystics predicted they would find. The Jewish mystics call this point Kether and the physicists call it c. Using wildly deferring paths mystics and physicists have arrived at exactly the same place. The Heisenberg lines have crossed.

The mind created matter so that matter can create mind. A paradox if there ever was one. Logic breaks down here just as it does for Schrödinger's cat. And trying to understand the one is as futile as trying to understand the other. For in the final analysis the world we live in is not founded upon logic. Logic is just one more aspect of that reality manifesting itself out of quantum weirdness. The epiphany that the world formed logic and not logic the world ultimately holds the key to truth.

It has to be more than chance that no matter how the problem of the nature of reality is approached the same conclusion emerges. If all roads lead to Rome, it becomes difficult to doubt the existence of Rome. In just this way all lines of inquiry leads to the importance of the role of the mind. With the Heisenberg lines all converging on the importance of the mind it makes doubt increasingly difficult. Running counter as it does to plain common sense this idea always has —and probably always will—generate controversy. All of this not withstanding, the case for the importance of the observers in creating reality, with all the implications thereof, must be considered proven.

The Goblin Universe

Since the first <u>Homo habilis</u> sat thoughtfully pondering a rock, mankind has struggled to understand the world and his place in it. Not just an intellectual game for the idle this search for realities true nature is the most vital and elusive quarry ever pursued. Coloring our every thought and our every action our understanding of how the world works is the foundation on which we build our lives. In this quest, man has followed many paths: rationalism, mystical ecstasy, theological reasoning and Divine revelation have all played their part. Evasive, mysterious, subtle, fleeting and frequently baffling truth remains as elusive today as ever.

If there is one theme that occurs often enough to make it worthy of note it is awareness, either explicit or implicit, of the importance of the mind. Modern physics has strengthened this idea. Of all the various avenues to knowledge it is upon this idea that the Heisenberg lines most often converge; whichever way you turn there is no getting around this idea.

In spite of empirical evidence in its support, society seems curiously afraid of this conclusion. All of this participator stuff is all right for mystics and quantum physicists, but it somehow does not apply to everyday life. This resistance comes not only as a natural consequence of the primary rule, but also lies in the belief that in a relative universe there can be no truths only opinions.

This belief comes about from a misunderstanding of the nature of truth for in a relative universe there is no absolute truth external to itself. Truth must be looked for within reality not outside of it. When one person measures the ruler as 12 inches long, that is the truth and when another measures it as 10 inches long that also is the truth. Like everything else truth has its mental component, but it is truth nonetheless.

Relativity is not just an accounting ploy of the physicists to make the numbers balance. It is a property of nature present wherever a mind exists. In the middle dimension, it primarily expresses itself as uncertainty for just as gravity underlies physical reality so uncertainty underlies life.

Science acknowledges the uncertain foundation of knowledge with Gödel's theorem, while for philosophy it is skepticism. This makes itself felt in everyday life as well. We all know that the only thing we can be certain of is that we can be certain of nothing. All of the various modes of being recognize this and each, in its own way, tries to deal with it. Science does this with statistics, for religion it is propitiatory prayer, magic tries to influence the course of events with power, while mystics greet it with calm acceptance; whatever the response all are attempts to manage the uncertainties of life.

The world is not then as complex as it first appears. Springing out of relativity, complexity is a result of combining the subjective nature of the mental component with the underlying space-time continuum. Once this is done, a world of subjective truth becomes inevitable. The world your mind generates is the world you live in and it is here that answers must be sought. Grant this and certain conclusions follow. For instance, it is only when a mind is observing that the concepts of cause and effect have any meaning. It is only then that entropy appears and with it the arrow of time. The conclusion is inescapable; existence and consciousness are two different manifestations of the same thing.

The Weltanschauung produced by this participating mind has its base in the bicameral structure of the brain. The interaction of reason and intuition kneads experience into the world we live in. The rational speaking left-brain contributes structure and by so doing, lifts the world out of chaos.

Endowing the world with meaning is the province of the intuitive right brain.

Left to itself the rational left-brain would produce a soulless world inhabited by automatons; while the intuitive right brain would produce a world pregnant with meaning, but lacking the structure needed for personal survival. Again, the interaction of the objective and subjective is seen. It is by balancing these two types of knowledge that a world worth living in is created.

For many this delicate balance has been lost. Defining our culture the scientific explanation now forms the mores of society. As has been shown this is too limited. To quote Huston Smith, ". . .the world is not as science says it is; it is as science, philosophy, religion, the arts and everyday speech says it is. Not science but the sum of man's symbol system, of which science is but one, is the measure of things." It is upon this truth that the Heisenberg lines rest.

The way of truth is a turbulent stream with eddies and currents and if you wish to raft through it is necessary to read the river and follow the flow. Just as the point where all currents come together is the place with the strongest current so too is the point where the currents of knowledge converge the place where the greatest understanding is to be found.

Realize this and it becomes easier to sort through the workings of reality and separate the wheat from the chaff. Those ideas that agree with the same points in other streams are likely to be right. Those that can find no agreement with other streams are more suspect.

As we have seen, the mind can interact with the noumena in one of three ways. In the first, the mind can directly affect the outcome of what is being observed. By choosing one's methods light can be made a wave or a particle. By choosing the speed of the airliner, the length of the ruler can be made any length from

12 inches to almost zero and by choosing the speed of the rocket one can fine-tune the age difference of the twins.

In the second case, there is no direct control but it is possible to arrive at a definite answer through observation. You can open the box and see if the cat is alive or dead. While in the third case, you are faced with two or more probability waves with no way of ever opening the box. When this happens, what is left is belief and on such questions belief must substitute for physical observation. What is important to remember is that a reality created by belief can be just as 'real' as any other.

Stop and look around you. The world you are experiencing is the noumena translated by the mind into the middle dimension. From the choices the mind makes the paradigm is constructed with different people arriving at different answers of what that should be. With no one paradigm being more true than another the decision of which is best becomes a pragmatic one. Whether you are trying to fix the toaster or save your immortal soul success follows from the proper frame of mind.

Flying in the face of common sense as it does this is a difficult idea for many people to grasp. Yet, once again, appearances are deceiving for this is really one of the most common and widely accepted ideas in Western thought. It is nothing less than the foundation of the Christian religion as embodied in the concept of the Trinity. For Christian's there are the Father, the Son and the Holy Spirit, yet there is only one God. Each manifestation has different attributes with which He is being dependent upon how the mind perceives Him. Worship God the Father and He is the Father, worship God the Son and He is the Son.

So what does all of this mean? What does it have to say about who we are, where we came from and where we are going? Does life have a meaning greater than itself or does it only have the meaning we give it? The fact that no answer acceptable to all has ever been found must place this question in the can never be answered category. Kant was right; the most anyone can do is to lead their life "as if" there was meaning. When you do this you have done all it is possible to do and, in a paradoxical way, you have created a meaning greater than yourself.

Nowhere does the different possibilities inherent in the different paradigms show up more clearly than in their understanding of immortality. And in this statement lies hope for struggling humanity for in the illogic of reality can be found an escape clause. No longer are we confined to one destiny. The preachers were right, what you believe does matter. After all, it can only be a point of hope that out of four modes of being, three specifically allow for an afterlife and even the sensory mode does not absolutely forbid it. These are pretty good odds.

Who and what we are now takes on a new meaning. For if the boundary of death is an artificial one then the boundary of birth must be so as well. Take the abortion-pro-life controversy as an example. If death is not the end of life and birth is not its beginning then the essence that is you is more than a biological unit. From the instant that an egg and sperm unite to form a single cell zygote until you die of senility at 103 that is you. And the fact that for a short time you were attached to your mother has no more relevance than when you are on life support at the end.

Yet the sensory mode is not wrong when it says that life is a biological unit upon which limits can be set. Within such diametrically opposite views, no one answer can be truer than another can. The answer then becomes a subjective one based on the beliefs of the individual to which no absolute truths can ever be found. The final answer can only be solved by the political will of the opponents and to try and answer it in any absolute sense is and exercise in futility.

Beginning in the cradle the proper description of what the world should look like is beaten into us until it becomes second nature. So thoroughly is this learned that any other possibility becomes inconceivable. All of which affects our relationship with ourselves and with others. Raised within a particular paradigm we know what is right and that any deviation from this is wrong. Whether due to arrogance, error or ignorance it is a failure and a sin. Failure in others leads to feelings of righteous indignity or virtuous superiority. Carried to excess these can degenerate into feelings of intolerance, bigotry and hatred. Disharmony reigns.

A well-rounded, well-balanced person requires the nourishment of all aspects of the psyche. Breaking the hold of the primary rule is the first step in achieving this. Only in this way can the full range of the human experience be brought to bear. No longer confined to a single point of view the mind is now free to switch programs as the situation demands. By acknowledging the validity of other peoples point of view energy now wasted on anger, resentment and bitterness can be directed to more positive goals. Tolerance is harmony in action.

Lenience, patience, kindheartedness and mercy, all of these are marks of a happy, well-adjusted person. Flowing with the rhythms of life rather than continually fighting them such people are what the Taoist's call "superior." It is no accident that all of the world's great spiritual leaders have these very qualities. Flowing with the rhythm of life like a leaf floating down a stream these are the people who have found the secret of life.

Apply the concept of harmony to life styles and a guideline for what constitutes an acceptable one is established. No lifestyle can be acceptable that advocates the willful harming of others. Bringing disharmony to ones life or the lives of others is the only true sin. Relativity can never be used to justify destructive or bigoted behavior of any kind.

As an aside, it may be noted that harmony and the rhythms of life are not the same thing as pacifism. When a lion kills a deer, it is flowing with the rhythms of life. Contrary to what most people think, even Jesus was not a pacifist. It is true He taught that one should "turn the other cheek", but he also drove the moneychangers out of the temple. Harmony does not mean never using violence, but rather in knowing when to use it. "Take what you need and leave the rest."

As we have seen of all extant beings, our own existence must be that in which we have the most confidence. "I think therefore I am." Of the existence of others, we are slightly less sure. This uncertainty lies in the fact that we can never know what or even if, anyone else is thinking. They too could be part of the hologram without any noumenal base.

Pass beyond the bounds of biological organisms and the insubstantial beings of the Fortean Universe are encountered. These entities actually do lack the noumena base that we assume to be present in others. Taken together the life forms that inhabit this planet can be thought of as forming a gradient from the most substantial to the least.

Our senses tell us that we have a solid body. Faith healing shows that this is not so. Reality is a composite of the three ways the mind interacts with reality with that part generated by belief providing its elasticity. This belief-generated part makes faith healing, visualization and miracles possible. Both the reason these things can be changed and the reason they are so hard to change now become clear.

Reality, then, can be thought of as a circle of existence based upon mental activity. The world and thought is the same thing. Whether that thought emanates from the mind of God or the mind of man is a personal choice. Humanity can be thought of as a thought-form manifested by the mind of God, which now has evolved to the point where it can—in a small way—manifest life forms of its own. John Napier had it wrong. We do not have to plunge into the Goblin Universe because we already live in it.

One of the facts of the world we live in is the primary rule. So intricately is this rule build into our thinking that the possibility of it being wrong simply does not occur. Yet wrong it is. Understand this and a much richer and more varied world opens up.

Multiple paradigms multiply the available choices by just that much. And it is in our ability to make choices that our humanity rest. Animals have few choices we have many. This is the defining characteristic of intelligence. This allows a human being to lead a life of happiness or despair impossible for any animal

Ecologists understand the importance of saving the snail darter and the spotted owl as intricate parts of the web of life. This knowledge has been translated into action only with the greatest difficulty. What is lacking is not knowledge of what is wrong but the will to fix it. Motives that engage the emotions enough to stimulate the will are not the sensory modes long suit.

Motives in the sensory mode tend to be of the profit and loss variety. Any higher ideals must be sought in other modes. When Chief Seattle made his famous statement about the earth being our mother whom no one can own he was standing squarely in the mythic mode of being. All of this about the earth as a loving mother makes no sense to a mathematician; it makes perfect sense to a shaman.

To the modern mind, a thing becomes real when it can be physically demonstrated that it is real. It is for this reason that religion has lost ground in today's world. With no physical evidence ever found to prove God's reality and no theory to explain the idea of the Divine within the rules of the dominate mode of being God has been downgraded from the central fact of life to a hypothesis we have no need of. But stop trying to shove God into the sensory mode, return Him to the transpsychic mode where he belongs, and He regains His rightful place in our lives.

With our new understanding, some philosophical questions now become comprehensible. Take the problem of whether monism, pluralism or dualism is the correct way of viewing reality. With the answer being, of course, that they all are. Monism, pluralism and dualism are simply the world looked at from different places on the boardwalk. Moreover, this is not a play on words and it is not a cop out. This is the answer there is nothing more.

Nowhere can the affect language has on the creation of reality be seen more clearly than right here. The world is usually presented as a strange and mysterious place full of paradoxes that defy reason. However, change the word paradox to the word complementarity and suddenly the world is a much friendlier place. The two ages of the twins are not a paradox but only complementary ways of viewing reality. In a relative universe, there are no paradoxes only different places to stand on the boardwalk.

Relative truth leads to a world of increased options for confronting life, properly used the relativistic nature of reality yields a greater number of choices, more confidence in ones judgments, more variety in life's directions and more tolerance for the views of others.

Improperly used it leads to nihilism. If anything is possible then one can believe in nothing. This leads to lawlessness, mob rule and terrorism. If there are no truths and nothing to believe in what is left but a completely selfish existence at best, or striking out in anger and despair against a meaningless existence at worst.

What we have tried to find here is a reasonable explanation of the human condition in line with known human abilities. Concocted out of the common ingredients of all branches of the human experience the theory relies on no powers, higher vibrations or astral forces of any kind. A proper theory must explain these things not presuppose them.

That the world is observer created and amendable to change through belief can answer many questions. By understanding the role of subjectivity in phenomena at the periphery of life, they become explainable. Still it should be remembered that understanding this is the easy part. Using this knowledge to modify reality to ones own advantage is the hard part. After all, they do not call such happenings miracles for nothing.

Knowledge, they say, is power and herein lays great power; power to do yourself good or to do yourself harm. Still it is easier to win the game if you know the rules. By understanding that you can be right without the other person being wrong knowledge can be utilized in a more sophisticated manner. The gain this gives in the sum of human knowledge may be marginal; yet how often has the price of survival been marginal? How much difference was there after all between Neanderthal and Cro-Magnon man? Multiple paradigms mean multiple choices, take what you need from each, and ignore the others at your peril.

There will be some who find here a truth, something they have long felt. For others it will be complete nonsense. If you have stayed with me this far you must have found something of interest. Whether your reaction was an epiphany, benign interest or outrage you have been compelled to think, surely no bad thing in our multi-media age. For this short time, your thoughts have risen above sex, clothes, the sports channel and computers to grapple with some of life's most fundamental questions. "I firmly believe it takes but a little philosophy to make a man happy in whatever state fortune may place him."[14]

Philosophy is what raises us above the level of the animals. Yet in our modern tendency to subordinate everything to making money and looking good we begin to bear more than a little resemblance to a colony of ants. In just the same way that cutting down virgin forests to create jobs is humanity cutting its own throat so too is a failure to utilize our full potential in grappling with life a failure. If we are to maintain our humanity intact it is to places like this that we must look. The present theory cannot tell you how to live your life. What it can do is show the available paths. Finding the one that is right for you now becomes the problem. This requires more than just thinking about it, intuition must also play its part. For it is only by the combination of reason and intuition that your full potential can be brought to bear.

As don Juan told Carlos Castaneda, "Any path is only a path, and there is no affront to oneself or to others, in dropping it if that is what your heart tells you . . . Look at every path closely and deliberately. Try it as many times as you think necessary. Then ask yourself, and yourself alone, one question . . . Does this path have a heart? If it does the path is good; if it doesn't it is of no use." Namaste.

---

[14] Daniel Boone

Selected Bibliography

Allen, Benedict. *Last of the Medicine Men.* Dorling Kindersley, 2000.
Here you are taken on a trip to find the last of the world's shamans in the far-flung corners of the world and in so doing you are given a glimpse into what the world as seen in the mythic mode looks like.

Bucke, Richard Maurice. *Cosmic Consciousness: A Study in the Evolution of the Human Mind.* E.P. Dutton & Co., 1923.
A classic since it was first published Burke takes a journey into the world of the mystic mode of being by examining the life of some of the world's greatest mystics.

Capra, Fritijof. *The Tao of Physics.* Shambhala, 2000.
The best book out there to exam the relationship being the findings of modern science and the world as seen by the mystics.

Castaneda, Carlos. *Journey to Ixtlan. Pocket Books, 1972.*
Carlos Castaneda wrote many books about his adventures with the Yagui sorcerer don Juan, this is the best.

Frazer, James G. *The Golden Bough.* Collier Books, 1950.
A must for anyone interested in understanding the mythic mode of being this is the definitive work on the nature and meaning of magic.

Heuvelmans, Bernard. *On the Track of Unknown Animals.* Hill
& Wang 1958.
Heuvelmans takes you on trip through the world of
cryptozoology, a field he founded. If the only unknowns you
know are Bigfoot and the Loch Ness Monster you will find this
an eye-opener and it is fun reading too.

James, William. *The Varieties of Religious Experience: A Study
in Human Nature.* Modern Library, 1929.
The transpsychic mode gets its turn in William James' landmark
study of the religious experience in human life.

LeShan, Lawrence. *Alternate Realities.* Ballantine Books, 1976.
One of the finest treatments of paradigms and their role in
creating the world we live in and the inspiration for this work. A
must for anyone interested in this subject.

Napier, John. *Bigfoot.* E.P.Dutton & Co., Inc., 1973.
There are many books on Bigfoot out there but none treats the
subject with more intelligence and wit than Dr. Napier.

Owen, Iris M., with Margaret Sparrow, *Conjuring Up Philip, A
Adventure in Psychokinesis.* Harper & Row Publishers, 1976.
If you are seriously interested in trying to understand the
concept of functional entities this is a good place to start.

Penrose, Roger, *The Emperor's New Mind.* Penguin Books, 1989.
If you are into mathematics and like your books a little more technical than the present one this is the book for you.

Randi, James. *Flim Flam!* Prometheus Books, 1982.
When one begins talk about faith healing, PK happenings and even fortean events one enters an area rich in chicanery. In this book James Randi (a practicing stage magician) takes a walk through these fields and gives some practical advice on recognizing double-dealings when you see them.

Russell, Bertrand, *A History of Western Philosophy.* Simon & Schuster, 1972.
More technical than most books recommended here this is a good book for any serious student of philosophy.

Schatzman, Morton, M.D. *The Story of Ruth.* G.P. Putman's Sons, 1980. To understand how a functional entity can be created it is first necessary to know a little about hallucinations. Dr. Schatzman gives you that very knowledge in a manner most people can understand.

Smith, Adam. *Powers of the Mind.* Random House, 1978.
Adams Smith's tongue-in-cheek tour of the mind and its purported abilities is insightful, witty, entertaining and as relevant today as ever and a good read too.

CPSIA information can be obtained at www.ICGtesting.com
Printed in the USA
LVOW011801211212

312808LV00019B/675/P